THE
EVERYTHING.
EASY
INSTANT POT®
COOKBOOK

Dear Reader,

Unless you have been living your life without social media, you probably
know about the Instant Pot®—the countertop electric pressure cooker
that does it all! From roast dinners in an hour or less to homemade
yogurt, fluffy rice, and more, the Instant Pot® has revolutionized how
meals are planned and prepared. I have had my Instant Pot® for a few
years now, and I can't imagine my life without it. Say, for example, I am
having a stressful day, and I want some fall-off-the-bone beef short ribs
to soothe my weary soul. With the Instant Pot® I can stop by the market
in the afternoon to buy fresh short ribs and have them ready for dinner, along with some perfectly tender potatoes and carrots, with time to
spare!

The Instant Pot® is the ultimate culinary multitasker. It has replaced
my slow cooker, rice cooker, and yogurt maker and has introduced me to
a universe of quick-cooked meals that taste even better than their slow-
cooked counterparts. The best part is that in most cases my Instant Pot®
liner is the only thing I need to wash, so I don't have to spend time soaking and scrubbing pots and pans. I approve of less scrubbing in my life.

So, unpack your Instant Pot® and get ready because you have a
whole new world of cooking adventures ahead!

Kelly Jaggers

Welcome to the EVERYTHING® Series!

These handy, accessible books give you all you need to tackle a difficult project, gain a new hobby, comprehend a fascinating topic, prepare for an exam, or even brush up on something you learned back in school but have since forgotten.

You can choose to read an Everything® book from cover to cover or just pick out the information you want from our four useful boxes: e-questions, e-facts, e-alerts, and e-ssentials.

We give you everything you need to know on the subject, but throw in a lot of fun stuff along the way too.

We now have more than 400 Everything® books in print, spanning such wide-ranging categories as weddings, pregnancy, cooking, music instruction, foreign language, crafts, pets, New Age, and so much more. When you're done reading them all, you can finally say you know Everything®!

QUESTION

Answers to common questions

FACT

Important snippets of information

ALERT

Urgent warnings

ESSENTIAL

Quick handy tips

PUBLISHER Karen Cooper

MANAGING EDITOR Lisa Laing

COPY CHIEF Casey Ebert

ASSOCIATE PRODUCTION EDITOR Jo-Anne Duhamel

ACQUISITIONS EDITOR Zander Hatch

DEVELOPMENT EDITOR Sarah Doughty

EVERYTHING® SERIES COVER DESIGNER Erin Alexander

Visit the entire Everything® series at www.everything.com

THE EVERYTHING® EASY INSTANT POT® COOKBOOK

Learn to master your Instant Pot®
with these 300 delicious—and super
simple—recipes!

Kelly Jaggers

Adams Media
New York London Toronto Sydney New Delhi

To my family.

Adams Media
An Imprint of Simon & Schuster, Inc.
57 Littlefield Street
Avon, Massachusetts 02322

An Everything® Series Book.
Everything® and everything.com® are registered trademarks of Simon & Schuster, Inc.

First Adams Media trade paperback edition
December 2018

ADAMS MEDIA and colophon are trademarks of Simon & Schuster.

For information about special discounts for bulk purchases, please contact Simon & Schuster Special Sales at
1-866-506-1949 or business@simonandschuster.com.

The Simon & Schuster Speakers Bureau can bring authors to your live event. For more information or to book an event contact the Simon & Schuster Speakers Bureau at 1-866-248-3049 or visit our website at www.simonspeakers.com.

Cover photographs by James Stefiuk

Interior photographs by Kelly Jaggers; © Getty Images/istetiana, zia_shusha, bhofack2

Manufactured in the United States of America

10 9 8 7 6 5 4

Library of Congress Cataloging-in-Publication Data
Jaggers, Kelly, author.
The Everything® Easy Instant Pot® Cookbook / Kelly Jaggers.
Avon, Massachusetts: Adams Media, 2018.
Series: Everything.
Includes index.
LCCN 2018037091 | ISBN 9781507209400 (pb) | ISBN 9781507209417 (ebook)
Subjects: LCSH: Pressure cooking. | Quick and easy cooking. | One-dish meals. | LCGFT: Cookbooks.
Classification: LCC TX840.P7 J34 2018 | DDC 641.5/12--dc23
LC record available at https://lccn.loc.gov/2018037091

ISBN 978-1-5072-0940-0
ISBN 978-1-5072-0941-7 (ebook)

Contents

Acknowledgments

I want to send a special thank you to my mother, Carol. You are amazing, and without you I would not be the food lover I am today. I also appreciate your continued work as a recipe tester! You are amazing! To my brother, Wayne, I could not be happier to have you as a part of my life. I am happy you are home. To my friends, Tori, Novia, Tanisha, Sonya, and Jodi, thank you for listening to me, supporting me, and making sure I take care of myself when I forget to. What would I do without you?

Finally, to my husband, Mark, you are perhaps the best person I know, and I love you so very, very much. No one else I know would work as hard as you do, and put up with as much as you do, for nothing more than my love and devotion. I adore you.

Introduction

YOU HAVE PROBABLY HEARD the buzz around the Instant Pot®, the one appliance that can replace a multitude of kitchen tools and make cooking faster and easier. So, does it live up to the hype? What exactly *is* an Instant Pot®?

Well, the Instant Pot® is an electric countertop pressure multifunction appliance that, depending on the model, is a pressure cooker, slow cooker, rice cooker, steamer, sauté pan, yogurt maker, and more. All this may feel a little overwhelming, but never fear! *The Everything® Easy Instant Pot® Cookbook* is here to assist you with helpful tips and 300 delicious recipes for mastering the Instant Pot® in no time.

In *The Everything® Easy Instant Pot® Cookbook*, you will find easy recipes for all occasions. From Cheesy Artichoke Dip and Garlicky Green Beans to Kimchi Chicken Wings and Shrimp and Lobster Bisque, you are covered from tasty sides and weeknight meals to dishes for special occasions. The recipes are arranged to get you through your day, starting with breakfast and ending with dessert and drinks! And, once you become familiar with your Instant Pot® you will be able to convert your favorite recipes cooked in the oven, on the stovetop, or in the slow cooker.

An Instant Pot® is versatile, easy to use, and will transform the way you cook. With most recipes cooked in an hour or less, you can make any night special by cooking meals that might otherwise be saved for weekends. Some of the best parts of Instant Pot® cooking are the fun you can have experimenting with recipes, learning new techniques, and feeding the ones you care about the most delicious, nutritious meals. Enjoy!

CHAPTER 1

Instant Pot® 101

The Instant Pot® is the smart-cooking superstar that is a pressure cooker, slow cooker, steamer, sauté pan, rice cooker, yogurt maker, and warming pot all in one. While there is a lot of satisfaction in long, slow cooking on, say, a Sunday afternoon before a busy week ahead, there are other days when you want delicious food quickly with less cleanup, more energy savings, and all the same great textures and flavors. If you are imagining perfectly cooked meals for your friends and family at the touch of a button, the Instant Pot® is the key to culinary success. Like with any new kitchen tool, you will need to learn a bit more about your new culinary best friend. From functions and safety to tips and tricks for cooking success, this chapter will help you learn more about what your Instant Pot® can do and how to use it masterfully.

Equipment and Set-Up

First things first, you have a new Instant Pot®. Congratulations! It's time to unbox and inspect. You need to check out your Instant Pot® and everything that comes with it to make sure it is in good condition. If you have not done so already, take a moment to become familiar with your model's safety features and its operating, cleaning, and maintenance instructions. The manual contains a lot of very useful information, and you will have greater success if you take the time to read it. Be sure to keep the manual in a handy place so you can reference it when needed. While accessories may vary by model, there are a few things that are common to each Instant Pot®, such as a measuring cup for rice, a small ladle, a rice paddle, and a small rack for elevating items off the bottom of the inner pot. This section will cover the features and elements of the Instant Pot® in greater detail.

FACT

Instant Pot® makes a variety of pressure cookers in different sizes and with different functions. The recipes in this book were created and tested in a 6-quart Duo model, so you may need to adjust the recipes depending on the size of your particular machine.

Inner Pot

The inner pot (or liner) of your Instant Pot® should be shiny and dent-free and should fit securely in the body of the machine. On the inside of the liner you will see measurement lines. These lines are designed to help you measure the amount of liquid in the pot, and they are especially handy when making rice or soup. The liner is dishwasher safe, so cleanup is easy, but if there is any stubborn food stuck inside, it helps to soak the liner with warm water and dish detergent and then scour the pot gently with a soft brush or scrubbing sponge. Always be sure the liner is dry before inserting it into the machine, and never insert the liner into the machine if there is any food, grease, or debris on the outside of the pot.

Lid and Sealing Ring

The lid has a lot of important parts that will need to be checked on a regular basis so your Instant Pot® will work properly. Before your first use inspect the lid carefully. Make sure it fits the machine and locks into place with ease. When the machine is plugged in, you will hear a musical sound when the lid is locked and unlocked, letting you know you have successfully opened or closed the lid. Next, flip the lid over and check the sealing ring around the outside of the lid. The ring can be removed if it becomes very dirty or greasy or if food or grease get under the ring. It should fit snugly into the lid when replaced. After you cook with your Instant Pot® you will want to make sure the lid and seal are clean and that the sealing ring fits securely around the rim of the lid.

ALERT

The inner pot should never be filled more than ⅔ of the way with food such as meats, vegetables, soups, or stews. Foods that expand while cooking, like pasta, rice, and dry beans, should not fill the pot more than halfway. As pressure builds, the food in the pot will expand. You need to make sure there is plenty of room so your food will cook properly.

Float Valve, Condensation Collector, and Steam Release

On the top of the lid are the float valve and steam release, and to the side of these is the condensation collector. The float is a small round valve that will pop up when the machine comes to full pressure and will sink when pressure is released. Make sure the valve area is clean and free from grease or debris. Next, check out the steam release. If it is not already installed, you will want to insert it following your manual's directions. The steam release should move smoothly from Sealing to Venting. This release can be used to quickly release the pressure in your Instant Pot®; just be sure when turning the valve that your fingers, hands, and face are clear of the steam. Finally, there is a small cup attached to the side of the machine that collects any condensation that develops while the machine is coming up to pressure. It easily snaps onto the machine and can be removed to be drained and cleaned.

Power Cord

You may notice that the power cord on your Instant Pot® seems short. This is by design for safety. The short cord helps prevent tangling with other appliances and also helps prevent the machine from being pulled or dragged by the cord if it is draped off the side of a counter. The plug is a 3-pronged grounded plug and should be used with a grounded outlet. Make sure the cord is completely intact and securely attached to the machine before use. Never hang the power cord off the edge of a counter or leave it where it could be pulled or tugged. It is also recommended that you never use your Instant Pot® with an extension cord.

Pressure Functions

The Instant Pot® can be used manually, allowing you to select your preferred pressure and cook time. It also comes with a number of preprogrammed function buttons that have been calibrated for specific types of foods. When you first look at all of these options it can be a little intimidating and confusing. How do you know which one to use? How can you adjust things if your recipe calls for something different? What about all the other buttons? Well, never fear! This section will demystify the Instant Pot® functions and programs and offer hints on how to use these functions successfully.

Manual Pressure Cooking

The Manual/Pressure button allows you to set your own pressure and time for cooking. This may be the button you use most when pressure cooking, as it is the easiest to customize for precision cooking. The Manual/Pressure setting will automatically default to high pressure, but you can manually set the pressure by pressing the -/+ buttons from Low to High depending on what you are cooking. Once you seal the pot, you will need to set your timer using the -/+ buttons. The Instant Pot® will take about 10–15 minutes to come to full pressure. Once it reaches full pressure, the countdown timer will start and all you need to do is sit back, relax, and let the Instant Pot® do all the work! Remember, never open the lid while the machine is coming to pressure, and do not try to open the lid once the machine has reached full pressure. It is incredibly difficult to do in any case, because the machine is designed with safety in mind. If for any reason you need to end cooking early or stop the machine as it is coming to pressure, press Cancel and let any pressure release naturally.

Be sure you add the appropriate amount of liquid for your particular mode, in most cases ½–1 cup of liquid. The liquid is what will create the pressure, and if there is not enough liquid in the machine, it will not be able to come to the appropriate pressure—so don't forget it!

Preset Cooking Functions

If you choose, you can use one of the many preset functions programmed into your Instant Pot®. These functions are programmed with suggested cooking times for certain foods in certain volumes, as tested by the manufacturer. These can be a handy place to start, but please be aware that the Instant Pot® does not know if you are starting with fresh or frozen foods or how much food you are cooking by weight or volume, so some manual adjustments may be needed to ensure thorough cooking. These buttons are meant to get you close to your desired cooking time, so they can be very convenient as a place to start when you are unsure what pressure level and time you should use. Your owner's manual has information about each of your specific model's programmed functions, including pressure level and cooking time, so please review this. While each model is different, some of the most common programmed functions include Soup/Broth, Meat/Stew, Bean/Chili, Rice, Poultry, and Steam.

Nonpressure Functions

If you are thinking that the Instant Pot® is only a pressure cooker, think again! It's true, you may use your Instant Pot® primarily for pressure cooking, but it can do so much more! The Instant Pot® has a number of nonpressure cooking options that make it a reliable replacement for things like slow cookers, warming pots, yogurt makers, electric sauté pans, and rice cookers. This section will dive a little deeper into some of the most common nonpressure functions and how they can make your cooking easier!

Sauté

Sautéing is the process of cooking food over fairly high heat with a small amount of fat such as oil or butter added to the pan. The Instant Pot® Sauté function allows you to brown meats, soften vegetables, and thicken sauces all inside the inner pot. This function may be the one you depend on most because browned meats and vegetables give your food more flavor, and doing it all in the same pot will add even more flavor to your finished dishes. To sauté, simply plug in your machine and press or use the dial to set it to the Sauté function. Depending on your model, the temperature of the Sauté setting can be changed by pressing either the Adjust button or the -/+ buttons. The machine is ready when the display reads Hot. You can also use Sauté after pressure cooking to reduce soups, stews, and pan juices or to thicken gravy. The Sauté feature times out after 30 minutes for safety, and you should never place the lid on the machine while in Sauté mode to avoid building pressure.

Slow Cook

When you use this function, your Instant Pot® will behave just like a traditional slow cooker. The default time for most models is 4 hours but can be adjusted to suit your recipe. You can also adjust the temperature to Low, Normal, or High. Your owner's manual has more details on exact cooking temperatures and how to make these adjustments, but in general, Low is 180°F–190°F (to keep food warm), Normal is 190°F–200°F (like a traditional slow cooker's Low setting), and High is 200°F–210°F (like a traditional slow cooker's High setting). Be sure to add about 1–2 cups of liquid to the Instant Pot® when using it as a slow cooker to help evenly distribute the heat. The lid can be used with this function, but be sure the steam release is set to Venting to avoid pressure buildup.

Yogurt

There is nothing quite like homemade yogurt, but the process can seem intimidating. With the Instant Pot® homemade yogurt is nearly impossible to mess up. You can make both dairy and nondairy yogurts, so you can produce yogurt for most diets. All you need is the milk of your choice and either a live yogurt culture or unsweetened, prepared yogurt with a live active culture. Store-bought plain yogurt can be used for an initial batch, then you can reserve a small amount of your own homemade yogurt to use in the future. It is important to note that your yogurt must contain an active culture. Be sure to sanitize your liner before starting to avoid any off flavors or bad bacteria overtaking your yogurt culture. The simplest way to sanitize is to fill the liner with boiling water, allow it to stand for a few minutes, then discard the water and allow the liner to air-dry. You have the option to make the yogurt directly in the pot or in smaller heatproof jars. If you opt for the jars, you need to be sure they are also sanitized, and you will need to place them on a rack and use a small amount of water in the pot to generate heat and steam for incubating your yogurt culture.

Keep Warm

Keep Warm does exactly what the name suggests: it holds your food at a safe temperature until you are ready to serve. Keep Warm will start automatically after any programmed or manual cooking ends, so if your food is ready but you are not, your food will be kept warm until you're ready to eat. Keep Warm will hold food at 145°F–172°F and will display "L" along with a count-up timer that shows you how long your food has been on Keep Warm. Keep Warm will automatically shut off after 10 hours if you do not turn the machine off. However, if you open and close the lid, it will not turn Keep Warm off—so you can use your Instant Pot® as a warming pot for a potluck or party. When making rice in your Instant Pot® you may want to consider turning the Keep Warm function off after cooking, as the rice may become dry or even burnt.

Other Buttons

Along with the buttons that set cooking settings, there are a number of buttons that allow you to make adjustments and customizations to these settings. You may need to adjust the pressure you use for a certain cut of meat or increase the cooking time for rice, oats, or other foods. These settings may vary by model, but in general they include the following options.

Pressure Level/Pressure

You may need to adjust the pressure used for cooking based on your recipe. When that happens, you will need to press the Pressure or Pressure Level button within 10 seconds of selecting your cooking program and then select the pressure you prefer. This button works to adjust the pressure for manual cooking and the preset cooking programs. You can select between high pressure (10–12 psi) and low pressure (5.5–7 psi). High pressure will heat the food to a higher temperature of 240°F–245°F, while low pressure cooks at 230°F –233°F. In general, you will use high pressure more often than low pressure. Most electric pressure cooker recipes are formulated using high pressure, so when it doubt use high pressure. The one major exception is eggs, which come out better when cooked using low pressure.

Delay Start/Timer

This feature can be used for pressure and nonpressure cooking. Load the Instant Pot® with your ingredients, then press the cooking function you want or use your Manual/Pressure button and set to your desired cooking time and pressure. Then, within 10 seconds, press the Delay Start or Timer button and set the time to wait before beginning cooking. You will first set the hours, then press Delay Start or Timer a second time to set the minutes. To cancel this feature, you simply press the Keep Warm/Cancel button. It is important to note that you should not use this feature with temperature-sensitive foods like meat and seafood, as you run the risk of incubating harmful bacteria that lead to foodborne illness. This function is best for things like grains, oats, beans, and vegetables.

Keep Warm and Keep Warm/Cancel

While there is a Keep Warm function, there is also a Keep Warm button—and on some models, a combined Keep Warm/Cancel button. The Cancel button on the Instant Pot® will cancel a program you have selected. Keep Warm will set your food to the Keep Warm function. If you are in the middle of a nonpressure cooking function such as Sauté or you want to make an adjustment after a cooking program has started but has not yet come to pressure, you can press Keep Warm/Cancel to end that function. You can then select a new program and make any adjustments you desire. If you have food in the pot you want to keep hot, you can press the button to activate the Keep Warm function. In some models, you can also prevent your machine from going into Keep Warm mode after a cooking program ends. You can press the Keep Warm button twice within 10 seconds of selecting your desired program, and the light on the Keep Warm/Cancel button will turn off. This indicates that Keep Warm has been cancelled. Check your owner's manual to see if your model has this feature.

Adjust

This button has a lot of different functions depending on what kind of cooking you are doing. When pressure cooking, you can press Adjust to change the cook times of the programmed cooking functions, such as Soup and Poultry, but not other functions, like Rice, that are fully automatic. If you press Adjust after pressing Sauté or Slow Cook, you can adjust the temperature of those features to Low, Normal, and High. Finally, Adjust can select different programs in the Yogurt setting. All of these functions are fully explained in your owner's manual, and you should read about them to see exactly how this feature works for your particular model.

QUESTION

How is natural release different from quick-release?
Natural release happens when the pressure cooking time is up. As the machine cools, the pressure will slowly release until the lid unlocks. This process can take 10–20 minutes. Quick-release happens when you turn the steam release handle from Sealing to Venting. This will release a lot of steam, so stand clear once released. Quick-release takes 1–2 minutes.

Cooking Under Pressure

Knowing your Instant Pot® is one thing, but how can you really use all of the fancy features to make delicious meals? Well, this section will cover tips for success, information on some foods that can be a little tricky, and also ideas for converting family-favorite recipes that were not originally designed for an electric pressure cooker—so you can enjoy them with all the amazing benefits that pressure cooking has to offer.

Preparing Foods for Pressure Cooking

When you are preparing foods for cooking in the Instant Pot®, you want to consider a few things. First, will the item you want to cook fit in the pot? Larger roasts might not fit well if left whole, so it is sometimes better to slice larger cuts of meat into small pieces. This also has the benefit of reducing the cooking time, as smaller pieces cook faster than larger ones. Certain cuts of meat that include bones should be checked for fit. You may need to remove larger bones. Second, will the pot or pan you plan to use inside the Instant Pot® fit without touching the sides of the liner? It is important to make sure your pot or pan does not touch the sides of the liner, as this will affect the ability of the steam to circulate evenly through the Instant Pot®. When cooking cheesecake, bread, or any other item cooked inside a second vessel, you'll want to place it in on a metal rack inside the pot and check that there is space around the edges of the pot. Third, do you have any vegetables that could be cut into more equal pieces? It is a good idea to cut vegetables of a similar density into similar sizes so they cook uniformly. When cooking firm and soft vegetables at the same time, it is a good idea to cut the firm vegetables into smaller pieces than the softer ones.

The Importance of Browning

Browned food, particularly meat, simply tastes better. When browned, the food is more appealing on the plate and has a richer, deeper flavor. While you can skip the browning step to save time and still have plenty of great flavor, browning foods before pressure and slow cooking adds that extra layer of flavor that takes your cooking to the next level. Since the Instant Pot® has the Sauté function, you can sear and brown meats and soften vegetables with ease and without dirtying a second pan. This works best for fresh meats and vegetables. You will want to thaw frozen meat before you brown it in your Instant Pot® for the best, most even sear. Don't clean out the pot after browning; instead, add a little of the cooking liquid to the hot pot. This will add even more flavor!

ALERT

Starchy foods like pasta, beans, barley, and cereals can cause starchy foam to form in the Instant Pot®, which can be released when you release the steam from the pot. This foam can clog your steam release, and it can also cause a mess in your kitchen! For some of these foods (like pasta), a little fat, such as a tablespoon of olive oil or butter, added to the pot can help minimize the foam.

Cooking Rice

How you like your rice is a matter of personal preference, so when you first start cooking rice in the Instant Pot® you may need to experiment to get it just right. Different types of rice and deciding how much to cook at one time will also require some finessing, such as adjusting the ratio of dry rice to water. In general, dry rice needs a 1:1.25 ratio of rice to water. So, for every cup of dry white rice you should add 1¼ cups of water. Brown rice is a little different due to its increased fiber content, so it uses a ratio of 1:1.5 rice to water. If you rinse and then soak your rice prior to cooking, you should try a 1:1 ratio of rice to water. When measuring rice and water, use the same vessel for both. So, if you use the included measuring cup and you add one level scoop of dry rice, add 1¼ level measuring cups of water. Adding a little fat to the pot will also help reduce starch in the rice, which is helpful if you quick-release the steam after cooking. Rice is best if the pressure is allowed to release naturally so it can absorb all of the cooking liquid, and it is better still if you let it rest on the Keep Warm setting for 5–10 minutes more to help ensure the rice comes out perfectly tender.

Cooking Pasta

Want to make homemade macaroni and cheese in the same time it takes to make the boxed kind? How about a giant spaghetti and meatballs dinner that is bursting with flavor—and all cooked at one time in one pot? With the Instant Pot® you can! When making pasta in an electric pressure cooker, you should remember a few simple tricks. First, for every 4 ounces of pasta, you will need approximately 2 cups of liquid. So, for a full pound (16 ounces) of pasta, you will need 8 cups of water. Second, you will need to add a little fat, such as olive oil or butter, to help reduce the starchy foam that will form and that may be released when you release the steam after cooking. Finally, most regular pasta takes about 4 minutes to cook after coming to pressure. Other types of pasta, such as whole wheat or whole grain, may take longer. You can always start with 4 minutes, then release the pressure and check. If it is not cooked to your liking, you can reseal and set for another 1–2 minutes.

Converting Recipes

Say you want to make Aunt Sally's famous pot roast, but you don't have 4 hours. Your Instant Pot® is here to help! In most cases you can simply verify that the volume of food does not exceed the amount recommended for filling your particular model and make sure it fits inside the pot properly and that you have sufficient liquid to bring the machine to pressure. Once you have checked all these things, the easiest course of action is to check out the cooking time charts included in the back of this book. Please note that these charts are designed using high pressure. It is best to lean on the side of undercooking, as you can always clamp the lid back on and cook the food longer. Another option is to try one of the programmed cooking functions.

Instant Pot® Maintenance and Safety

Maintaining your Instant Pot® will ensure you have many happy years of cooking ahead of you. Your Instant Pot® owner's manual will include specific information for care and maintenance of your particular model, but in general there are a few basic things you can do to make sure your machine is in good working order. Review this information before you start cooking.

FACT

When you receive your Instant Pot®, it is important to note any safety precautions from the manufacturer. One item to pay particular attention to is the seal in the lid to be sure it fits properly. An ill-fitting seal will not allow the lid to trap steam, and the machine will not be able to come to pressure.

Cleaning

The most valuable maintenance you can do is to properly and thoroughly clean your Instant Pot® after each use (once it is completely cooled!). This includes wiping the inner and outer body of the machine, cleaning the lid and sealing ring with warm water and mild detergent, making sure the steam release and float valve areas are clean, and cleaning the inner pot thoroughly. Never immerse the body of the Instant Pot® in water. Use a damp cloth to clean off any food or debris.

Safety

Always unplug your Instant Pot® when it is not in use, inspecting the power cord on a regular basis for damage, discoloration, or other defects. Wipe down the power cord and prongs to remove any dust or debris on a regular basis. Never use the Instant Pot® if it has a burning smell or is heating abnormally. If the power cord is ever hot, carefully unplug it and do not use the machine. If there is ever any damage, if you notice any changes to the lights and sounds of the machine, or if it is not cooking properly, you should discontinue use and contact the Instant Pot® support center for assistance.

CHAPTER 2

Light and Healthy Breakfasts

Hard-Boiled Eggs

These Hard-Boiled Eggs come out perfectly every time when you use the Instant Pot®! You can find egg holders designed to fit inside your Instant Pot® online, or you can just use the rack that comes with your machine.

INGREDIENTS | YIELDS 12 EGGS

12 large eggs

1 cup water

Large bowl ice water

1. Place rack or egg holder in Instant Pot®. Arrange eggs on rack or holder, then add water. Close lid and set steam release to Sealing. Press Manual and adjust cook time to 5 minutes.

2. Once cooking is complete let machine sit on Keep Warm 5 minutes, then quick-release any remaining pressure. Carefully remove eggs and place into bowl of ice water. Let stand in ice water 10 minutes, then remove, peel shells, and serve, or store in refrigerator until ready to use, up to one week.

PER SERVING Calories: 72 | Fat: 4.5g | Protein: 6g | Sodium: 71mg | Fiber: 0g | Carbohydrates: 0g | Sugar: 0g

Quinoa Yogurt Breakfast Bowls

These breakfast bowls are wonderful warm, but you can also prepare them in advance, layering the quinoa and fruit into jars for breakfasts on the go. Mix up the fruit and nuts for more flavors!

INGREDIENTS | SERVES 6

2 cups quinoa, rinsed and drained

4 cups water

1 teaspoon vanilla extract

¼ teaspoon salt

2 cups plain Greek yogurt

2 cups fresh blueberries

1 cup toasted almonds

½ cup pure maple syrup

1. Place quinoa, water, vanilla, and salt in Instant Pot®. Close lid and set steam release to Sealing. Press Rice and adjust cook time to 12 minutes.

2. Once cooking is complete allow pressure to release naturally, about 20 minutes. Once pressure has released, remove lid and fluff quinoa.

3. Stir in yogurt. Serve warm in six bowls, topped with berries, almonds, and maple syrup.

PER SERVING Calories: 495 | Fat: 18g | Protein: 16g | Sodium: 146mg | Fiber: 8g | Carbohydrates: 70g | Sugar: 25g

Poached Eggs

Silicone cupcake liners, or a silicone egg poaching tray designed to fit in your Instant Pot®, are all you need for easy, perfectly poached eggs for any occasion.

INGREDIENTS | YIELDS 6 EGGS

1 tablespoon unsalted butter, melted

6 large eggs

1 cup water

Is It Really Poached?

Technically, a steamed egg is not really poached. To poach, you need to add a whole egg to simmering water and cook until it is as done as you like. The Instant Pot® will technically steam your eggs, but this method yields similar results to traditional poaching, plus all your eggs are cooked at the same time, and to the same level of doneness.

1. Brush silicone cupcake liners or poaching tray with melted butter. Crack eggs into cups.

2. Place rack in Instant Pot® and add water. Place cups or poaching tray onto rack. Close lid and set steam release to Sealing. Press Steam and adjust cook time to your desired level of doneness—2 minutes for very soft eggs, 3 minutes for firm whites with runny yolks, 4 minutes for firm whites and yolks just starting to set, or 5 minutes for firm whites and yolks.

3. Once cooking is complete quick-release steam and remove lid. Remove eggs carefully and slide from silicone cups onto serving plates. Serve immediately.

PER SERVING Calories: 71 | Fat: 4.5g | Protein: 6g | Sodium: 71mg | Fiber: 0g | Carbohydrates: 0g | Sugar: 0g

Basic Steel-Cut Oats

Steel-cut oats are less processed than rolled oats, and when cooked on the stove, they require a lot of babysitting. These steel-cut oats take about the same time to make as the stovetop version, but here you just press a button and walk away!

INGREDIENTS | SERVES 4

2 cups steel-cut oats

5 cups water

1 tablespoon unsalted butter

¼ teaspoon salt

1. Place all ingredients in Instant Pot®. Stir well. Close lid and set steam release to Sealing. Press Manual and adjust cook time to 4 minutes.

2. Once cooking is complete allow pressure to release naturally, about 20 minutes, then remove lid and stir well. Serve hot.

PER SERVING Calories: 178 | Fat: 5.5g | Protein: 5g | Sodium: 157mg | Fiber: 4g | Carbohydrates: 27g | Sugar: 0g

No-Crust Vegetable Quiche

This vegetarian and gluten-free breakfast is great for brunch and holidays and can be made ahead of time. Just warm slices in the oven or microwave for a hot breakfast anytime!

INGREDIENTS | SERVES 6

1 tablespoon unsalted butter

1 medium yellow onion, peeled and chopped

1 medium green bell pepper, seeded and chopped

2 cups sliced button mushrooms

2 cups fresh baby spinach

1 cup water

2 cups shredded sharp Cheddar cheese

8 large eggs

½ cup whole milk

2 tablespoons chopped fresh chives

½ teaspoon salt

½ teaspoon ground black pepper

½ teaspoon hot sauce

Utensil Hacks

You can fashion an aluminum foil sling for easy retrieval if you don't have a pair of plate retriever tongs. Fold a 10" × 10" square of aluminum foil in half. Place sling under the bowl or pan before cooking so that you can easily lift up the heated dish by the foil when cooking is complete.

1. Press Sauté on Instant Pot®. Once machine indicates Hot, add butter and let heat 30 seconds, then add onion, bell pepper, and mushrooms. Cook until tender, about 8 minutes.

2. Add spinach and stir until wilted, about 3 minutes. Press Cancel and transfer vegetables to a large bowl to cool. Wipe out inner pot to remove any large pieces left behind.

3. Place rack in Instant Pot® and add water. Fold a long piece of aluminum foil in half. Lay foil over rack to form a sling.

4. Spray an 8" × 8" baking dish with nonstick cooking spray. Add vegetables and cheese to prepared baking dish. Mix well.

5. In a separate large bowl mix eggs, milk, chives, salt, black pepper, and hot sauce until well combined. Pour over vegetable mixture and gently place dish in Instant Pot®. Cover loosely with aluminum foil to protect quiche from condensation inside pot.

6. Close lid and set steam release to Sealing. Press Manual and adjust cook time to 30 minutes. Once cooking is complete allow pressure to release naturally, about 15 minutes. Remove lid. Let stand 15 minutes before carefully removing dish from pot using sling.

7. Run a thin knife around edge of quiche, then turn out onto a serving platter. Serve warm.

PER SERVING Calories: 322 | Fat: 23g | Protein: 21g | Sodium: 592mg | Fiber: 1g | Carbohydrates: 6g | Sugar: 3g

Basic Oatmeal

Nothing is more comforting than a simple bowl of oatmeal in the morning. This method takes you away from the stove, so you can get on with your morning while your breakfast cooks on its own!

INGREDIENTS | SERVES 4

4 cups water

2 cups rolled oats

1 tablespoon unsalted butter

¼ teaspoon salt

Adding Extra Flavor

When you think of adding flavor to oatmeal, you may think of things you add to the top or mix in, but adding flavor starts with your plain raw oats. Instead of just tossing all ingredients into your pot, try toasting your oats first. Melt butter on Sauté, then add oats and toast until they are fragrant, about 5 minutes. Then, add your liquid and proceed as usual.

1. Place all ingredients in Instant Pot®. Stir well. Close lid and set steam release to Sealing. Press Manual and adjust cook time to 4 minutes.

2. Once cooking is complete quick-release steam and remove lid. Stir well, then serve.

PER SERVING Calories: 178 | Fat: 5.5g | Protein: 5g | Sodium: 155mg | Fiber: 4g | Carbohydrates: 27g | Sugar: 0g

Cinnamon Apple Oats

In the summer you can make these oats with fresh peaches and serve with a little heavy cream and a drizzle of honey!

INGREDIENTS | SERVES 4

3 tablespoons unsalted butter

1 crisp apple (Granny Smith, Honeycrisp, or Pink Lady), peeled, cored, and diced

½ teaspoon ground cinnamon

1 cup steel-cut oats

4 cups water

1 cup apple juice

½ teaspoon salt

1. Press Sauté on Instant Pot®. Once machine indicates Hot, add butter and let heat 30 seconds until melted and foaming, then add apples and cinnamon and cook until apples are fragrant, about 2 minutes. Press Cancel.

2. Place remaining ingredients in pot. Stir well. Close lid and set steam release to Sealing. Press Manual and adjust cook time to 5 minutes.

3. Once cooking is complete allow pressure to release naturally 10 minutes, then quick-release remaining pressure. Remove lid and stir well. Serve hot.

PER SERVING Calories: 200 | Fat: 10g | Protein: 3g | Sodium: 302mg | Fiber: 3g | Carbohydrates: 25g | Sugar: 10g

Pumpkin Spice Oatmeal

Nothing says autumn like pumpkin spice. This recipe combines pumpkin purée with the warm spices of fall for a hearty, healthful breakfast!

INGREDIENTS | SERVES 4

2 tablespoons unsalted butter

2 cups rolled oats

½ teaspoon pumpkin pie spice

3 cups water

1 cup pumpkin purée

¼ cup packed light brown sugar

¼ teaspoon salt

Homemade Pumpkin Pie Spice

Sure, you can buy ready-mixed pumpkin pie spice, but making your own is easy and allows for customization. Start by combining 1 tablespoon ground cinnamon, ¾ teaspoon each of ground allspice and ground cloves, and ½ teaspoon ground nutmeg. Mix well and store in an airtight container for up to six months.

1. Press Sauté on Instant Pot®. Once machine indicates Hot, add butter and let heat 30 seconds until melted and foaming, then add oats and cook until oats are fragrant, about 4 minutes. Add pumpkin pie spice and cook 30 seconds until very fragrant. Press Cancel.

2. Place remaining ingredients in pot. Stir well. Close lid and set steam release to Sealing. Press Manual and adjust cook time to 4 minutes.

3. Once cooking is complete allow pressure to release naturally 10 minutes, then quick-release remaining pressure. Remove lid and stir well. Serve hot.

PER SERVING Calories: 246 | Fat: 8g | Protein: 6g | Sodium: 156mg | Fiber: 4g | Carbohydrates: 38g | Sugar: 9g

Vanilla Almond Steel-Cut Oats

If you want to ramp up the almond flavor, you can use 5 cups of almond milk in this recipe. You can also use vanilla almond milk for even more flavor! If you use sweetened almond milk, just be sure to skip the sugar, as it might be too sweet.

INGREDIENTS | SERVES 4

2 cups steel-cut oats

3 cups water

2 cups unsweetened almond milk

¼ cup granulated sugar

2 tablespoons unsalted butter

¼ teaspoon salt

½ cup sliced toasted almonds, cooled

½ teaspoon vanilla extract

1. Place oats, water, almond milk, sugar, butter, and salt in Instant Pot®. Stir well. Close lid and set steam release to Sealing. Press Manual and adjust cook time to 4 minutes.

2. Once cooking is complete allow pressure to release naturally, about 20 minutes, then remove lid, add sliced almonds and vanilla, and stir well. Serve hot.

PER SERVING Calories: 423 | Fat: 19g | Protein: 13g | Sodium: 216mg | Fiber: 7g | Carbohydrates: 51g | Sugar: 18g

Ham and Broccoli Omelet

Leftover spiral ham is perfect in this dish, as is chopped-up ham lunch meat that you want to use up. You can also use frozen broccoli—just be sure to drain it well after steaming.

INGREDIENTS | SERVES 6

2 cups fresh broccoli florets

2 tablespoons plus 1 cup water, divided

2 cups shredded Swiss cheese

2 cups cubed ham

8 large eggs

½ cup half-and-half

½ teaspoon salt

½ teaspoon ground black pepper

½ teaspoon hot sauce

1. Place broccoli and 2 tablespoons water into a large microwave-safe bowl. Cover with plastic wrap, a damp towel, or a microwave-safe lid. Cook 3 minutes until broccoli is bright green and tender. Remove cover and let cool.

2. Place rack in Instant Pot® and add remaining water. Fold a long piece of aluminum foil in half. Lay foil over rack to form a sling.

3. Spray an 8" × 8" baking dish with nonstick cooking spray. Add in broccoli, cheese, and ham. Mix well.

4. In a large bowl mix eggs, half-and-half, salt, pepper, and hot sauce until well combined. Pour over vegetable mixture and gently place dish in Instant Pot®. Cover loosely with aluminum foil to protect quiche from condensation inside pot.

5. Close lid and set steam release to Sealing. Press Manual and adjust cook time to 30 minutes.

6. Once cooking is complete allow pressure to release naturally, about 15 minutes. Remove lid. Let stand 15 minutes before carefully removing dish from pot with sling.

7. Run a thin knife around edge of quiche, then turn out onto a serving platter. Serve warm.

PER SERVING Calories: 375 | Fat: 24g | Protein: 30g | Sodium: 933mg | Fiber: 1g | Carbohydrates: 7g | Sugar: 2g

Sweet Potato Breakfast Bowl

This is a perfect breakfast after an intense morning workout. The flavor-filled protein and good-for-you vegetables will help you tackle the day!

INGREDIENTS | SERVES 4

6 large eggs

1 tablespoon Italian seasoning

½ teaspoon sea salt

½ teaspoon ground black pepper

½ pound ground pork sausage

1 large sweet potato, peeled and cubed

1 small yellow onion, peeled and diced

2 cloves garlic, peeled and minced

1 medium green bell pepper, seeded and diced

2 cups water

1. Lightly coat a 7-cup glass bowl with nonstick cooking spray.

2. In a medium bowl whisk together eggs, Italian seasoning, salt, and pepper. Set aside.

3. Press Sauté on Instant Pot®. Once machine indicates Hot, stir-fry sausage, sweet potato, onion, garlic, and bell pepper until onions are translucent, about 5 minutes. Press Cancel.

4. Transfer sausage mixture to greased bowl. Pour whisked eggs over sausage mixture.

5. Add water to pot and insert rack. Place dish on rack. Close lid and set steam release to Sealing. Press Manual and adjust cook time to 5 minutes.

6. Once cooking is complete quick-release steam, then remove lid. Remove dish from pot and let sit 10 minutes to allow eggs to set. Serve.

PER SERVING Calories: 362 | Fat: 24g | Protein: 23g | Sodium: 471mg | Fiber: 2g | Carbohydrates: 11g | Sugar: 3g

Honey Walnut Quinoa

Top this breakfast treat with additional coconut milk and a drizzle of honey. If you are not a fan of walnuts, feel free to substitute pecans or almonds or omit the nuts entirely.

INGREDIENTS | SERVES 4

1½ cups quinoa, rinsed and drained
2 cups unsweetened almond milk
1⅓ cups water
⅓ cup honey
1 teaspoon vanilla extract
½ teaspoon ground cinnamon
¼ teaspoon salt
1 cup toasted chopped walnuts

1. Place all ingredients except walnuts in Instant Pot®. Close lid and set steam release to Sealing. Press Rice and adjust cook time to 12 minutes.

2. Once cooking is complete allow pressure to release naturally, about 20 minutes. Once pressure has released, remove lid.

3. Add walnuts and fluff quinoa. Serve warm.

PER SERVING Calories: 555 | Fat: 24g | Protein: 17g | Sodium: 195mg | Fiber: 7g | Carbohydrates: 70g | Sugar: 24g

Cocoa Quinoa Breakfast Bowl

This recipe is great for kids because they can decorate their bowls with their favorite toppings! Sliced bananas, strawberries, raspberries, and toasted nuts are all excellent choices, as is an extra splash of coconut milk!

INGREDIENTS | SERVES 6

2 cups quinoa, rinsed and drained
1 (15-ounce) can unsweetened full-fat coconut milk
2 cups water
¼ cup packed light brown sugar
3 tablespoons cocoa powder
1 teaspoon vanilla extract
¼ teaspoon salt
¼ cup semisweet chocolate chips

1. Place all ingredients except chocolate chips in Instant Pot®. Close lid and set steam release to Sealing. Press Rice and adjust cook time to 12 minutes.

2. Once cooking is complete allow pressure to release naturally, about 20 minutes. Once pressure has released, remove lid, add chocolate chips, and mix until chocolate is melted. Serve warm.

PER SERVING Calories: 413 | Fat: 21g | Protein: 10g | Sodium: 114mg | Fiber: 5g | Carbohydrates: 50g | Sugar: 10g

Coconut Quinoa Porridge

Quinoa has a delightfully nutty flavor that pairs well with the flavor of coconut. Adding a garnish of freshly toasted shredded coconut to the porridge would be the perfect flourish for special occasions.

INGREDIENTS | SERVES 4

1½ cups quinoa, rinsed and drained

1 (15-ounce) can unsweetened full-fat coconut milk

1½ cups water

¼ cup packed light brown sugar

1 teaspoon vanilla extract

½ teaspoon cardamom

¼ teaspoon salt

1. Place all ingredients in Instant Pot®. Close lid and set steam release to Sealing. Press Rice and adjust cook time to 12 minutes.

2. Once cooking is complete allow pressure to release naturally, about 20 minutes. Once pressure has released, remove lid.

3. Fluff quinoa and serve warm.

PER SERVING Calories: 479 | Fat: 26g | Protein: 11g | Sodium: 167mg | Fiber: 4.5g | Carbohydrates: 52g | Sugar: 8g

Eggs Poached in Chili Sauce

These eggs are cooked in a homemade chili sauce, but you can also swap the homemade sauce out for your favorite bottled chili sauce. This dish is spectacular over grits or toasted crusty bread covered in plenty of butter.

INGREDIENTS | SERVES 6

2 tablespoons unsalted butter

1 medium yellow onion, peeled and chopped

1 clove garlic, peeled and minced

1 (15-ounce) can tomato purée

2 medium tomatoes, seeded and diced

¼ cup packed light brown sugar

3 tablespoons apple cider vinegar

1 tablespoon horseradish

¼ teaspoon ground allspice

½ teaspoon salt

½ teaspoon ground black pepper

6 large eggs

1. Press Sauté on Instant Pot®. Once machine indicates Hot, add butter and let heat 30 seconds, then add onion. Cook until onion is tender, about 5 minutes, then add garlic and cook until fragrant, about 30 seconds. Add tomato purée, diced tomatoes, brown sugar, vinegar, horseradish, allspice, salt, and pepper and stir well. Once mixture starts to bubble, about 5 minutes, press Cancel.

2. Carefully crack eggs into sauce, making sure eggs are spaced out evenly. Close lid and set steam release to Sealing. Press Manual, set pressure to Low, and adjust cook time to 0 minutes.

3. Once cooking is complete quick-release steam, open lid, and serve.

PER SERVING Calories: 172 | Fat: 8g | Protein: 8g | Sodium: 411mg | Fiber: 2g | Carbohydrates: 16g | Sugar: 11g

Instant Pot® Yogurt

Homemade yogurt is wonderful for many reasons, not least of which is how inexpensive it is to make! Use this yogurt for breakfast bowls or for making cakes, sauces, or marinades! Just be sure to sterilize all equipment, including your digital thermometer, whisk, storage jars, and the inner pot beforehand with boiling water.

INGREDIENTS | SERVES 6

8 cups whole milk

Large bowl ice water

2 tablespoons plain yogurt with live active cultures

Greek Yogurt

You can transform your traditional Instant Pot® Yogurt into Greek-style yogurt by transferring the prepared and cooled yogurt into a fine-mesh strainer lined with a few layers of cheesecloth or a coffee filter. Place strainer over a bowl, cover with plastic wrap, and refrigerate overnight. The next day transfer the thickened yogurt to an airtight container and discard water and cheesecloth.

1. Place milk in Instant Pot®. Close lid and set steam release to Sealing. Press Yogurt and press Adjust until Boil is indicated.

2. Once cooking is complete quick-release steam, then remove lid. Check temperature with digital thermometer to ensure it is at 180°F.

3. Remove any skin on milk. Place inner pot into large bowl of ice water, whisking occasionally without scraping the bottom or sides of pot, until milk reaches 110°F, about 7 minutes. Lift pot from ice bath and dry thoroughly.

4. In a medium bowl add 1 cup milk to prepared yogurt and whisk well. Stir mixture into remaining milk. Place inner pot back into machine and close lid. Press Yogurt and adjust cook time to 10 hours for thicker yogurt or 8 hours for thinner yogurt.

5. Once cooking is complete remove lid and transfer yogurt to storage containers and refrigerate until well chilled, about 4 hours.

PER SERVING Calories: 198 | Fat: 10g | Protein: 10g | Sodium: 139mg | Fiber: 0g | Carbohydrates: 15g | Sugar: 16g

Instant Pot® Coconut Yogurt

This homemade yogurt is perfect for people on vegan diets or for those who are avoiding dairy. It has a mild, tangy coconut flavor. If you are unable to find coconut cream, you can substitute unsweetened full-fat coconut milk. The texture will be a little thinner, so you can thicken with agar or xanthan gum if you like.

INGREDIENTS | SERVES 6

2 (15-ounce) cans unsweetened coconut cream

Large bowl ice water

1 teaspoon (about 4 capsules) probiotic powder

Yogurt Culture

This recipe uses probiotic supplement capsules because they are easy to source in almost every drugstore and grocery store. Many health food stores and nutrition markets also have yogurt culture available. You can use yogurt culture here if you prefer; just follow the directions on the package for the volume of coconut cream called for in this recipe.

1. Place coconut cream in Instant Pot®. Press Sauté and cook, whisking often, until coconut cream reaches 180°F, about 8 minutes.

2. Place inner pot into large bowl of ice water, whisking occasionally without scraping the bottom or sides of pot, until coconut cream reaches 110°F, about 7 minutes, on a digital thermometer. Lift pot from ice bath and dry thoroughly.

3. In a medium bowl add 1 cup coconut cream to probiotic powder and whisk well. Stir mixture into remaining cream in inner pot and place back into machine and close lid. Press Cancel, then press Yogurt and adjust cook time to 10 hours for thicker yogurt or 8 hours for thinner yogurt.

4. Once cooking is complete remove lid and transfer yogurt to storage containers and refrigerate until well chilled, about 4 hours.

PER SERVING Calories: 322 | Fat: 33g | Protein: 3g | Sodium: 21mg | Fiber: 3g | Carbohydrates: 7g | Sugar: 4.5g

Millet and Oat Porridge

Millet is a staple grain used around the world for meals all day long—from breakfast to dinner. With its mild flavor, millet is an excellent canvas for letting other flavors shine!

INGREDIENTS | SERVES 4

½ cup millet
½ cup rolled oats
2½ cups unsweetened almond milk
2 tablespoons packed light brown sugar
1 tablespoon unsalted butter
¼ teaspoon ground cinnamon
¼ teaspoon salt
½ teaspoon vanilla extract

1. Place all ingredients except vanilla in Instant Pot®. Stir well. Close lid and set steam release to Sealing. Press Manual and adjust cook time to 6 minutes.

2. Once cooking is complete allow pressure to release naturally, about 20 minutes, then remove lid, add vanilla, and stir well. Serve hot.

PER SERVING Calories: 227 | Fat: 7g | Protein: 8.5g | Sodium: 202mg | Fiber: 4g | Carbohydrates: 32g | Sugar: 5g

Cheesy Steamed Egg Bites

These are similar to the egg bites served at popular coffee and breakfast chains. Feel free to customize them to your taste with sautéed vegetables, diced meat, or mixed cheeses. If you want, you can also make these ahead and warm them in the oven or microwave.

INGREDIENTS | YIELDS 6 EGGS

1 tablespoon unsalted butter, melted
½ cup shredded Gruyère cheese
6 large eggs
1 tablespoon chopped fresh chives
¼ teaspoon ground black pepper
1 cup water

1. Brush silicone cupcake liners or silicone poaching tray with melted butter. Divide cheese into prepared cups.

2. In a medium bowl with a pour spout combine eggs, chives, and pepper. Mix well.

3. Place rack in Instant Pot® and add water. Place prepared cupcake liners or poaching tray onto rack. Pour egg mixture into cups. Close lid and set steam release to Sealing. Press Steam and adjust cook time to 5 minutes.

4. Once cooking is complete quick-release steam and remove lid. Remove eggs carefully and slide from silicone cups onto serving plates. Serve warm.

PER SERVING Calories: 134 | Fat: 10g | Protein: 9.5g | Sodium: 151mg | Fiber: 0g | Carbohydrates: 0g

Buckwheat Porridge

Buckwheat groats are the hulled seed of the buckwheat plant. You can use buckwheat groats in salads, mixed into stuffings and dressings, or milled into flour for baking.

INGREDIENTS | SERVES 4

1 cup rinsed raw buckwheat groats

3 cups unsweetened almond milk

½ cup raisins

3 tablespoons packed light brown sugar

1 tablespoon unsalted butter

¼ teaspoon ground cinnamon

¼ teaspoon salt

½ teaspoon vanilla extract

1. Place all ingredients except vanilla in Instant Pot®. Stir well. Close lid and set steam release to Sealing. Press Manual and adjust cook time to 6 minutes.

2. Once cooking is complete allow pressure to release naturally, about 20 minutes, then remove lid, add vanilla, and stir well. Serve hot.

PER SERVING Calories: 309 | Fat: 7g | Protein: 10g | Sodium: 218mg | Fiber: 6g | Carbohydrates: 54g | Sugar: 18g

Korean-Style Steamed Eggs

This Korean egg dish is often served with rice for breakfast, lunch, or dinner. You can dress up this recipe by adding a variety of different fillings, such as diced red bell peppers, mushrooms, zucchini, and onions.

INGREDIENTS | SERVES 4

4 large eggs

1¾ cups water, divided

1 teaspoon soy sauce

¼ teaspoon red pepper flakes

1 green onion, peeled and thinly sliced

¼ teaspoon toasted sesame seeds

1. In a heat-safe ceramic bowl that fits inside your Instant Pot®, whisk together eggs, ¾ cup water, soy sauce, red pepper, and green onion until foamy, about 20 seconds.

2. Place rack in Instant Pot® and add remaining 1 cup water. Place bowl with egg mixture onto rack, close lid and set steam release to Sealing. Press Steam and adjust cook time to 4 minutes.

3. Once cooking is complete quick-release steam. Remove lid and carefully remove eggs from pot, top with sesame seeds, and serve hot.

PER SERVING Calories: 73 | Fat: 4.5g | Protein: 6g | Sodium: 74mg | Fiber: 0g | Carbohydrates: 0g | Sugar: 0g

CHAPTER 3

Hearty Breakfasts

Cheese Grits

Cheese Grits are a staple of the Southern table and can be found there morning, noon, and night. Leftover grits can be reheated in the microwave or cut and panfried for grits cakes.

INGREDIENTS | SERVES 6

4 tablespoons unsalted butter

½ medium yellow onion, peeled and chopped

1 cup corn grits

3 cups water

¼ cup heavy whipping cream

1 cup shredded sharp Cheddar cheese

Benefits of Fresh-Shredded Cheese

Ready-shredded cheese at the grocery store is certainly convenient, but it also has added anti-caking agents to keep the cheese from clumping. These agents can have a negative effect on your recipes, giving the finished product a slightly gritty texture. It may take a few more minutes, but using fresh-shredded cheese will yield a better texture and flavor.

1. Press Sauté on Instant Pot®. Once machine indicates Hot, about 3 minutes, add butter and melt 30 seconds, then add onion. Cook, stirring often until tender, about 3 minutes.

2. Add grits and cook 1 minute, then add water and stir well. Press Cancel, close lid, and set steam release to Sealing. Press Manual and adjust cook time to 7 minutes.

3. Once cooking is complete allow pressure to release naturally, about 10 minutes. Remove lid and add cream and shredded cheese. Stir until smooth. Serve hot.

PER SERVING Calories: 294 | Fat: 19g | Protein: 8g | Sodium: 150mg | Fiber: 0.5g | Carbohydrates: 23g | Sugar: 1g

Brown Sugar and Butter Grits

Sweet grits make a tasty breakfast and a nice change of pace from other breakfast porridges. Serve these grits with extra brown sugar, butter, and fresh cream for topping.

INGREDIENTS | SERVES 6

5 tablespoons unsalted butter

1 cup corn grits

3 cups water

⅓ cup packed light brown sugar

½ teaspoon salt

½ cup heavy whipping cream

1. Add all ingredients except cream to Instant Pot® and stir well. Close lid and set steam release to Sealing. Press Manual and adjust cook time to 7 minutes.

2. Once cooking is complete allow pressure to release naturally, about 10 minutes. Remove lid and stir in cream. Serve hot.

PER SERVING Calories: 282 | Fat: 17g | Protein: 3g | Sodium: 208mg | Fiber: 0.5g | Carbohydrates: 30g | Sugar: 8.5g

Sausage Gravy

Sausage gravy makes a welcome addition to any breakfast table. You can use it to smother biscuits or top eggs or as a dipping side for breakfast potatoes.

INGREDIENTS | SERVES 6

1 pound breakfast sausage

¼ cup all-purpose flour

½ teaspoon salt

½ teaspoon ground black pepper

2 cups whole milk

1. Press Sauté on Instant Pot®. Once machine indicates Hot, about 3 minutes add sausage. Cook, browning well and crumbling, about 10 minutes.

2. Add flour, salt, and pepper to pot and mix until flour is completely moistened with sausage drippings, about 1 minute. Press Cancel and whisk in milk.

3. Close lid and set steam release to Sealing. Press Manual and adjust cook time to 2 minutes. Once cooking is complete quick-release pressure, remove lid, and stir well. Serve warm.

PER SERVING Calories: 244 | Fat: 16g | Protein: 15g | Sodium: 706mg | Fiber: 0g | Carbohydrates: 9g | Sugar: 4g

Giant Blueberry Pancake

This Japanese-style pancake tastes like your traditional pancake, but it is much fluffier and has a slightly crisp, browned top. Feel free to substitute chocolate chips, strawberries, raspberries, or chopped nuts for the blueberries.

INGREDIENTS | SERVES 6

2 cups all-purpose flour

2½ teaspoons baking powder

2 tablespoons granulated sugar

¼ teaspoon salt

2 large eggs

1½ cups whole milk

½ teaspoon vanilla extract

½ cup blueberries

6 tablespoons unsalted butter

½ cup pure maple syrup

Sinking Berries?

Do you find when baking that ingredients like blueberries, chocolate chips, and nuts sink to the bottom? There is a simple trick to help prevent this. Just coat the ingredient you are planning to mix into your batter in a little all-purpose flour. For each cup of additions, you will need about 1 tablespoon of flour. Coat the ingredients well and then mix in as usual!

1. Spray inside of Instant Pot® liner with nonstick cooking spray.

2. In a medium bowl combine flour, baking powder, sugar, and salt. Whisk well to combine.

3. In a separate medium bowl combine eggs, milk, and vanilla. Mix well. Pour wet ingredients into dry ingredients and stir until just mixed, about six strokes. Add blueberries and fold to combine.

4. Pour batter into liner, close lid, and set steam release to Sealing. Press Manual, set pressure to Low, and adjust cook time to 45 minutes.

5. Once cooking is complete allow pressure to release naturally and remove lid. Pancake should spring back in center when gently pressed. Gently loosen pancake from sides of pot, then turn out onto serving platter. Serve hot with butter and syrup.

PER SERVING Calories: 409 | Fat: 15g | Protein: 8.5g | Sodium: 355mg | Fiber: 1.5g | Carbohydrates: 59g | Sugar: 24g

French Toast Casserole

You can fold in diced apples, raisins, or chopped nuts to make this breakfast treat your own. Maple syrup, confectioners' sugar, or even freshly whipped cream make excellent toppings.

INGREDIENTS | SERVES 6

1 cup water

7 cups cubed stale bread

1 cup whole milk

¼ cup heavy cream

⅓ cup packed light brown sugar

2 large eggs

2 tablespoons unsalted butter, melted

½ teaspoon ground cinnamon

½ teaspoon vanilla extract

Best Bread for French Toast

You can make French toast with just about any bread, but some breads are a little better than others. For extradecadent French toast use stale brioche bread or croissants. For an extra burst of flavor, you can use cinnamon raisin or chocolate chip bread. If you want a little more texture, try a crusty bread like ciabatta or a baguette.

1. Spray an 8" × 8" baking dish with nonstick cooking spray.

2. Place rack inside Instant Pot® and add water. Fold a long piece of aluminum foil in half. Lay foil over rack to form a sling.

3. In a large bowl add bread cubes. Set aside.

4. In a separate large bowl combine milk, cream, brown sugar, eggs, butter, cinnamon, and vanilla. Whisk well, then pour over bread cubes. Gently mix to coat. Let stand 10 minutes, turning mixture once after 5 minutes.

5. Transfer bread mixture to prepared dish. Loosely cover with another piece of aluminum foil and place in Instant Pot®. Close lid and set steam release to Sealing, then press Manual and adjust cook time to 30 minutes.

6. Once cooking is complete allow pressure to release naturally, about 15 minutes. Press Cancel and allow casserole to cool 20 minutes uncovered. Carefully remove casserole from pot with sling and turn out onto a serving dish. Serve warm.

PER SERVING Calories: 311 | Fat: 14g | Protein: 21g | Sodium: 324mg | Fiber: 3.5g | Carbohydrates: 94g | Sugar: 17g

Butter Pecan French Toast Casserole

The butter and pecan topping of this French toast dish melts while cooking. Some soaks into the bread, but some stays on top, making a buttery, sweet sauce!

INGREDIENTS | SERVES 6

1 cup water

7 cups cubed stale bread

¾ cup whole milk

½ cup heavy cream

¼ cup granulated sugar

2 large eggs

2 tablespoons unsalted butter, melted

½ teaspoon vanilla extract

3 tablespoons unsalted butter, chilled and cubed

3 tablespoons packed light brown sugar

½ cup chopped pecans

¼ teaspoon ground cinnamon

Pecans

Did you know that pecans are not a nut? They are a drupe, which means they're related to apricots, mangoes, olives, plums, cherries, and peaches! As the pecan develops, the soft outer layer of the fruit splits into four sections, exposing the hard inner shell containing the pecan. Pecans are harvested in the late fall and are not picked but rather gathered from the ground.

1. Spray an 8" × 8" baking dish with nonstick cooking spray.

2. Place rack inside Instant Pot® and add water. Fold a long piece of aluminum foil in half. Lay foil over rack to form a sling.

3. In a large bowl add bread cubes. Set aside.

4. In a separate large bowl combine milk, cream, granulated sugar, eggs, melted butter, and vanilla. Whisk well, then pour over bread cubes. Gently mix to coat. Let stand 10 minutes, turning over once after 5 minutes.

5. While bread soaks, combine cubed butter, brown sugar, pecans, and cinnamon in a small bowl with a fork until crumbly. Set aside.

6. Transfer bread mixture to prepared dish. Top with pecan mixture. Loosely cover with another piece of aluminum foil and place in pot. Close lid and set steam release to Sealing, then press Manual and adjust cook time to 30 minutes.

7. Once cooking is complete allow pressure to release naturally, about 15 minutes. Press Cancel and allow casserole to cool 20 minutes uncovered. Carefully remove casserole from pot with sling and spoon into six bowls. Serve warm.

PER SERVING Calories: 393 | Fat: 26g | Protein: 8g | Sodium: 203mg | Fiber: 1.5g | Carbohydrates: 33g | Sugar: 16g

Denver Omelet

Instead of making multiple omelets for a crowd and working at the stove all morning, impress your guests with a giant fluffy, sliceable omelet that frees you up to relax!

INGREDIENTS | SERVES 4

1 tablespoon unsalted butter

1 medium yellow onion, peeled and chopped

1 medium green bell pepper, seeded and chopped

1 cup diced cooked ham

1 cup water

2 cups shredded sharp Cheddar cheese

8 large eggs

½ cup whole milk

2 tablespoons chopped fresh chives

½ teaspoon salt

½ teaspoon ground black pepper

½ cup sour cream

½ cup salsa

1. Press Sauté on Instant Pot®. Once machine indicates Hot, add butter and let heat 30 seconds, then add onion, bell pepper, and ham. Cook until tender and ham is lightly browned, about 8 minutes. Press Cancel and transfer mixture to a medium bowl to cool. Wipe out inner pot to remove any large pieces left behind.

2. Place rack in pot and add water. Fold a long piece of aluminum foil in half. Lay foil over rack to form a sling.

3. Spray an 8" × 8" baking dish with nonstick cooking spray. Add vegetable mixture to dish, then top with cheese.

4. In a large bowl mix eggs, milk, chives, salt, and black pepper until well combined. Pour over vegetable mixture and gently place in pot. Cover loosely with aluminum foil to protect eggs from condensation inside pot.

5. Close lid and set steam release to Sealing, then press Manual and adjust cook time to 30 minutes. Once cooking is complete allow pressure to release naturally, about 15 minutes. Remove lid. Let stand 15 minutes before carefully removing dish from pot with sling.

6. Run a thin knife around edge of dish, then turn out onto a serving platter. Serve warm with sour cream and salsa.

PER SERVING Calories: 585 | Fat: 43g | Protein: 37g | Sodium: 1,587mg | Fiber: 1.5g | Carbohydrates: 11g | Sugar: 6g

Ham and Cheese Mini-Omelets

Silicone cupcake liners make these omelets perfectly single portion–sized. Kids and adults alike will love these cheesy on-the-go breakfasts! You can also replace the ham with cooked bacon, sausage, or leftovers from the night before.

INGREDIENTS | YIELDS 6 OMELETS

1 tablespoon unsalted butter, melted

¼ cup shredded Swiss cheese

¼ cup shredded Cheddar cheese

½ cup cubed cooked ham

6 large eggs

¼ teaspoon salt

¼ teaspoon ground black pepper

1 cup water

Silicone Baking Dishes

Silicone baking dishes are perfect for the Instant Pot® since they are heat-safe. While they are also naturally nonstick, it is still a good idea to brush them with a little melted butter or oil. Better safe than sorry! You can find a full range of silicone baking dishes and baking cups for your Instant Pot® at most home goods stores.

1. Brush six silicone muffin cups with melted butter. Divide cheese and ham into prepared cups.

2. In a large bowl with a pour spout combine eggs, salt, and pepper.

3. Place rack in Instant Pot® and add water. Place prepared muffin cups onto rack. Pour egg mixture into cups. Close lid and set steam release to Sealing. Press Steam and adjust cook time to 5 minutes.

4. Once cooking is complete quick-release steam and remove lid. Remove eggs carefully and slide from silicone cups onto serving plates. Serve warm.

PER SERVING Calories: 150 | Fat: 11g | Protein: 11g | Sodium: 357mg | Fiber: 0g | Carbohydrates: 1g | Sugar: 0g

Roasted Vegetable and Swiss Omelet

This recipe calls for frozen roasted peppers, thawed, but you can also use leftover vegetables from dinner the night before, or you can buy roasted vegetables from your deli or salad bar too!

INGREDIENTS | SERVES 4

1 tablespoon unsalted butter

1 medium white onion, peeled and chopped

2 cups frozen roasted pepper blend, thawed

1 clove garlic, peeled and minced

1 cup water

2 cups shredded Swiss cheese

8 large eggs

½ cup half-and-half

½ teaspoon smoked paprika

½ teaspoon salt

½ teaspoon ground black pepper

1. Press Sauté on Instant Pot®. Once machine indicates Hot, add butter and let heat 30 seconds, then add onion. Cook until tender, about 8 minutes. Add thawed peppers and garlic and cook until garlic is fragrant, about 1 minute. Press Cancel and transfer mixture to a medium bowl to cool. Wipe out inner pot to remove any large pieces left behind.

2. Place rack in pot and add water. Fold a long piece of aluminum foil in half. Lay foil over rack to form a sling.

3. Spray an 8" × 8" baking dish with nonstick cooking spray. Add vegetable mixture to prepared dish, then top with cheese.

4. In a large bowl mix eggs, half-and-half, paprika, salt, and pepper until well combined. Pour over vegetable mixture and gently place in pot. Cover loosely with aluminum foil to protect eggs from condensation inside pot.

5. Close lid and set steam release to Sealing. Press Manual and adjust cook time to 30 minutes. Once cooking is complete allow pressure to release naturally, about 15 minutes. Remove lid. Let stand 15 minutes before carefully removing dish from pot with sling.

6. Run a thin knife around edge of dish, then turn out onto a serving platter. Serve warm.

PER SERVING Calories: 472 | Fat: 34g | Protein: 31g | Sodium: 494mg | Fiber: 0g | Carbohydrates: 8g | Sugar: 3g

Sticky Bun Oatmeal

This decadent breakfast treat is topped with cream cheese drizzle, caramel sauce, and extra cinnamon. If you like nuts, you can add toasted pecans or walnuts as a fun, crunchy topping!

INGREDIENTS | SERVES 4

4 cups water

2 cups rolled oats

3 tablespoons unsalted butter

½ teaspoon plus ¼ teaspoon ground cinnamon, divided

¼ teaspoon salt

1 (8-ounce) package cream cheese

¼ cup salted butter, room temperature

½ cup confectioners' sugar

½ teaspoon vanilla extract

½ cup caramel sauce

1. Place water, oats, unsalted butter, ½ teaspoon cinnamon, and salt in Instant Pot®. Stir well. Close lid and set steam release to Sealing. Press Manual and adjust cook time to 4 minutes.

2. While oatmeal cooks combine cream cheese, salted butter, sugar, and vanilla in a medium bowl. Mix until smooth.

3. Once cooking is complete quick-release steam and remove lid. Stir well. Top bowl of hot oatmeal with cream cheese mixture, caramel, and remaining cinnamon. Stir and serve hot.

PER SERVING Calories: 658 | Fat: 32g | Protein: 7g | Sodium: 355mg | Fiber: 4g | Carbohydrates: 88g | Sugar: 61g

Basic Grits

No need to stand at the stove and slave over grits. These grits are great for breakfast, or they can be served with shrimp, sausage, or short ribs for a hearty dinner side dish.

INGREDIENTS | SERVES 6

4 tablespoons unsalted butter

1 cup corn grits

3 cups water

½ teaspoon salt

1. Add all ingredients to Instant Pot® and stir well. Close lid and set steam release to Sealing. Press Manual and adjust cook time to 7 minutes.

2. Once cooking is complete allow pressure to release naturally, about 10 minutes. Remove lid and stir. Serve hot.

PER SERVING Calories: 166 | Fat: 8g | Protein: 2.5g | Sodium: 198mg | Fiber: 0g | Carbohydrates: 21g | Sugar: 0g

Cheesy Potatoes and Eggs

If you prefer, you can use frozen shredded hash browns here; just be sure to defrost them and drain off any excess liquid. For extra flavor, you can brown the hash browns in a little butter before assembling the casserole.

INGREDIENTS | SERVES 6

½ pound breakfast sausage

½ medium yellow onion, peeled and chopped

1 cup peeled shredded russet potatoes

1 cup shredded Cheddar cheese, divided

8 large eggs

¼ cup heavy cream

¼ teaspoon salt

¼ teaspoon ground black pepper

1 tablespoon chopped fresh chives

1 cup water

Keeping Potatoes White

Just like apples, potatoes will turn brown if you cut them and let them sit too long, as they contain an enzyme that oxidizes rapidly when exposed to air. The easiest way to stop cut or shredded potatoes from turning brown is to put them into cold water. With this trick, you can cut or shred potatoes up to a day ahead of your recipe.

1. Press Sauté on Instant Pot®. Once machine indicates Hot, about 3 minutes, add sausage. Cook, crumbling, until no pink remains, about 5 minutes. Add onion and cook until sausage is browned and onion is tender, about 2 minutes. Press Cancel.

2. Spray an 8" × 8" baking dish with nonstick cooking spray. Transfer sausage mixture to prepared dish and clean out inner pot. Top mixture with potatoes and ½ cup cheese.

3. In a large bowl combine eggs, cream, salt, and pepper. Mix well, then add chives and whisk to mix. Pour egg mixture over sausage mixture.

4. Place rack in Instant Pot® and add water. Fold a long piece of aluminum foil in half. Lay foil over rack to form a sling. Place dish on rack and cover loosely with foil. Close lid and set steam release to Sealing, then press Manual and adjust cook time to 30 minutes.

5. Once cooking is complete allow pressure to release naturally, about 15 minutes. Remove lid. Let stand 15 minutes before carefully removing dish from pot with sling.

6. Run a thin knife around edge of dish, then turn out onto a serving platter and top with reserved cheese. Serve warm.

PER SERVING Calories: 330 | Fat: 24g | Protein: 20g | Sodium: 578mg | Fiber: 0.5g | Carbohydrates: 7g | Sugar: 1g

Layered Breakfast Taco Casserole

You can add a variety of different meats to this casserole to use up leftovers, including shredded chicken, taco meat, brisket, or shredded pork. This dish is also perfect if you like breakfast for dinner!

INGREDIENTS | SERVES 6

1 (3-ounce) can green chilies

6 large eggs

¼ cup heavy cream

¼ teaspoon salt

¼ teaspoon ground black pepper

1 cup shredded pepper jack cheese

1 cup shredded Cheddar cheese

8 (6") corn tortillas, quartered

1 cup water

Make It for Dinner!

Make this a hearty dinner by adding your favorite cooked shredded or crumbled meat substitute; 1–2 cups is plenty. For a vegetarian option, try adding soy crumbles, sautéed mushrooms and bell peppers, or rinsed and drained canned beans. Never add raw meat to this dish, as the cooking time is not long enough to cook it to a safe temperature.

1. In a medium bowl combine green chilies, eggs, cream, salt, and pepper. Whisk well. In a small bowl combine pepper jack and Cheddar cheeses and mix well.

2. Spray an 8" × 8" baking dish with nonstick cooking spray. In prepared dish layer tortilla pieces, cheese, and egg mixture.

3. Place rack in Instant Pot® and add water. Fold a long piece of aluminum foil in half. Lay foil over rack to form a sling. Place dish on rack and cover loosely with aluminum foil to protect eggs from condensation inside pot. Close lid and set steam release to Sealing, then press Manual and adjust cook time to 30 minutes.

4. Once cooking is complete allow pressure to release naturally, about 15 minutes. Remove lid. Let stand 15 minutes before carefully removing dish from pot with sling.

5. Run a thin knife around edge of dish, then turn out onto a serving platter. Serve warm.

PER SERVING Calories: 360 | Fat: 24g | Protein: 19g | Sodium: 471mg | Fiber: 2g | Carbohydrates: 16g | Sugar: 1.5g

Chorizo and Eggs for Tacos

If you are a vegetarian or cooking for nonmeat eaters, you can use soy chorizo. It can be found in most grocery stores in either the vegetarian refrigerated section or with the regular chorizo.

INGREDIENTS | SERVES 4

1 tablespoon vegetable oil

6 ounces Mexican chorizo

1 medium yellow onion, peeled and chopped

6 large eggs

¼ cup heavy cream

¼ teaspoon salt

¼ teaspoon ground black pepper

1 cup shredded queso quesadilla cheese, divided

1 cup water

4 (8") flour tortillas

½ cup salsa

¼ cup roughly chopped fresh cilantro

1. Spray an 8" × 8" baking dish with nonstick cooking spray.

2. Press Sauté on Instant Pot®. Once machine indicates Hot, about 3 minutes, add oil and let heat 30 seconds, then add chorizo. Cook, crumbling well, until cooked through, about 8 minutes. Add onion and cook until tender, about 5 minutes. Press Cancel and transfer mixture to prepared dish. Clean out inner pot.

3. In a large bowl combine eggs, cream, salt, and pepper. Whisk well. Pour eggs over chorizo and top with ½ cup cheese.

4. Place rack in Instant Pot® and add water. Fold a long piece of aluminum foil in half. Lay foil over rack to form a sling. Place dish on rack and cover loosely with foil to protect eggs from condensation inside pot. Close lid and set steam release to Sealing, then press Manual and adjust cook time to 20 minutes.

5. Once cooking is complete allow pressure to release naturally, about 15 minutes. Remove lid. Let stand 15 minutes before carefully removing dish from pot with sling.

6. Scoop egg mixture into tortillas and top with reserved cheese, salsa, and cilantro. Serve warm.

PER SERVING Calories: 673 | Fat: 46g | Protein: 32g | Sodium: 1,579mg | Fiber: 2g | Carbohydrates: 31g | Sugar: 5g

Mashed Potato Breakfast Casserole

If you do not have leftover mashed potatoes, you can buy ready-made mashed potatoes from the deli of your local market or ready-to-steam frozen potatoes from the freezer section.

INGREDIENTS | SERVES 6

4 cups prepared mashed potatoes

1 cup shredded Cheddar cheese, divided

8 strips thick-cut bacon, cooked crispy and chopped

1 tablespoon chopped fresh chives

¼ teaspoon salt

¼ teaspoon ground black pepper

6 large eggs

1 cup water

1. Spray an 8" × 8" baking dish with nonstick cooking spray.

2. In a large bowl combine mashed potatoes, ½ cup cheese, bacon, chives, salt, and pepper. Mix well, then transfer to prepared dish.

3. Use a spoon to press six indentations into potatoes. Crack eggs into indentations.

4. Place rack in Instant Pot® and add water. Fold a long piece of aluminum foil in half. Lay foil over rack to form a sling. Place dish on rack and cover loosely with foil to protect eggs from condensation inside pot. Close lid and set steam release to Sealing, then press Manual and adjust cook time to 5 minutes.

5. Once cooking is complete quick-release pressure. Remove lid.

6. Top dish with reserved cheese, then let stand 10 minutes before carefully removing dish from pot with sling. Serve warm.

PER SERVING Calories: 423 | Fat: 26g | Protein: 18g | Sodium: 1,102mg | Fiber: 2g | Carbohydrates: 25g | Sugar: 2g

Baked Eggs with Ham and Kale

Creamy kale, poached eggs, and browned ham make this a dish perfect for company but also easy enough for every day! You can use a pound of sliced mushrooms in place of the ham to make the dish vegetarian.

INGREDIENTS | SERVES 6

1 tablespoon olive oil

2 cups diced ham

1 medium yellow onion, peeled and chopped

2 pounds chopped kale

½ cup heavy cream

1 (8-ounce) package cream cheese

¼ teaspoon salt

¼ teaspoon ground black pepper

⅛ teaspoon ground nutmeg

6 large eggs

1 cup water

1. Spray an 8" × 8" baking dish with nonstick cooking spray.

2. Press Sauté on Instant Pot®. Once machine indicates Hot, add oil and let heat 30 seconds, then add ham. Cook until ham is starting to brown, about 5 minutes. Add onion and cook until tender, about 5 minutes, then add kale and cook until wilted, about 5 minutes.

3. Add cream, cream cheese, salt, pepper, and nutmeg and stir until cream cheese is melted and mixture thickens, about 5 minutes. Press Cancel and transfer mixture to prepared dish. Clean out pot.

4. Use a spoon to press 6 indentations into kale mixture. Crack eggs into indentations.

5. Place rack in Instant Pot® and add water. Fold a long piece of aluminum foil in half. Lay foil over rack to form a sling. Place dish on rack and cover loosely with aluminum foil to protect eggs from condensation inside pot. Close lid and set steam release to Sealing, then press Manual and adjust cook time to 5 minutes.

6. Once cooking is complete quick-release pressure. Remove lid. Let stand 5 minutes before carefully removing dish from pot with sling. Serve warm.

PER SERVING Calories: 316 | Fat: 19g | Protein: 21g | Sodium: 830mg | Fiber: 5.5g | Carbohydrates: 16g | Sugar: 5g

Breakfast Casserole with Drop Biscuit Dumplings

Cassava flour is a gluten-free, grain-free, and all-natural product that enables people with gluten sensitivities and those on a paleo lifestyle to enjoy biscuits and dumplings. If you prefer you can use your favorite traditional drop biscuit recipe here.

INGREDIENTS | SERVES 4

DROP BISCUIT DUMPLINGS

½ cup cassava flour
1 teaspoon baking powder
¼ teaspoon baking soda
⅛ teaspoon sea salt
1 large egg white, whisked
2 tablespoons ghee, melted

BREAKFAST CASSEROLE

1 pound breakfast pork sausage, cut from casings
½ medium yellow onion, peeled and diced
½ cup diced button mushrooms
4 large eggs
1 teaspoon ground black pepper
1 cup water

1. In a medium bowl combine dumpling ingredients. Set aside.

2. Press Sauté on Instant Pot®. Once machine indicates Hot, about 3 minutes, add sausage, onion, and mushrooms. Cook 3 minutes to render fat. Transfer mixture to a lightly greased 7-cup glass bowl. Press Cancel.

3. Whisk together eggs and pepper in a small bowl. Pour over sausage mixture in large bowl. Drop spoonfuls of dumpling mixture over casserole.

4. Place rack in Instant Pot® and add water. Fold a long piece of aluminum foil in half. Lay foil over rack to form a sling. Place dish on rack and cover loosely with aluminum foil to protect eggs from condensation inside pot. Close lid and set steam release to Sealing, then press Manual and adjust cook time to 5 minutes.

5. Once cooking is complete quick-release pressure. Remove lid. Let stand 5 minutes before carefully removing dish from pot with sling. Serve warm.

PER SERVING Calories: 635 | Fat: 46g | Protein: 21g | Sodium: 382mg | Fiber: 1g | Carbohydrates: 21g | Sugar: 2g

Condiments and Sauces

Apple Butter

Homemade Apple Butter is delicious on toast or a bagel for breakfast, but it is also lovely with ham, turkey, or roast pork. Consider giving a jar as a gift. It makes a thoughtful host or hostess gift or a cute thank-you for a teacher.

INGREDIENTS | YIELDS 8 CUPS

5 pounds tender apples, such as McIntosh, Cortland, or Liberty, peeled and sliced

¾ cup packed light brown sugar

¼ cup apple juice

2 teaspoons ground cinnamon

¼ teaspoon ground nutmeg

¼ teaspoon ground cloves

¼ teaspoon salt

1 teaspoon vanilla extract

1. Place apples, sugar, apple juice, cinnamon, nutmeg, cloves, and salt in Instant Pot®. Close lid and set steam release to Sealing, then press Manual and adjust cook time to 8 minutes.

2. Once cooking is complete allow pressure to release naturally, about 15 minutes. Press Cancel and remove lid. Let stand 10 minutes before carefully puréeing apples with immersion blender or transferring to blender or food processor and blending until smooth.

3. Press Sauté on pot and adjust temperature to Less. Return apple mixture to pot and cook, stirring constantly, until apple butter is thickened to your preferred consistency, about 7 minutes. Stir in vanilla.

4. Press Cancel and allow apple butter to cool to room temperature, about 45 minutes. Transfer to jars and store in refrigerator up to two weeks.

PER SERVING Calories: 191 | Fat: 0.5g | Protein: 1g | Sodium: 77mg | Fiber: 4g | Carbohydrates: 50g | Sugar: 42g

Cranberry Sauce

The holidays are hardly complete without cranberry sauce, but this year skip the canned food aisle and make your own from scratch. Leftover Cranberry Sauce makes an excellent sandwich spread, and it also tastes great on toast with butter for breakfast.

INGREDIENTS | YIELDS 1 CUP

24 ounces fresh whole cranberries

Zest of 1 orange (about 1 tablespoon)

¾ cup pulp-free orange juice

1 cup granulated sugar

¼ teaspoon salt

1 cinnamon stick

Fresh Cranberries

When choosing your cranberries, remember these tips: First, good cranberries will bounce when dropped. Second, they will be firm to the touch and not mushy or squishy. Finally, they will be a bright, vibrant red. If you can't find good-quality fresh cranberries, you can swap with frozen whole cranberries.

1. Place cranberries, orange zest, orange juice, sugar, salt, and cinnamon stick in Instant Pot®. Close lid and set steam release to Sealing, then press Manual and adjust cook time to 6 minutes.

2. Once cooking is complete allow pressure to release naturally, about 15 minutes. Press Cancel and remove lid.

3. Press Sauté on pot and adjust temperature to Less. Cook, mashing berries gently, until sauce is your preferred consistency. If it is too thick, add in a little water. Press Cancel and allow cranberry sauce to cool to room temperature. Transfer to jars and store in refrigerator up to two weeks.

PER SERVING (2 tablespoons) Calories: 148 | Fat: 0g | Protein: 0.5g | Sodium: 2mg | Fiber: 4g | Carbohydrates: 38g | Sugar: 30g

Blueberry Maple Syrup

If you love pancakes, waffles, or crepes, then this sauce is right up your alley! If the fresh blueberries in the produce section of your grocery store look less than tempting, you can use frozen whole blueberries.

INGREDIENTS | YIELDS 2 CUPS

1½ cups fresh blueberries

1 cup pure maple syrup

1 teaspoon lemon zest

1 teaspoon vanilla extract

1. Place blueberries, maple syrup, and lemon zest in Instant Pot®. Stir well. Close lid and set steam release to Sealing, then press Manual and adjust cook time to 4 minutes.

2. Once cooking is complete quick-release pressure. Remove lid. Stir in vanilla. Serve warm or store covered in refrigerator up to one week.

PER SERVING (2 tablespoons) Calories: 60 | Fat: 0g | Protein: 0g | Sodium: 3mg | Fiber: 0.5g | Carbohydrates: 15g | Sugar: 13g

Caramel Cream Sauce

Also known as dulce de leche, this is a two-ingredient recipe, but the transformation in the Instant Pot® is nothing short of magical. You can serve this sauce with fresh fruit for dipping, stir it into hot coffee, or drizzle it over cakes or cookies.

INGREDIENTS | YIELDS 14 OUNCES

1 (14-ounce) can sweetened condensed milk

8 cups water

Add Extra Flavors

Want to add a little pizzazz to your caramel sauce? You can do so by adding a little vanilla extract and salt. When the caramel is cool, stir in up to 1 teaspoon of vanilla. It may look curdled, but keep stirring. Then add ¼ teaspoon of sea salt and stir well.

1. Remove lid and label from milk can. Wrap top of can tightly in aluminum foil.

2. Place rack in Instant Pot® and put can on rack. Slowly pour water in pot until it reaches about halfway up can. Close lid and set steam release to Sealing, then press Manual and adjust cook time to 40 minutes.

3. Once cooking is complete quick-release pressure. Turn off machine and let stand 30 minutes before removing can from pot. Stir well, then transfer to storage container. Do not store in can. Serve warm or at room temperature, or store in refrigerator up to one week.

PER SERVING (1 ounce) Calories: 89 | Fat: 2.5g | Protein: 2g | Sodium: 39mg | Fiber: 0g | Carbohydrates: 15g | Sugar: 15g

Fresh Tomato Sauce

When tomatoes are in season, there is nothing like fresh tomato sauce—but it can be quite a production to cook the tomatoes to perfection. The Instant Pot® speeds things up, so you can enjoy your tomato sauce in record time!

INGREDIENTS | SERVES 4

¼ cup olive oil

1 medium yellow onion, peeled and chopped

4 cloves garlic, peeled and minced

8 large tomatoes, peeled and cut into big chunks

1 bay leaf

1 tablespoon granulated sugar

¼ cup chopped fresh basil

1 teaspoon dried oregano

1 teaspoon dried fennel

1 teaspoon salt

½ teaspoon ground black pepper

Best Tomatoes for Tomato Sauce

When making tomato sauce, you want to use paste tomatoes. These tomatoes have few seeds and a firm texture. They are perfect for sauce, as they cook down to a thick and hearty mixture. Roma tomatoes are a good choice that can be found in most stores, though a San Marzano tomato variety is ideal if your market carries them.

1. Press Sauté on Instant Pot®. Once machine indicates Hot, add olive oil and let heat 30 seconds, then add onion. Cook until onion is soft, about 5 minutes, then add garlic and cook until fragrant, about 30 seconds.

2. Add tomatoes and bay leaf and cook 5 minutes until tomatoes start to release their juice. Press Cancel and add sugar, basil, oregano, fennel, salt, and pepper. Stir once, then close lid and set steam release to Sealing. Press Manual and adjust cook time to 5 minutes.

3. Once cooking is complete quick-release pressure and turn off machine. Let sauce cool 10 minutes, then discard bay leaf and purée sauce with an immersion blender, or transfer sauce to blender and purée until smooth. If you prefer a thicker sauce, you can also press Sauté on pot and cook, stirring constantly, until desired thickness is reached. Serve warm, or refrigerate covered up to one week.

PER SERVING Calories: 203 | Fat: 14g | Protein: 4g | Sodium: 601mg | Fiber: 5g | Carbohydrates: 18g | Sugar: 10g

Bolognese Sauce

Rich and meaty, Bolognese originated in Bologna, Italy; however, its power has won the world's heart. Make a jar on food-prep day and enjoy the tasty sauce during the week, served over spaghetti, spiralized zucchini or carrots, or whatever else you like to spriralize!

INGREDIENTS | YIELDS 6 CUPS

2 tablespoons ghee

2 ribs celery, finely diced

1 medium carrot, peeled and finely diced

½ medium yellow onion, peeled and finely diced

4 cloves garlic, peeled and quartered

1 pound ground Italian sausage

2 slices bacon, diced

1 (28-ounce) can crushed tomatoes, including juice

½ cup beef broth

2 tablespoons chopped fresh basil

2 tablespoons fresh thyme leaves

1 teaspoon sea salt

½ teaspoon ground black pepper

½ cup unsweetened almond milk

1. Press Sauté on Instant Pot®. Once machine indicates Hot, add ghee and let heat 30 seconds, then add celery, carrot, and onion and cook 3 minutes until onions are tender.

2. Add garlic, Italian sausage, and bacon. Cook, stirring constantly, until sausage is just cooked through, about 5 minutes. Drain off and discard any excess fat.

3. Stir in tomatoes, including juice, and scrape up the bits from the sides and bottom of pot. Add broth, basil, thyme, salt, and pepper. Press Cancel. Close lid and set steam release to Sealing, then press Manual and adjust cook time to 10 minutes.

4. Once cooking is complete allow pressure to release naturally 5 minutes. Quick-release any remaining pressure and then open lid. Stir in almond milk.

5. Simmer uncovered 3 minutes. Pour sauce into a storage container or jar and refrigerate until ready to use. Sauce keeps up to five days.

PER SERVING (1 cup) Calories: 295 | Fat: 22g | Protein: 15g | Sodium: 1,176mg | Fiber: 3.5g | Carbohydrates: 9g | Sugar: 4.5g

Easy Chocolate Hazelnut Syrup

Drizzle this delicious new favorite over ice cream, pancakes, waffles, and fresh fruit!

INGREDIENTS | YIELDS 1 CUP

½ cup pure maple syrup

1 tablespoon cocoa powder

⅓ cup chocolate hazelnut spread

2 tablespoons unsalted butter

1. Place all ingredients except butter in Instant Pot® and whisk until combined. Close lid and set steam release to Sealing, then press Manual and adjust cook time to 2 minutes.

2. Once cooking is complete quick-release pressure. Turn off machine and add butter. Whisk 30 seconds until melted. Serve warm or at room temperature. Store in refrigerator up to two weeks.

PER SERVING (2 tablespoons) Calories: 142 | Fat: 8g | Protein: 2.5g | Sodium: 48mg | Fiber: 0.5g | Carbohydrates: 16g | Sugar: 13g

Buttery Tomato Sauce

When fresh tomatoes are not in season, it can be tempting to buy sauce in a jar. Well, put that jar down! This sauce may not be traditional, but it produces a rich flavor that is almost addicting—all from canned tomatoes. Don't knock it until you try it!

INGREDIENTS | SERVES 6

1 (28-ounce) can crushed tomatoes

4 tablespoons salted butter

2 teaspoons ground fennel

2 teaspoons dried oregano

½ teaspoon dried thyme

¼ teaspoon crushed red pepper flakes

¼ teaspoon ground black pepper

1. Place all ingredients in Instant Pot®. Stir well. Close lid and set steam release to Sealing, then press Manual and adjust cook time to 5 minutes.

2. Once cooking is complete quick-release steam, press Cancel, remove lid, and stir well. If you prefer a thicker sauce, press Sauté and cook, stirring constantly, until desired thickness is reached. Serve warm, or refrigerate covered up to one week.

PER SERVING Calories: 90 | Fat: 8g | Protein: 1g | Sodium: 211mg | Fiber: 2.5g | Carbohydrates: 5g | Sugar: 3g

Garden Marinara Sauce

If you have your own vegetable garden, what better dish is there to show it off than this Garden Marinara Sauce? The portion of fennel is kept low here, at just ½ teaspoon, as it might be an unfamiliar flavor to some, especially in a savory dish. Fennel lovers can add more!

INGREDIENTS | SERVES 4

2 tablespoons olive oil

1 large Vidalia onion, peeled and diced

1 small red bell pepper, seeded and diced

1 large carrot, peeled and grated

4 cloves garlic, peeled and minced

1 tablespoon dried parsley leaves

½ teaspoon dried ground fennel

1 teaspoon dried basil leaves

1 bay leaf

⅛ teaspoon dried red pepper flakes

¼ teaspoon salt

1 (14.5-ounce) can diced tomatoes, with juice

½ cup vegetable broth

1. Press Sauté on Instant Pot®. Once machine indicates Hot, add oil and let heat 30 seconds, then add onion, bell pepper, and carrot and sauté 3 minutes. Stir in garlic and cook an additional 30 seconds.

2. Add remaining ingredients to pot. Press Cancel. Close lid and set steam release to Sealing, then press Manual and adjust cook time to 10 minutes.

3. Once cooking is complete quick-release pressure and remove lid. Stir sauce and discard bay leaf. If desired, use an immersion blender to purée sauce in pot. Store remaining mixture in an airtight container and refrigerate up to three days, or freeze up to one week.

PER SERVING Calories: 110 | Fat: 7g | Protein: 2g | Sodium: 279mg | Fiber: 3.5g | Carbohydrates: 11g | Sugar: 6g

Ketchup

Homemade ketchup is like nothing else, but it takes a lot of work if you make it on the stove—and it takes even longer in the slow cooker. You can cut the time down to a mere fraction by using your Instant Pot®!

INGREDIENTS | SERVES 6

1 (28-ounce) can crushed tomatoes

½ small sweet yellow onion, peeled and diced

½ cup apple cider vinegar

¼ cup raisins

2 teaspoons salt

1 teaspoon paprika

½ teaspoon ground black pepper

½ teaspoon celery seed

⅛ teaspoon ground allspice

Flavored Ketchup

Give boring ol' ketchup a makeover! To ¼ cup ketchup, mix in any of the following: ¼ teaspoon curry powder and ⅛ teaspoon lime juice; 1 tablespoon sweet barbecue sauce; 1 teaspoon sriracha and ½ teaspoon honey; 1 tablespoon Thai sweet chili sauce; 1 teaspoon finely chopped chipotle in adobo sauce. Mix additives in advance and chill 30 minutes to an hour to let flavors develop.

1. Place tomatoes in Instant Pot®. Using a potato masher, crush tomatoes until juices begin to run. Add remaining ingredients. Close lid and set steam release to Sealing, then press Manual and adjust cook time to 10 minutes.

2. Once cooking is complete quick-release pressure. Remove lid and stir. Carefully purée mixture with an immersion blender or transfer to a blender to purée and then return to pot.

3. Press Cancel, then press Sauté and cook, stirring often, until ketchup is thickened, about 15 minutes. Mixture may splatter, so use a splatter shield if desired. Once ketchup is thick, press Cancel and let cool to room temperature, about 1 hour. Transfer to storage container and refrigerate at least 4 hours before serving. Ketchup keeps in refrigerator up to one month.

PER SERVING Calories: 49 | Fat: 0.5g | Protein: 1.5g | Sodium: 928mg | Fiber: 3g | Carbohydrates: 10g | Sugar: 7g

Barbecue Sauce

This is a ketchup-based sauce, so feel free to use store-bought ketchup or your own homemade Ketchup from this chapter. Slather this sauce on brisket, ribs, chicken, or even smoked tofu and vegetables!

INGREDIENTS | SERVES 6

1 (15-ounce) can crushed tomatoes
1½ cups ketchup
½ cup packed dark brown sugar
½ cup apple cider vinegar
¼ cup molasses
½ teaspoon liquid smoke
½ teaspoon salt
½ teaspoon paprika
¼ teaspoon garlic powder
¼ teaspoon onion powder
⅛ teaspoon ground allspice

1. Place all ingredients in Instant Pot®. Close lid and set steam release to Sealing, then press Manual and adjust cook time to 10 minutes.

2. Once cooking is complete quick-release pressure. Remove lid and stir. Press Cancel, then press Sauté and cook, stirring often, until sauce is thickened, about 15 minutes. Mixture may splatter, so use a splatter shield if desired.

3. Once desired thickness is reached, press Cancel and let cool to room temperature, about 1 hour. Transfer to storage container and refrigerate for at least 4 hours before serving. Keeps up to two weeks in refrigerator.

PER SERVING Calories: 171 | Fat: 0g | Protein: 1g | Sodium: 900mg | Fiber: 1.5g | Carbohydrates: 43g | Sugar: 38g

Quick Pickled Peppers

Peppers in a pinch, these are great for topping steak sandwiches or nachos or for adding to casseroles. You can also use this recipe with thin slices of cucumbers, onions, or carrots.

INGREDIENTS | SERVES 6

1 pound jalapeños, sliced
1½ cups apple cider vinegar
1 teaspoon pickling salt
1 teaspoon granulated sugar
2 cloves garlic, peeled and crushed

1. Place all ingredients in Instant Pot®. Close lid and set steam release to Sealing, then press Manual and adjust cook time to 1 minute.

2. Once cooking is complete allow pressure to release naturally, about 15 minutes. When float valve releases press Cancel. Transfer peppers into sterile jars. Peppers keep up to one month in refrigerator.

PER SERVING Calories: 38 | Fat: 0g | Protein: 0.5g | Sodium: 392mg | Fiber: 2g | Carbohydrates: 6g | Sugar: 4g

Bacon Jam

Sweet and salty, this glorious concoction will give new life to several meals. On top of a burger, alongside your scrambled eggs in the morning, or even licked off a kitchen spoon, Bacon Jam will be your new favorite condiment.

INGREDIENTS | YIELDS 2 CUPS

1 tablespoon coconut oil

1 pound center-cut bacon, diced

1 large yellow onion, peeled and chopped

4 cloves garlic, peeled and halved

¼ cup apple cider vinegar

½ cup pure maple syrup

1 chipotle in adobo sauce

1 teaspoon adobo sauce from chipotle jar

1 teaspoon smoked paprika

1 tablespoon instant espresso powder

½ cup water

1. Press Sauté on Instant Pot®. Once machine indicates Hot, add oil and let heat 30 seconds, then add bacon and onion and cook until bacon is just cooked, about 4 minutes. Add garlic and cook 1 minute.

2. Discard all but 1 tablespoon bacon grease from pot. Add remaining ingredients. Press Cancel. Close lid and set steam release to Sealing, then press Manual and adjust cook time to 10 minutes.

3. Once cooking is complete quick-release pressure. Remove lid. Use an immersion blender to blend mixture in pot until preferred consistency is reached. Spoon jam into a jar and refrigerate up to two weeks until ready to use.

PER SERVING (2 tablespoons) Calories: 156 | Fat: 11g | Protein: 3.5g | Sodium: 187mg | Fiber: 0g | Carbohydrates: 8g | Sugar: 6g

Quick Pickles

These pickles are great on burgers and sandwiches and are also great finely chopped and folded into tuna or egg salad. You can also just eat them straight from the jar!

INGREDIENTS | SERVES 6

1 pound pickling cucumbers, sliced

1½ cups apple cider vinegar

½ cup granulated sugar

1 teaspoon pickling salt

1 teaspoon mustard seeds

½ teaspoon celery seeds

2 cloves garlic, peeled and crushed

1. Place all ingredients in Instant Pot®. Close lid and set steam release to Sealing, then press Manual and adjust cook time to 1 minute.

2. Once cooking is complete allow pressure to release naturally, about 15 minutes. When float valve releases press Cancel. Transfer pickles to sterile jars. Pickles keep up to one month in refrigerator.

PER SERVING Calories: 92 | Fat: 0g | Protein: 0.5g | Sodium: 392mg | Fiber: 0.5g | Carbohydrates: 20g | Sugar: 18g

Ricotta Cheese

Homemade ricotta is easier than you think, and it tastes amazing! You can use this ricotta for Italian cooking, with fresh berries and a drizzle of balsamic vinegar, or as a topper for bruschetta with pesto, diced tomatoes, and fresh basil.

INGREDIENTS | YIELDS 2 CUPS

8 cups (½ gallon) whole milk

½ teaspoon salt

⅓ cup freshly squeezed lemon juice

Uses for Whey

Whey is the cloudy liquid left in the cheese-making process after straining out the cheese. You may be tempted to discard this liquid, but it is packed with flavor and enzymes that you don't want to just toss away. Some more common uses for whey are as a buttermilk substitute in baking, a base for a liquid marinade, or an addition to smoothies for extra nutrition.

1. Add milk and salt to Instant Pot®. Stir well. Close lid and set steam release to Sealing, then press Yogurt and press Adjust until Boil is indicated.

2. Once cooking is complete remove lid and stir milk. Use a thermometer to check milk has reached 190°F. If milk is not at 190°F, press Cancel and then Sauté and simmer until correct temperature is reached. Press Cancel.

3. Stir in lemon juice. Let mixture stand 10 minutes without stirring, then pour into a colander lined with a double layer of cheesecloth. Drain until desired consistency is reached. For a creamier, spreadable ricotta strain only 30 minutes. For a firmer, dryer ricotta strain up to 1 hour.

4. Transfer ricotta to storage container. Use immediately or store up to one week in refrigerator.

PER SERVING (½ cup) Calories: 297 | Fat: 15g | Protein: 15g | Sodium: 500mg | Fiber: 0g | Carbohydrates: 23g | Sugar: 24g

Mango Chutney

This Indian condiment is often served alongside spicy curry dishes, but you can use it for so much more! Spread it on grilled cheese sandwiches, use it anywhere you would use ketchup in a recipe, or pour it over cream cheese and serve it with crackers.

INGREDIENTS | SERVES 6

1 tablespoon olive oil

1 teaspoon cumin seeds

3 whole cloves

3 cardamom pods, crushed

1 whole red chili, minced

2 mangoes, peeled and finely chopped

¼ cup granulated sugar

¼ cup freshly squeezed lime juice

½ teaspoon salt

1. Press Sauté on Instant Pot®. Once machine indicates Hot, add oil and let heat 30 seconds, then add cumin, cloves, and cardamom. Cook, stirring constantly, until spices are well toasted, about 1 minute. Press Cancel.

2. Place remaining ingredients in pot. Close lid and set steam release to Sealing, then press Manual and adjust cook time to 5 minutes.

3. Once cooking is complete allow pressure to release naturally, about 15 minutes. When float valve releases press Cancel. Transfer chutney to sterile jars. Chutney keeps up to one month in refrigerator.

PER SERVING Calories: 123 | Fat: 2.5g | Protein: 1g | Sodium: 196mg | Fiber: 2g | Carbohydrates: 25g | Sugar: 24g

Vegan Nacho Cheese Sauce

If you are a vegan or are avoiding dairy for health or diet reasons, this satisfyingly cheesy-tasting nacho sauce is for you! This sauce is great poured over steamed vegetables, used as a dip with chips, or tossed with pasta for vegan mac and cheese.

INGREDIENTS | SERVES 8

2 cups water

2 cups cubed Yukon Gold potatoes

1 cup peeled sliced carrots

½ medium Vidalia onion, peeled and chopped

3 whole cloves, chopped

½ cup raw cashews

½ cup nutritional yeast

2 tablespoons miso paste

1 teaspoon smoked paprika

1 teaspoon apple cider vinegar

1 teaspoon salt

1. Place all ingredients in Instant Pot®. Close lid and set steam release to Sealing, then press Manual and adjust cook time to 5 minutes.

2. Once cooking is complete quick-release pressure. Press Cancel and open lid. Transfer mixture into blender and process 30 seconds, stir, then blend again 30 seconds until smooth. Serve hot, or refrigerate covered up to one week.

PER SERVING Calories: 163 | Fat: 5g | Protein: 7.5g | Sodium: 1,030mg | Fiber: 6.5g | Carbohydrates: 20g | Sugar: 2.5g

Enchilada Sauce

Dried peppers are the key to a smooth sauce with depth of flavor. Oven roasting the peppers will bring out the flavor and make your sauce deliciously toasty. Leftover sauce can be refrigerated covered for up to one week, or frozen for up to one month.

INGREDIENTS | SERVES 8

12 dried chilies (Anaheim, pasilla, New Mexico, or guajillo)

2 cups boiling water

3 whole cloves, chopped

1 teaspoon ground cumin

½ teaspoon ground coriander

½ teaspoon paprika

1 teaspoon salt

2 tablespoons lard

1. Preheat oven to 350°F. Place chilies on an ungreased baking sheet and bake 4 minutes until just fragrant. Cool to room temperature, about 20 minutes, then cut off stems and remove seeds.

2. Place chilies in a large bowl and cover with boiling water. Soak 30 minutes. Drain, reserving soaking liquid.

3. Place remaining ingredients except lard in Instant Pot®. Add soaked chilies and 1 cup reserved soaking liquid to pot. Close lid and set steam release to Sealing, then press Manual and adjust cook time to 3 minutes.

4. Once cooking is complete quick-release pressure. Press Cancel and open lid. Transfer mixture into blender and process 30 seconds, stir, then blend again 30 seconds until smooth. If mixture is too thick to blend into a smooth sauce, add additional soaking liquid.

5. Press Sauté on pot and add lard. Once lard is melted, about 30 seconds, add purée to pot. Cook, stirring constantly, 3 minutes. Mixture may splatter, so use a splatter shield if desired. Press Cancel and use sauce immediately, or let sauce cool to room temperature, about 1 hour, and transfer to a storage container. Sauce will keep in refrigerator up to one week, or in freezer up to one month.

PER SERVING Calories: 86 | Fat: 5g | Protein: 2g | Sodium: 328mg | Fiber: 4.5g | Carbohydrates: 13g | Sugar: 4g

CHAPTER 5

Dips and Appetizers

Cheeseburger Dip

Slices of crusty bread are the perfect dipper for this, but you can also serve with thick tortilla chips. If you like, place the dip topped with the reserved cheese under the broiler for 4 minutes to create a browned, crusty top.

INGREDIENTS | SERVES 8

1 pound ground beef

1 medium white onion, peeled and chopped

½ teaspoon salt

½ teaspoon ground black pepper

2 tablespoons all-purpose flour

1 cup whole milk

1 cup shredded American cheese, divided

2 (8-ounce) packages cream cheese, cubed

¼ cup yellow mustard

¼ cup ketchup

¼ cup dill pickle relish

Burger Bun Dippers

Want to get the full cheeseburger experience from your Cheeseburger Dip? Cut your favorite buttery rolls into cubes about 2 inches in size. Toss the cubes with melted butter, spread them on a baking sheet, and bake at 350°F until toasted and browned, about 15–20 minutes, making sure to turn the bread frequently.

1. Press Sauté on Instant Pot®. Once machine indicates Hot, about 3 minutes, add beef and cook, crumbling well with a wooden spoon, until browned, about 5 minutes. Add onion, salt, and pepper and cook until onion is tender, about 3 minutes.

2. Sprinkle flour over meat mixture and stir to combine. Slowly stir in milk and cook until mixture thickens, about 8 minutes. Press Cancel and stir in ½ cup American cheese along with cream cheese.

3. Close lid and set steam release to Sealing, then press Manual and adjust cook time to 2 minutes.

4. Once cooking is complete quick-release pressure. Open lid and stir well. Press Cancel and transfer to a serving dish. Top immediately with reserved cheese, and garnish with mustard, ketchup, and relish. Serve hot.

PER SERVING Calories: 292 | Fat: 18g | Protein: 19g | Sodium: 761mg | Fiber: 0.5g | Carbohydrates: 11g | Sugar: 4.5g

Taco Dip

This is a fantastic complement to a game-day spread and is a welcome addition to any tailgate, potluck, or party. This dip can also be used to fill large tortillas—along with some refried beans—for a quick burrito!

INGREDIENTS | SERVES 8

1 pound ground beef

1 medium yellow onion, peeled and chopped

1 jalapeño, seeded and chopped

1 (10-ounce) can diced tomatoes with green chilies, drained

1 (1.25-ounce) packet taco seasoning

1 cup water

1 cup shredded Mexican-style cheese, divided

2 (8-ounce) packages cream cheese, cubed

¼ cup chunky salsa

¼ cup chopped fresh cilantro

Taco Seasoning Mix

Homemade taco seasoning mix is a breeze! For one pound of ground beef combine 1 tablespoon chili powder, 1 teaspoon ground cumin, 1 teaspoon cornstarch, ½ teaspoon dried oregano, ½ teaspoon paprika, ½ teaspoon salt, ¼ teaspoon ground black pepper, ¼ teaspoon garlic powder, ¼ teaspoon onion powder, and ⅛ teaspoon cayenne pepper in a small bowl with a lid. Shake well to mix.

1. Press Sauté on Instant Pot®. Once machine indicates Hot, about 3 minutes, add beef and cook, crumbling well with a wooden spoon, until browned, about 5 minutes. Add onion, jalapeño, and diced tomatoes with green chilies and cook until onion is tender, about 3 minutes.

2. Sprinkle taco seasoning over meat mixture and stir to combine, then add water to meat mixture and cook, stirring often, until it thickens, about 8 minutes. Press Cancel.

3. Stir in ½ cup shredded cheese along with cream cheese. Close lid and set steam release to Sealing, then press Manual and adjust cook time to 3 minutes.

4. Once cooking is complete quick-release pressure. Open lid and stir well. Press Cancel and transfer to a serving dish. Top immediately with reserved cheese and garnish with salsa and cilantro. Serve hot.

PER SERVING Calories: 293 | Fat: 21g | Protein: 17g | Sodium: 631mg | Fiber: 1.5g | Carbohydrates: 7g | Sugar: 3g

Jalapeño Popper Dip

All the flavors of the bar food favorite, but in dip form? Yes, please! Scoop-shaped tortilla chips are best with this dip, as you will want a lot of it with each bite! You can even serve the dip already divided into the scoop chips for finger food.

INGREDIENTS | SERVES 8

½ pound bacon, chopped

1 medium yellow onion, peeled and chopped

2 jalapeños, seeded and chopped

2 cloves garlic, peeled and chopped

1 teaspoon ground cumin

½ teaspoon ground coriander

½ teaspoon smoked paprika

¼ teaspoon salt

1 cup shredded Mexican-style cheese, divided

2 (8-ounce) packages cream cheese, cubed

½ cup mayonnaise

Make It a Meal!

Want to transform your dip into a family-pleasing meal? Simply stir in 2 cups of shredded rotisserie chicken, or leftover beef or chicken fajita meat, before cooking. Then, when cooking is complete, top with the reserved cheese and serve! If you want, you can also transfer the recipe to a baking dish and broil on high for 4 minutes for a browned top.

1. Press Sauté on Instant Pot®. Once machine indicates Hot, about 3 minutes, add bacon and cook with a wooden spoon until browned and crisp, about 5 minutes. Add onion, jalapeño, and garlic and cook until onion is tender, about 3 minutes.

2. Add cumin, coriander, paprika, and salt and stir to combine. Press Cancel and stir in ½ cup shredded cheese, along with cream cheese and mayonnaise. Close lid and set steam release to Sealing, then press Manual and adjust cook time to 1 minute.

3. Once cooking is complete quick-release pressure. Open lid and stir well. Press Cancel and transfer to a serving dish. Top immediately with reserved cheese. Serve hot.

PER SERVING Calories: 391 | Fat: 37g | Protein: 9.5g | Sodium: 549mg | Fiber: 0.5g | Carbohydrates: 4g | Sugar: 2g

Cheesy Artichoke Dip

This dip will make guests think you slaved over it, but it takes mere moments to put together! It may seem a little runny once cooked, but as it cools it will thicken nicely.

INGREDIENTS | SERVES 8

1 tablespoon unsalted butter

1 medium white onion, peeled and chopped

2 cloves garlic, peeled and minced

1 (10-ounce) package frozen spinach, thawed and excess water removed

1 (9-ounce) package frozen artichoke hearts, thawed and drained

¼ cup vegetable broth

½ cup sour cream

¼ cup mayonnaise

1 (8-ounce) package cream cheese, cubed

1 cup shredded mozzarella cheese

1. Press Sauté on Instant Pot®. Once machine indicates Hot, add butter and let heat 30 seconds, then add onion and cook, stirring frequently, until tender, about 3 minutes. Add garlic and cook until fragrant, about 30 seconds. Press Cancel.

2. Add spinach, artichoke hearts, and broth to pot. Stir well, then close lid and set steam release to Sealing. Press Manual and adjust cook time to 4 minutes.

3. Once cooking is complete quick-release pressure. Stir in sour cream, mayonnaise, cream cheese, and mozzarella cheese. Close lid and let stand 5 minutes, then stir again until all cheese is combined. Serve hot.

PER SERVING Calories: 227 | Fat: 18g | Protein: 7g | Sodium: 282mg | Fiber: 3g | Carbohydrates: 10g | Sugar: 3g

Buffalo Chicken Meatballs

Frozen chicken meatballs are the time-saving all-star of this recipe. If you want, you can also use regular beef, pork, or turkey meatballs. This recipe also makes for delicious buffalo meatball sliders on toasted dinner rolls.

INGREDIENTS | SERVES 8

2 pounds frozen chicken meatballs

1 cup buffalo wing sauce

1 cup ranch dressing

½ cup crumbled blue cheese

Homemade Chicken Meatballs

Combine 1½ pounds ground chicken, 1 medium peeled and chopped white onion, 2 peeled and minced cloves garlic, 1 cup panko bread crumbs, 1 egg, and ½ teaspoon each of salt and pepper. Combine and roll into about twenty-four 1" balls.

1. Add meatballs, wing sauce, and ranch dressing to Instant Pot®. Stir well. Close lid and set steam release to Sealing, then press Manual and adjust cook time to 5 minutes.

2. Once cooking is complete allow pressure to release naturally. Open lid and stir well. Top with crumbled blue cheese. Serve hot.

PER SERVING (2 meatballs) Calories: 292 | Fat: 19g | Protein: 26g | Sodium: 453mg | Fiber: 0g | Carbohydrates: 2g | Sugar: 1g

Loaded Game-Day Queso

When you have a rowdy crowd of sports fans over, the last thing you want is for them to go hungry! This hearty queso dip is packed with meat and vegetables to fill them up, and the flavor will have them coming back again and again!

INGREDIENTS | SERVES 12

2 tablespoons unsalted butter

1 medium yellow onion, peeled and chopped

2 jalapeños, seeded and diced

1 medium red bell pepper, seeded and diced

2 cups shredded cooked chicken

1 tablespoon taco seasoning

1 (32-ounce) package Velveeta, cubed

1 (14.5-ounce) can diced tomatoes with green chilies, drained

1 cup shredded Mexican-style cheese

1. Press Sauté on Instant Pot®. Once machine indicates Hot, about 3 minutes, add butter and melt 30 seconds. Add onion, jalapeño, and bell pepper and cook until onion is tender, about 3 minutes.

2. Add shredded chicken, taco seasoning, cheese cubes, and diced tomatoes with green chilies. Stir well. Press Cancel. Close lid and set steam release to Sealing, then press Manual and adjust cook time to 2 minutes.

3. Once cooking is complete quick-release pressure. Open lid, add shredded cheese, and stir well. Serve hot.

PER SERVING Calories: 373 | Fat: 32g | Protein: 15g | Sodium: 425mg | Fiber: 0g | Carbohydrates: 6g | Sugar: 4g

Instant Pot® Salsa

If you like your salsa hot and spicy, you can switch up the peppers and substitute one or more of the jalapeños with habanero peppers. If you don't want any heat, you can omit the jalapeños and substitute a bell pepper in its place.

INGREDIENTS | SERVES 12

12 cups seeded diced tomatoes

6 ounces tomato paste

2 medium yellow onions, peeled and diced

6 jalapeños, seeded and minced

4 cloves garlic, peeled and minced

¼ cup white vinegar

¼ cup freshly squeezed lime juice

2 tablespoons granulated sugar

2 teaspoons salt

¼ cup chopped fresh cilantro

1. Add all ingredients except cilantro to Instant Pot® and stir well. Close lid and set steam release to Sealing. Press Manual and adjust cook time to 20 minutes.

2. Once cooking is complete quick-release pressure. Remove lid, stir in cilantro, and press Cancel.

3. Let salsa cool to room temperature, about 40 minutes, then transfer to a storage container and refrigerate overnight. Salsa keeps up to two weeks in refrigerator.

PER SERVING Calories: 62 | Fat: 0.5g | Protein: 2.5g | Sodium: 508mg | Fiber: 3g | Carbohydrates: 14g | Sugar: 9g

Queso Blanco

This white cheese dip makes a nice alternative to traditional yellow queso. If you can find fresh green chilies, you can sauté them with some butter in place of the canned chilies.

INGREDIENTS | SERVES 12

2 tablespoons unsalted butter

1 medium yellow onion, peeled and chopped

2 serrano peppers, seeded and diced

1 (3-ounce) can diced green chilies

½ teaspoon ground cumin

2 tablespoons all-purpose flour

2 cups whole milk

2 (8-ounce) packages cream cheese, cubed

2 cups shredded Monterey jack cheese

¼ teaspoon salt

1. Press Sauté on Instant Pot®. Once machine indicates Hot, about 3 minutes, add butter and melt 30 seconds. Once melted add onion and peppers. Cook until onion is tender, about 3 minutes.

2. Add green chilies and cumin and cook 30 seconds until fragrant, then sprinkle flour over top. Stir until combined and no dry flour remains, about 1 minute.

3. Stir in milk, scraping up any bits of flour from bottom of pot, and cook until mixture thickens, about 5 minutes. Press Cancel until Keep Warm is indicated. Stir in cheeses and salt, close lid, set steam release to Venting, and let stand 10 minutes. Open lid and stir well. Serve hot.

PER SERVING Calories: 175 | Fat: 14g | Protein: 7g | Sodium: 244mg | Fiber: 0g | Carbohydrates: 5g | Sugar: 3g

Cheesy Corn Dip

To make sure your corn stays crisp, use frozen or fresh only. Canned corn can get a little mushy, and you want your corn firm so it really pops as you eat.

INGREDIENTS | SERVES 12

1 cup water

2 (8-ounce) packages cream cheese

1 cup mayonnaise

2 cups shredded Cheddar cheese, divided

1 cup shredded Monterey jack cheese

1 teaspoon Worcestershire sauce

½ teaspoon ground mustard

½ teaspoon onion powder

½ teaspoon dried dill weed

¼ teaspoon garlic powder

¼ teaspoon salt

1 (10-ounce) can diced tomatoes and green chilies, drained

1 tablespoon unsalted butter

1 medium white onion, peeled and chopped

1 medium red bell pepper, chopped

1 (10-ounce) bag frozen corn, thawed

1. Spray an 8" × 8" baking dish with nonstick cooking spray.

2. Place rack in Instant Pot® and add water. Fold a long piece of aluminum foil in half. Lay foil over rack to form a sling.

3. In a large bowl combine cream cheese, mayonnaise, 1 cup Cheddar cheese, Monterey jack cheese, Worcestershire sauce, mustard, onion powder, dill, garlic powder, and salt. Mix until everything is thoroughly combined. Fold in diced tomatoes and green chilies and set aside.

4. Press Sauté on Instant Pot®. Once Machine indicates Hot, about 3 minutes, add butter. Once butter foams, about 30 seconds, add onion and bell pepper. Cook, stirring often, until onion and pepper begin to soften, about 5 minutes. Add corn and toss to coat, then press Cancel.

5. Add cooked vegetables to cream cheese mixture. Fold to combine. Pour mixture into prepared baking dish and spread out evenly. Top with remaining cheese and place onto rack, covering with aluminum foil. Close lid and set steam release to Sealing, then press Manual and adjust cook time to 5 minutes.

6. Once cooking is complete quick-release pressure. Open lid, press Cancel, and let dip stand 10 minutes before carefully removing from pot with sling. Serve warm.

PER SERVING Calories: 312 | Fat: 30g | Protein: 9g | Sodium: 435mg | Fiber: 0.5g | Carbohydrates: 2g | Sugar: 1g

Black Bean Dip

Most bean dishes call for many hours of soaking before you can even begin cooking the beans. The Bean setting on your Instant Pot® takes care of that in a fraction of the time. To give this dip a little kick, you can substitute canned or bottled jalapeño pepper slices for the mild green chilies or add 2 teaspoons of chipotle powder.

INGREDIENTS | SERVES 12

1 tablespoon olive oil

1 small yellow onion, peeled and diced

3 cloves garlic, peeled and minced

1 cup dry black beans

2 cups water

1 (14.5-ounce) can diced tomatoes

2 (4-ounce) cans mild green chilies, finely chopped

1 teaspoon chili powder

½ teaspoon dried oregano leaves

¼ cup finely chopped fresh cilantro

1 cup shredded vegan Monterey jack cheese

1. Press Sauté on Instant Pot®. Once machine indicates Hot, add oil and let heat 30 seconds, then add onion and cook 3 minutes until soft. Add garlic and cook 30 seconds. Transfer onions and garlic to a small bowl and set aside. Press Cancel.

2. Add beans, water, tomatoes, chilies, chili powder, and oregano to pot. Stir well, then close lid and set steam release to Sealing. Press Manual and adjust cook time to 30 minutes.

3. Once cooking is complete quick-release pressure, then remove lid. Transfer mixture to a food processor or blender. Add onion mixture, cilantro, and cheese to processor and blend until smooth. Transfer dip to a serving bowl. Serve warm.

PER SERVING Calories: 189 | Fat: 5g | Protein: 6g | Sodium: 182mg | Fiber: 4g | Carbohydrates: 17g | Sugar: 3g

Classic Grape Jelly Meatballs

Need these meatballs in a hurry? Feel free to substitute your favorite frozen or ready-cooked meatballs!

INGREDIENTS | SERVES 8

½ pound uncooked smoked bacon, cut into 1" pieces

1 pound ground beef

½ cup panko bread crumbs

½ medium yellow onion, peeled and chopped

1 large egg

1 teaspoon salt

½ teaspoon ground fennel

½ teaspoon dried oregano leaves

½ teaspoon smoked paprika

¼ teaspoon ground black pepper

1 cup chili sauce

1 cup grape jelly

1. Pulse bacon in a food processor until ground but not a paste, about thirty pulses. Transfer bacon to a large bowl along with beef, bread crumbs, onion, egg, salt, fennel, oregano, paprika, and pepper. Mix well and roll into about twenty-four 1" meatballs.

2. Press Sauté on Instant Pot®. Once machine indicates Hot, about 3 minutes, add meatballs 1" apart. Cook 2 minutes per side, about 6 minutes total, until browned. Once browned transfer meatballs to a large plate and repeat with remaining meatballs. Press Cancel.

3. Add meatballs, chili sauce, and jelly to pot. Close lid and set steam release to Sealing, then press Manual and adjust cook time to 10 minutes.

4. Once cooking is complete allow pressure to release naturally. Open lid and stir well. Serve hot.

PER SERVING (2 meatballs) Calories: 401 | Fat: 17g | Protein: 17g | Sodium: 1,041mg | Fiber: 3g | Carbohydrates: 40g | Sugar: 24g

Sweet Chili Cocktail Sausages

Thai sweet chili sauce is available in the Asian foods section of most grocery stores. It is sweet and garlicky, with a little hint of heat. If you are unable to find it, you can use a favorite pepper jelly with a little extra fresh garlic added for flavor.

INGREDIENTS | SERVES 8

1 (28-ounce) package cocktail sausages

1 cup Thai sweet chili sauce

¼ cup apricot preserves

2 tablespoons freshly squeezed lime juice

2 tablespoons sriracha sauce

1. Add all ingredients to Instant Pot® and stir well. Close lid and set steam release to Sealing, then press Manual and adjust cook time to 5 minutes.

2. Once cooking is complete quick-release pressure. Transfer sausages to a serving bowl, leaving sauce behind.

3. Press Cancel on pot, then press Sauté and cook sauce 8 minutes until thick. Pour over sausages and turn to coat. Serve hot.

PER SERVING Calories: 291 | Fat: 17g | Protein: 16g | Sodium: 1,087mg | Fiber: 2g | Carbohydrates: 15g | Sugar: 8g

Texas Caviar

This is a great dish filled with flavor, and it's great for a party. It takes a little time, and it is worth planning ahead so that it can be served chilled. Prepare up to two days in advance and store in a covered container in the refrigerator. Texas Caviar is said to have first been served on New Year's Eve at the Houston Country Club around 1940!

INGREDIENTS | YIELDS 5 CUPS

1 cup dry black-eyed peas

4 cups water

1 pound cooked corn kernels

½ medium red onion, peeled and diced

½ medium green bell pepper, seeded and diced

1 pickled jalapeño, finely chopped

1 medium tomato, diced

2 tablespoons chopped fresh cilantro

¼ cup red wine vinegar

2 tablespoons extra-virgin olive oil

1 teaspoon salt

½ teaspoon ground black pepper

½ teaspoon ground cumin

1. Add black-eyed peas and water to Instant Pot®. Close lid and set steam release to Sealing, then press Manual and adjust cook time to 30 minutes.

2. Once cooking is complete allow pressure to release naturally, about 15 minutes, and remove lid. Drain peas and transfer to a large mixing bowl. Add remaining ingredients and stir until thoroughly combined. Refrigerate covered 2 hours before serving.

PER SERVING (1 cup) Calories: 262 | Fat: 6.5g | Protein: 11g | Sodium: 483mg | Fiber: 7g | Carbohydrates: 43g | Sugar: 7g

Pineapple Teriyaki Pork Meatballs

You can use fresh pineapple in this recipe, but you will need juice for the meatball sauce. If you're using fresh pineapple, be sure to chop it into small pieces and do not include any of the core, which will not become tender.

INGREDIENTS | SERVES 8

1 pound ground pork

½ cup panko bread crumbs

½ medium sweet onion, peeled and chopped

1 large egg

1 teaspoon salt

¼ teaspoon ground black pepper

2 tablespoons olive oil

1 (15-ounce) can pineapple tidbits in juice, drained and juice reserved

½ cup teriyaki sauce

¼ teaspoon crushed red pepper flakes

2 tablespoons sesame seeds

¼ cup sliced green onion tops

1. Add pork, bread crumbs, onion, egg, salt, and pepper to a large bowl. Mix well and roll into about twenty-four 1" meatballs.

2. Press Sauté on Instant Pot®. Once machine indicates Hot, add oil and let heat 30 seconds, then add meatballs, spaced 1" apart. Cook 2 minutes per side, about 6 minutes total, until browned. Once browned transfer to a plate and repeat with remaining meatballs. Press Cancel.

3. Add meatballs, pineapple, ½ cup pineapple juice, teriyaki sauce, and red pepper flakes to pot. Close lid and set steam release to Sealing, then press Manual and adjust cook time to 10 minutes.

4. Once cooking is complete allow pressure to release naturally. Open lid and stir well. Serve hot with sesame seeds and green onion for garnish.

PER SERVING (2 meatballs) Calories: 277 | Fat: 17g | Protein: 12g | Sodium: 1,071mg | Fiber: 1.5g | Carbohydrates: 17g | Sugar: 10g

Basic Hummus

Hummus, an ancient dish made with chickpeas and sesame seeds, can be enhanced with a variety of flavors. While hummus can be thrown together quite quickly in a food processor, the real contribution of the Instant Pot® here is to allow you to bring this dish together using dried beans instead of canned in just 30 minutes. Add roasted red peppers, roasted garlic, or sun-dried tomatoes to spice up this basic recipe.

INGREDIENTS | YIELDS 2 CUPS

1 cup dried chickpeas

4 cups water

1 tablespoon plus ¼ cup extra-virgin olive oil, divided

2 teaspoons ground cumin

¾ teaspoon ground black pepper

¾ teaspoon salt

⅓ cup freshly squeezed lemon juice

1 teaspoon peeled minced garlic

⅓ cup tahini

1. Add chickpeas, water, and 1 tablespoon oil to Instant Pot®. Close lid and set steam release to Sealing, then press Manual and adjust cook time to 30 minutes.

2. Once cooking is complete quick-release pressure and remove lid. Drain, reserving cooking liquid.

3. Place remaining ingredients, including cooked chickpeas, in a food processor and blend until creamy. If the consistency is too thick, add reserved cooking liquid a little at a time until hummus reaches your desired consistency. Serve chilled or at room temperature. Store in the refrigerator for up to one week.

PER SERVING (2 tablespoons) Calories: 108 | Fat: 7g | Protein: 3.5g | Sodium: 120mg | Fiber: 2g | Carbohydrates: 9g | Sugar: 1g

White Bean Hummus

White Bean Hummus can be dressed up just like traditional hummus, so you can add minced roasted red peppers, pesto, or just a drizzle of olive oil and smoked paprika to the top. Use vegetables like carrots and cucumbers for dippers.

INGREDIENTS | SERVES 8

⅔ cup dry white beans, picked through and rinsed

3 cloves garlic, peeled and crushed

4–6 cups cold water

¼ cup apricot olive oil

1 tablespoon freshly squeezed lemon juice

½ teaspoon salt

1. Add beans and garlic to Instant Pot® and stir well. Add enough cold water to cover ingredients. Close lid and set steam release to Sealing, then press Manual and adjust cook time to 30 minutes.

2. Once cooking is complete allow pressure to release naturally, about 20 minutes. Remove lid and use a fork to check beans are tender. Drain off excess water and transfer beans to food processor.

3. Add remaining ingredients to processor and pulse until mixture is smooth with some small chunks. Transfer to storage container and chill at least 4 hours. Serve cold or at room temperature. Store in the refrigerator for up to one week.

PER SERVING Calories: 111 | Fat: 6.5g | Protein: 3.5g | Sodium: 148mg | Fiber: 3g | Carbohydrates: 10g | Sugar: 1g

Baba Ghanoush

Often translated as "pampered daddy," baba ghanoush is a Middle Eastern dish that has captured the world's imagination for centuries. With just 12 minutes of cooking time, this dish is tailor-made for your Instant Pot®. Try it with toasted pita chips or as a vegetable dip.

INGREDIENTS | SERVES 4

1 tablespoon sesame oil

1 large eggplant, peeled and diced

4 cloves garlic, peeled and minced

½ cup water

3 tablespoons fresh Italian flat-leaf parsley

½ teaspoon salt

2 tablespoons freshly squeezed lemon juice

2 tablespoons tahini

1 tablespoon extra-virgin olive oil

1. Press Sauté on Instant Pot®. Once machine indicates Hot, add sesame oil and let heat 30 seconds, then add eggplant and cook until it begins to soften, about 5 minutes. Add garlic and cook until fragrant, about 30 seconds. Press Cancel.

2. Add water and close lid, then set steam release to Sealing. Press Manual and adjust cook time to 6 minutes.

3. Once cooking is complete quick-release pressure and then remove lid. Strain cooked eggplant and garlic and add to a food processor or blender along with parsley, salt, lemon juice, and tahini. Pulse to process. Add olive oil and process until smooth. Serve immediately or store in an airtight container in the refrigerator up to one week.

PER SERVING Calories: 144 | Fat: 11g | Protein: 3g | Sodium: 304mg | Fiber: 5g | Carbohydrates: 10g | Sugar: 5g

Warm Crab Dip

This dip is best when made with fresh lump crabmeat from your seafood department, but if all you can find is claw meat, that will work. Avoid canned or imitation crabmeat, as they won't have the best texture or flavor. Serve this dip with toasted baguette slices, butter crackers, or pita chips.

INGREDIENTS | SERVES 12

2 tablespoons unsalted butter

½ medium white onion, peeled and finely chopped

½ medium red bell pepper, seeded and finely chopped

2 cloves garlic, peeled and minced

½ teaspoon seafood seasoning

2 (8-ounce) packages cream cheese, room temperature

½ cup mayonnaise

1 cup shredded mozzarella cheese

1 cup shredded Monterey jack cheese

1 teaspoon Worcestershire sauce

½ teaspoon ground mustard

¼ teaspoon salt

1 pound lump crabmeat

1 cup water

Dip Variations

If you want, you can change up the seafood in this dip. Try adding chopped cooked shrimp or cooked lobster, or mix shrimp, crab, and lobster for a seafood lover's dream! You can also use imitation crab if you are looking for a budget-friendly substitute. It still tastes amazing!

1. Spray an 8" × 8" baking dish with nonstick cooking spray.

2. Press Sauté on Instant Pot®. Once machine indicates Hot, about 3 minutes, add butter and melt 30 seconds. Add onion and bell pepper and cook, stirring often, until tender, about 3 minutes. Add garlic and seafood seasoning and cook until fragrant, about 30 seconds. Press Cancel and transfer mixture to a large bowl.

3. Add cream cheese, mayonnaise, mozzarella cheese, Monterey jack cheese, Worcestershire sauce, mustard, and salt to onion mixture. Mix until well combined, then fold in crab. Spread crab mixture into prepared dish.

4. Place rack in Instant Pot® and add water. Fold a long piece of aluminum foil in half. Lay foil over rack to form a sling. Place dish on rack and cover with another piece of aluminum foil. Close lid and set steam release to Sealing, then press Manual and adjust cook time to 5 minutes.

5. Once cooking is complete quick-release pressure. Open lid, press Cancel, and let dip stand 10 minutes before carefully removing from pot with sling. Serve warm.

PER SERVING Calories: 226 | Fat: 18g | Protein: 12g | Sodium: 593mg | Fiber: 0g | Carbohydrates: 2g | Sugar: 1g

Zesty Pizza Dip

Pizza lovers will adore this hearty dip! Enjoy with garlic bread, a toasted baguette, or ciabatta bread.

INGREDIENTS | SERVES 12

1 pound bulk Italian sausage

½ cup chopped pepperoni

1 teaspoon pizza seasoning

1 cup seeded diced green bell peppers

1 cup peeled diced yellow onion

2 cups sliced button mushrooms

½ cup sliced black olives

1 clove garlic, peeled and minced

1 (28-ounce) jar marinara sauce

1 cup shredded mozzarella cheese

1. Press Sauté on Instant Pot®. Once machine indicates Hot, about 3 minutes, add sausage. Cook, crumbling well, until cooked through, about 8 minutes. Add pepperoni and pizza seasoning and cook 2 minutes until fat begins to render from pepperoni, then add pepper, onion, and mushrooms. Cook, stirring often, until onions and peppers are tender, about 5 minutes. Press Cancel.

2. Stir in olives, garlic, and marinara sauce. Close lid and set steam release to Sealing, then press Manual and adjust cook time to 3 minutes.

3. Once cooking is complete quick-release pressure. Open lid and top dip with cheese, then close lid and let stand 10 minutes until cheese is melted. Serve warm.

PER SERVING Calories: 189 | Fat: 12g | Protein: 10g | Sodium: 703mg | Fiber: 2g | Carbohydrates: 8g | Sugar: 5g

Asian Sesame Wings

These wings are sweet with a hot kick from the ginger. Serve these when you want to spice up your game-day menu or anytime you want a change from traditional wings.

INGREDIENTS | SERVES 8

4 pounds chicken wings, separated and tips discarded

1 teaspoon Chinese five-spice powder

½ teaspoon ground ginger

½ teaspoon garlic powder

1 cup water

1 cup teriyaki glaze

¼ cup toasted sesame seeds

1. In a large bowl combine wings, five-spice powder, ginger, and garlic powder. Toss to coat. Let stand 10 minutes.

2. Place steamer basket in Instant Pot® and add water. Arrange wings in basket. Close lid and set steam release to Sealing, then press Manual and adjust cook time to 5 minutes.

3. Heat broiler on high. Cover a baking sheet with aluminum foil and spray generously with nonstick cooking spray.

4. Once cooking is complete allow pressure to release naturally. Press Cancel and open lid. Transfer wings to a large clean bowl and add teriyaki glaze. Toss to coat, then arrange wings on prepared baking sheet. Broil, turning every 3 minutes, until wings are browned and sauce is bubbling and sticky, about 10 minutes. Garnish with sesame seeds. Serve hot.

PER SERVING Calories: 486 | Fat: 31g | Protein: 42g | Sodium: 1,569mg | Fiber: 0.5g | Carbohydrates: 7g | Sugar: 5g

Soup, Stew, and Chili

Speedy Chicken Soup

Making chicken soup from scratch can take hours. Here, the Instant Pot® slashes that time to a fraction, without losing the richness of the broth and tenderness of the vegetables. Be sure to finish seasoning the soup after it is prepared to avoid adding too much salt.

INGREDIENTS | SERVES 8

1 (3-pound) whole chicken

3 ribs celery, chopped

2 medium carrots, peeled and chopped

1 medium yellow onion, peeled and chopped

1 clove garlic, peeled and smashed

1 bay leaf

1 teaspoon poultry seasoning

½ teaspoon dried thyme leaves

1 teaspoon salt

¼ teaspoon ground black pepper

8 cups water

Rice and Noodle Variations

For chicken and rice soup add ½ cup dry long-grain rice to prepared soup and cook on Manual for 4 minutes, then allow pressure to release naturally. For chicken noodle soup, add 4 ounces dry egg noodles and cook on Manual for 4 minutes, then quick-release pressure.

1. Place all ingredients in Instant Pot®. Close lid and set steam release to Sealing, then press Soup.

2. Once cooking is complete allow pressure to release naturally, about 25 minutes. Press Cancel and open lid. Discard bay leaf.

3. Using tongs or a slotted spoon, transfer chicken to a cutting board. Carefully, as chicken is still hot, shred meat, discarding skin and bones. Return meat to pot and stir to combine. Serve hot.

PER SERVING Calories: 215 | Fat: 5g | Protein: 36g | Sodium: 450mg | Fiber: 1g | Carbohydrates: 4g | Sugar: 1.5g

Classic Beef Stew

Beef stew is the perfect way to use tough cuts of meat, sold often as stew meat in the market. You can have your butcher cut it up for you to save even more time.

INGREDIENTS | SERVES 6

1 pound beef stew meat, cut into 1" cubes

¼ cup all-purpose flour

1 teaspoon salt

1 teaspoon ground black pepper

3 tablespoons olive oil

2 tablespoons tomato paste

1 teaspoon dried thyme leaves

3 cups beef broth

1 teaspoon Worcestershire sauce

3 cloves garlic, peeled and minced

1 (8-ounce) container sliced button mushrooms

3 medium carrots, peeled and cut into ½" pieces

1 medium yellow onion, peeled and roughly chopped

1 large russet potato, peeled and cut into ½" cubes

1. In a resealable bag or airtight storage container, add beef, flour, salt, and pepper. Shake to coat beef cubes evenly.

2. Press Sauté on Instant Pot®. Once machine indicates Hot, about 3 minutes, add oil and heat for 15 seconds. Add beef to pot in an even layer, making sure there is space between beef cubes to prevent steam from forming. Brown 3 minutes on each side. Remove from pot and reserve on a plate. Repeat with remaining beef.

3. Add tomato paste and thyme to pot and cook 30 seconds, then add beef broth and scrape pot to release any browned bits. Press Cancel.

4. Add beef cubes and remaining ingredients to Instant Pot®. Close lid and set steam release to Sealing, then press Manual and adjust cook time to 35 minutes.

5. Once cooking is complete allow pressure to release naturally, about 20 minutes. Press Cancel, open lid, and stir well. If you prefer a thicker stew, press Sauté and let stew reduce to desired thickness. Serve hot.

PER SERVING Calories: 287 | Fat: 13g | Protein: 21g | Sodium: 954mg | Fiber: 3g | Carbohydrates: 23g | Sugar: 4g

Split Pea Soup

Split pea soup is perfect for when the weather starts to get chilly, and you can make it up ahead and have it for lunches and dinners all week. The flavor improves with time, so making this early in the week will reward you with extra flavor.

INGREDIENTS | SERVES 8

4 tablespoons unsalted butter

1 medium yellow onion, peeled and finely diced

2 ribs celery, finely diced

2 cups ham steak, diced

2 cloves garlic, peeled and minced

1 pound dry green split peas

6 cups chicken stock

1 bay leaf

½ teaspoon salt

½ teaspoon ground black pepper

Split Peas

Split peas are a type of field pea that is dried, hulled, and split. This process makes them easier to cook, and they do not require presoaking. They have plenty of fiber—26 grams per a 100-gram serving—so they will fill you up. Split peas come in green and yellow. Yellow peas are milder and a little starchier than the green variety.

1. Press Sauté on Instant Pot®. Once machine indicates Hot, about 3 minutes, add butter and melt 30 seconds. Once melted add onion, celery, and ham. Cook until onion and celery are just tender, about 3 minutes. Add garlic and cook until fragrant, about 30 seconds. Press Cancel.

2. Add remaining ingredients to pot. Close lid and set steam release to Sealing, then press Manual and adjust cook time to 20 minutes.

3. Once cooking is complete quick-release pressure. Press Cancel, open lid, and stir well. Remove and discard bay leaf. Serve hot.

PER SERVING Calories: 226 | Fat: 11g | Protein: 14g | Sodium: 862mg | Fiber: 3.5g | Carbohydrates: 17g | Sugar: 6g

Wild Rice Soup

This creamy soup is perfect for a cold, rainy day—or on a lazy weekend when you want something easy, hearty, and filling. Dress it up by using more exotic mushrooms such as hen of the woods, oyster, or shiitake.

INGREDIENTS | SERVES 8

2 tablespoons unsalted butter

4 medium carrots, peeled and chopped

4 ribs celery, chopped

1 medium white onion, peeled and chopped

1 (8-ounce) container sliced button mushrooms

2 cloves garlic, peeled and minced

½ teaspoon dried thyme leaves

1 teaspoon salt

½ teaspoon ground black pepper

1 cup wild rice

4 cups vegetable broth

⅓ cup water

2 tablespoons cornstarch

½ cup heavy cream

What Is Wild Rice?

Wild rice is a cousin of traditional white rice and is harvested in North America and across Asia. Wild rice is high in protein and fiber and is low in fat. It is also a good source of lysine, an amino acid that is good for your brain and gut!

1. Press Sauté on Instant Pot®. Once machine indicates Hot, about 3 minutes, add butter and melt 30 seconds. Once melted add carrot, celery, and onion. Cook until vegetables are just tender, about 5 minutes, then add mushrooms and cook until they start to release their juice, about 3 minutes.

2. Add garlic, thyme, salt, pepper, and rice to pot and cook until garlic is fragrant, about 1 minute. Press Cancel. Add broth, close lid, and set steam release to Sealing, then press Manual and adjust cook time to 45 minutes.

3. Once cooking is complete quick-release pressure, then open lid and stir well. Press Cancel, then press Sauté.

4. Whisk together water and cornstarch in a small bowl and add into pot. Bring mixture to a boil, stirring constantly, until thickened, about 4 minutes. Press Cancel and stir in cream. Serve hot.

PER SERVING Calories: 458 | Fat: 17g | Protein: 15g | Sodium: 1,003mg | Fiber: 3g | Carbohydrates: 63g | Sugar: 12g

Classic Beef Chili

Chili has always been a hotly debated dish. For some, chili isn't chili without beans, but for others you can't call it chili if there are beans in it. This chili does not call for beans, but if you are firmly in the "bean camp," feel free to stir in a can of rinsed and drained red beans after the chili has finished cooking.

INGREDIENTS | SERVES 8

2 pounds chuck roast

1 medium white onion, peeled and chopped

3 cloves garlic, peeled and minced

¼ cup chili powder

1 teaspoon ground cumin

2 tablespoons packed light brown sugar

½ teaspoon salt

½ teaspoon ground black pepper

2 cups beef broth

2½ cups water, divided

¼ cup corn masa

1 tablespoon freshly squeezed lime juice

Next-Level Chili

For next-level chili replace all but 1 tablespoon of the chili powder in this recipe with 1 cup of the Enchilada Sauce in Chapter 4. This will give you a richer chili flavor and more of the traditional Southwest chili taste. You may also want to add a teaspoon or two of vinegar at the end of cooking. The acid helps enhance the chili flavor.

1. Press Sauté on Instant Pot®. Once machine indicates Hot, about 3 minutes, add meat. Brown meat well, about 10 minutes. Once browned add onion, garlic, chili powder, cumin, brown sugar, salt, and pepper and cook until onions are just tender, about 10 minutes.

2. Add beef broth and 2 cups water and stir well. Press Cancel and close lid, then set steam release to Sealing and press Chili.

3. Once cooking is complete quick-release pressure, then open lid and stir well. Press Cancel, then press Sauté.

4. Whisk together reserved water and masa in a small bowl and then whisk into chili. Bring chili to a boil, stirring constantly, until it starts to thicken, about 5 minutes. Press Cancel, then add lime juice and serve hot.

PER SERVING Calories: 227 | Fat: 7g | Protein: 30g | Sodium: 570mg | Fiber: 2g | Carbohydrates: 9g | Sugar: 3g

Green Chicken Chili

*This delicious chicken chili gets a lot of rich flavor from the fat in the chicken thighs,
so it won't have the same robust flavor if you swap out for chicken breasts.*

INGREDIENTS | SERVES 8

2 tablespoons unsalted butter

1 medium yellow onion, peeled and chopped

½ pound poblano peppers, seeded and roughly chopped

½ pound Anaheim peppers, seeded and roughly chopped

½ pound tomatillos, husked and quartered

2 jalapeños, seeded and roughly chopped

2 cloves garlic, peeled and minced

1 teaspoon ground cumin

6 bone-in, skin-on chicken thighs, about 2½ pounds

2 cups chicken stock

2 cups water

⅓ cup roughly chopped fresh cilantro

3 (14.5-ounce) cans great northern beans, drained and rinsed

1. Press Sauté on Instant Pot®. Once machine indicates Hot, about 3 minutes, add butter and melt 30 seconds. Once melted add onion and cook until softened, about 3 minutes. Add poblano and Anaheim peppers, tomatillos, and jalapeños and cook 3 minutes, then add garlic and cumin and cook until fragrant, about 30 seconds. Press Cancel.

2. Add chicken thighs, chicken stock, and water to pot. Close lid, set steam release to Sealing, and press Chili.

3. Once cooking is complete quick-release pressure, then open lid and stir well. Press Cancel and remove chicken to a cutting board. Carefully remove skin from chicken and shred meat with two forks.

4. Use an immersion blender to purée sauce until smooth. Stir meat, cilantro, and beans into sauce. Serve warm.

PER SERVING Calories: 384 | Fat: 11g | Protein: 39g | Sodium: 681mg | Fiber: 8g | Carbohydrates: 31g | Sugar: 7g

Three-Bean Vegetarian Chili

This chili is great for vegans, but it will also satisfy any meat eaters in your group! You can use this on tortilla chips with Vegan Nacho Cheese Sauce (Chapter 4) for stadium-style nachos or smother it on a crisp baked potato for a filling vegan lunch or dinner!

INGREDIENTS | SERVES 8

1 cup dry pinto beans, soaked overnight

1 cup dry red beans, soaked overnight

1 cup dry black beans, soaked overnight

2 medium white onions, peeled and chopped

2 medium red bell peppers, seeded and chopped

2 ribs celery, chopped

1 (28-ounce) can diced tomatoes

1 (15-ounce) can tomato sauce

¼ cup chili powder

2 tablespoons smoked paprika

1 teaspoon ground cumin

1 teaspoon ground coriander

½ teaspoon salt

½ teaspoon ground black pepper

3 cups vegetable broth

1 cup water

1. Place all ingredients in Instant Pot®. Close lid, set steam release to Sealing, and press Chili.

2. Once cooking is complete quick-release pressure, then open lid and stir well. If chili is too thin, press Cancel and then press Sauté and let chili simmer, uncovered, until desired thickness is reached. Serve warm.

PER SERVING Calories: 398 | Fat: 8g | Protein: 18g | Sodium: 1,306mg | Fiber: 12g | Carbohydrates: 67g | Sugar: 16g

Quick Soaked Beans

You can speed-soak beans in your Instant Pot®! Just rinse them, put them in the pot, and add 4 cups of water for every 1 cup of dry beans. Press Sauté and bring beans to a boil, then press Cancel and close the lid. Set steam release to Sealing, press Manual, and adjust cook time to 2 minutes. Once done allow pressure to release naturally, drain, and proceed with your recipe!

Creamy Mushroom Bisque

Browning half of the fresh mushrooms in batches may take a little longer, but it ensures you get the most complex, rich flavor. If you choose, you can skip this step and still have amazing bisque!

INGREDIENTS | SERVES 8

1 (0.5-ounce) bag dry wild mushrooms

2 cups boiling water

3 tablespoons unsalted butter, divided

4 cups sliced cremini mushrooms

2 ribs celery, chopped

1 medium yellow onion, peeled and chopped

2 cloves garlic, peeled and minced

½ teaspoon dried thyme leaves

1 bay leaf

4 cups sliced button mushrooms

4 cups shiitake mushrooms, sliced into strips

2 cups vegetable broth

½ cup heavy cream

1. In a medium heatproof bowl add dry wild mushrooms and boiling water. Let stand until fully rehydrated, about 30 minutes. Strain mushrooms and reserve soaking liquid.

2. Press Sauté on Instant Pot®. Once machine indicates Hot, about 3 minutes, add 1 tablespoon butter and let melt, about 30 seconds. Add 2 cups cremini mushrooms and let stand, without stirring, 3 minutes until golden. Once golden stir well, then remove from pot. Add another tablespoon butter and melt 30 seconds, then add 2 more cups cremini mushrooms and repeat cooking. Remove from pot.

3. Add final tablespoon butter to pot and melt 30 seconds. Once melted add celery and onion. Cook until tender, about 5 minutes, then add garlic and thyme and cook 1 minute until fragrant.

4. Press Cancel and add soaked mushrooms, 1 cup of reserved soaking liquid, browned mushrooms, and remaining ingredients except cream. Stir well. Close lid and set steam release to Sealing, then press Manual and adjust cook time to 5 minutes.

5. Once cooking is complete quick-release pressure. Press Cancel and open lid. Stir well, discard bay leaf, and then purée soup with an immersion blender. Stir in cream. Serve hot.

PER SERVING Calories: 261 | Fat: 14g | Protein: 9g | Sodium: 347mg | Fiber: 2g | Carbohydrates: 26g | Sugar: 7g

Beer Cheese Soup

Beer adds a layer of flavor that really complements the cheese in this soup. Of course, you can skip the beer if you like and just add an equal amount of chicken or vegetable broth.

INGREDIENTS | SERVES 8

3 tablespoons unsalted butter

2 medium carrots, peeled and chopped

2 ribs celery, chopped

1 medium sweet onion, peeled and chopped

1 clove garlic, peeled and minced

1 teaspoon ground mustard

½ teaspoon smoked paprika

¼ cup all-purpose flour

1 (12-ounce) bottle lager or ale-style beer

2 cups chicken broth

½ cup heavy cream

2 cups shredded sharp Cheddar cheese

1 cup shredded Gouda cheese

Beer Soup

In central Europe, primarily Germany, medieval cooks would make a soup from thickened dark beer. It was served, often at breakfast, over bread as a filling meal. With time other ingredients were added to improve the flavor, including herbs, onions, and eventually cheese, to make it even more filling.

1. Press Sauté on Instant Pot®. Once machine indicates Hot, about 3 minutes, add butter and melt 30 seconds. Once melted add carrot, celery, and onion. Cook, stirring often, until softened, about 5 minutes. Add garlic and cook 30 seconds until fragrant, then add mustard and paprika and stir well.

2. Add flour to pot and stir well to combine, then cook 1 minute. Slowly stir in beer, scraping the bottom of pot well.

3. Add broth and press Cancel. Close lid and set steam release to Sealing, then press Manual and adjust cook time to 5 minutes.

4. Once cooking is complete allow pressure to release naturally, about 15 minutes. Open lid and purée mixture with an immersion blender until smooth.

5. Stir in cream, then stir in cheese 1 cup at a time, whisking each additional cup until completely melted before adding another. Serve hot.

PER SERVING Calories: 368 | Fat: 28g | Protein: 16g | Sodium: 467mg | Fiber: 1g | Carbohydrates: 9g | Sugar: 3g

Broccoli Cheese Soup

If you don't want larger chunks of broccoli in your soup, you can strain out some of the larger florets after cooking, purée, and then add them back in once the cheese has been added.

INGREDIENTS | SERVES 8

3 tablespoons unsalted butter

2 medium carrots, peeled and finely chopped

2 ribs celery, finely chopped

1 medium yellow onion, peeled and finely chopped

1 clove garlic, peeled and minced

½ teaspoon dried thyme leaves

2 cups fresh broccoli florets, chopped

¼ cup all-purpose flour

3 cups chicken broth

½ cup heavy cream

2 cups shredded medium Cheddar cheese

1 cup shredded Gruyère cheese

1. Press Sauté on Instant Pot®. Once machine indicates Hot, about 3 minutes, add butter and melt 30 seconds. Once melted add carrot, celery, and onion. Cook, stirring often, until softened, about 5 minutes. Add garlic and cook until fragrant, about 30 seconds, then stir in thyme and broccoli.

2. Add flour to pot and stir well to combine, then cook 1 minute. Slowly stir in broth, scraping the bottom of pot well. Press Cancel.

3. Close lid and set steam release to Sealing, then press Manual and adjust cook time to 5 minutes.

4. Once cooking is complete allow pressure to release naturally, about 15 minutes. Open lid and purée mixture with an immersion blender, leaving some chunks of broccoli behind.

5. Stir in cream, then stir in cheese 1 cup at a time, whisking each additional cup until completely melted before adding another. Serve hot.

PER SERVING Calories: 340 | Fat: 27g | Protein: 16g | Sodium: 382mg | Fiber: 1g | Carbohydrates: 9g | Sugar: 2g

Wild Mushroom Soup

*This broth-based mushroom soup makes a light but flavorful first course, and it is great
if you are feeling under the weather. If you are unable to find fresh wild mushrooms,
you can use whatever fresh mushrooms are available at your market.*

INGREDIENTS | SERVES 8

3 tablespoons unsalted butter

1 rib celery, finely chopped

1 medium carrot, peeled and finely chopped

½ medium yellow onion, peeled and finely chopped

1 clove garlic, peeled and minced

1 (8-ounce) container hen of the woods mushrooms, sliced

1 (8-ounce) container porcini or chanterelle mushrooms, sliced

2 cups sliced shiitake mushrooms

2 tablespoons dry sherry

4 cups vegetable broth

2 cups water

1 tablespoon chopped fresh tarragon

½ teaspoon salt

½ teaspoon ground black pepper

Wild Mushrooms

Wild mushrooms have flavors that range from mildly floral to meaty and earthy. If fresh varieties are unavailable, you can often find small bags of dried mushrooms that just need a quick soak in hot water to be ready. It is unadvisable to forage or pick mushrooms in the wild unless you are well trained or are with a mushroom expert, as some can be deadly.

1. Press Sauté on Instant Pot®. Once machine indicates Hot, about 3 minutes, add butter and melt 30 seconds. Once melted add celery, carrot, and onion. Cook, stirring often, until softened, about 5 minutes. Add garlic and cook 30 seconds until fragrant, then add mushrooms and cook until beginning to soften, about 5 minutes.

2. Add remaining ingredients to pot and stir well. Press Cancel. Close lid and set steam release to Sealing, then press Manual and adjust cook time to 5 minutes.

3. Once cooking is complete allow pressure to release naturally, about 15 minutes. Press Cancel, open lid, and stir well. Serve hot.

PER SERVING Calories: 136 | Fat: 6g | Protein: 5g | Sodium: 330mg | Fiber: 2g | Carbohydrates: 14g | Sugar: 4g

Lasagna Soup

Love lasagna but hate the work of layering everything and washing all the dishes?
This soup is for you. It has all of the delicious flavor with none of the stress!

INGREDIENTS | SERVES 8

1 pound bulk Italian sausage

1 medium yellow onion, peeled and diced

2 cloves garlic, peeled and minced

1 teaspoon Italian seasoning

¼ teaspoon crushed red pepper flakes

3 cups tomato sauce

1 (15-ounce) can crushed tomatoes

1 cup water

10 lasagna noodles, broken into 2" pieces

½ cup heavy cream

1 cup shredded mozzarella cheese

1. Press Sauté on Instant Pot®. Once machine indicates Hot, add sausage. Cook, crumbling, until browned, about 8 minutes. Add onion and cook until tender, about 3 minutes, then add garlic, Italian seasoning, and red pepper flakes and cook 30 seconds.

2. Add tomato sauce, crushed tomatoes, water, and noodles to pot. Press Cancel. Close lid and set steam release to Sealing, then press Manual and adjust cook time to 4 minutes.

3. Once cooking is complete quick-release pressure and open lid. Stir sauce, then add cream. Serve in eight bowls, topped with cheese.

PER SERVING Calories: 387 | Fat: 19g | Protein: 18g | Sodium: 961mg | Fiber: 3.5g | Carbohydrates: 36g | Sugar: 6g

Loaded Potato Soup

What could be better than baked potatoes? Why, potato soup, of course! Be careful not to overblend the soup, as the starch in the potatoes can get a little gluey if you purée too long.

INGREDIENTS | SERVES 8

4 tablespoons unsalted butter

1 medium yellow onion, peeled and chopped

3 tablespoons all-purpose flour

1 teaspoon salt

½ teaspoon ground black pepper

6 cups chicken broth

5 pounds russet potatoes, peeled and cubed

1 (8-ounce) package cream cheese

1 cup heavy cream

8 strips thick-cut bacon, cooked crisp and chopped

4 green onions, sliced

1 cup shredded Cheddar cheese

1 cup sour cream

1. Press Sauté on Instant Pot®. Once machine indicates Hot, add butter and melt 30 seconds. Once melted add onion and cook until tender, about 3 minutes. Add flour, salt, and pepper and mix until flour is moistened, about 1 minute. Slowly whisk in broth, then add potatoes. Press Cancel.

2. Close lid and set steam release to Sealing, then press Manual and adjust cook time to 10 minutes.

3. Once cooking is complete allow pressure to release naturally, about 15 minutes. Open lid and stir well, then use an immersion blender to purée soup until there are some large chunks of potato but soup is mostly smooth.

4. Add cream cheese and stir until melted, then add cream and stir well. Serve in eight bowls garnished with bacon, green onion, Cheddar cheese, and sour cream.

PER SERVING Calories: 694 | Fat: 43g | Protein: 19g | Sodium: 819mg | Fiber: 4g | Carbohydrates: 59g | Sugar: 5g

Cauliflower Soup with Cheddar and Chives

If you love potato soup but want to avoid the carbs, this soup is a dream come true. Fancy enough for guests, but easy enough to make anytime, this soup will quickly become a staple of your cooking repertoire!

INGREDIENTS | SERVES 6

4 tablespoons unsalted butter

1 medium yellow onion, peeled and chopped

1 rib celery, chopped

1 medium carrot, peeled and chopped

½ teaspoon dried thyme leaves

4 cups fresh cauliflower florets

2 cups chicken stock

1 cup heavy cream

1 (8-ounce) package cream cheese, room temperature

1½ cups shredded Cheddar cheese, divided

⅓ cup chopped fresh chives, divided

1. Press Sauté on Instant Pot®. Once machine indicates Hot, add butter and melt 30 seconds. Once melted add onion, celery, and carrot. Cook, stirring often, 3 minutes. Add thyme, cauliflower, and stock. Stir well, then press Cancel.

2. Close lid and set steam release to Sealing, then press Manual and adjust cook time to 5 minutes.

3. Once cooking is complete allow pressure to release naturally, about 15 minutes. Remove lid and use an immersion blender to purée soup until smooth.

4. Stir in cream and cream cheese. Process with blender until cream cheese is thoroughly incorporated. Stir in 1 cup Cheddar cheese and 3 tablespoons chives and mix until cheese is melted. Serve immediately in six bowls topped with remaining Cheddar cheese and chives.

PER SERVING Calories: 421 | Fat: 37g | Protein: 11g | Sodium: 380mg | Fiber: 2g | Carbohydrates: 11g | Sugar: 5g

Vegetable Barley Soup

A big pot of Vegetable Barley Soup is great to have on hand for lunches during the week with a sandwich or green salad.

INGREDIENTS | SERVES 8

2 tablespoons avocado oil

½ medium yellow onion, peeled and chopped

1 medium carrot, peeled and chopped

1 rib celery, chopped

2 cups sliced button mushrooms

2 cloves garlic, peeled and minced

½ teaspoon dried thyme leaves

½ teaspoon ground black pepper

1 russet potato, peeled and cut into ½" cubes

1 (14-ounce) can fire-roasted diced tomatoes, juice included

½ cup medium pearl barley

4 cups vegetable broth

2 cups water

1 (15-ounce) can corn, drained

1 (15-ounce) can cut green beans, drained

1 (15-ounce) can great northern beans, drained

½ teaspoon salt

1. Press Sauté on Instant Pot®. Once machine indicates Hot, add oil and let heat 30 seconds, then add onion, carrot, celery, and mushrooms. Cook until just tender, about 5 minutes. Add garlic, thyme, and pepper. Cook 30 seconds. Press Cancel.

2. Add potato, tomatoes, barley, broth, and water to pot. Close lid, set steam release to Sealing, and press Soup.

3. Once cooking is complete allow pressure to release naturally, about 15 minutes. Open lid and stir soup, then add corn, green beans, and great northern beans. Close lid and let stand on Keep Warm 10 minutes. Stir in salt. Serve hot.

PER SERVING Calories: 481 | Fat: 13g | Protein: 18g | Sodium: 1,052mg | Fiber: 8g | Carbohydrates: 77g | Sugar: 14g

Kitchen Sink Soup

Have you ever looked in the refrigerator and found you have half of a bell pepper, one quarter of a zucchini, a half cup of chopped squash, and perhaps a quarter of an onion? Vegetable soup is a perfect place to use up all of these odds and ends!

Shrimp and Lobster Bisque

Fresh lobster can be expensive, so stretch it with this satisfying bisque! Look for lobster or seafood stock in your local market in the canned food aisle or in the seafood section.

INGREDIENTS | SERVES 6

4 tablespoons unsalted butter

4 ribs celery, finely chopped

2 large carrots, peeled and finely chopped

1 medium yellow onion, peeled and finely chopped

2 cloves garlic, peeled and minced

¼ teaspoon ground white pepper

¼ cup all-purpose flour

3 cups seafood stock

1 bay leaf

1 pound raw shrimp, peeled and deveined

1 pound raw lobster tail meat, chopped

2 cups heavy cream

1 tablespoon dry sherry

Homemade Shellfish Stock

Save your lobster tails and shrimp shells for a delicious homemade seafood stock. Just combine 4 cups seafood shells with 3 minced garlic cloves, 1 each roughly chopped carrot, onion, and celery rib, and enough water to cover shells completely. Cook on Manual for 120 minutes, allow pressure to release naturally, and then strain into a storage container. Refrigerate covered up to three days, or freeze up to three months.

1. Press Sauté on Instant Pot®. Once machine indicates Hot, add butter and melt 30 seconds. Once melted add celery, carrot, and onion. Cook until tender, about 5 minutes. Add garlic and pepper and cook until fragrant, about 30 seconds.

2. Sprinkle flour over vegetables and stir to combine, then cook 1 minute until flour is moistened and no raw flour remains. Slowly add 1 cup stock, scraping bottom of pot well. Whisk in remaining stock and bay leaf. Press Cancel.

3. Close lid and set steam release to Sealing, then press Manual and adjust cook time to 5 minutes.

4. Once cooking is complete allow pressure to release naturally, about 15 minutes. Remove lid and stir well, remove bay leaf, then use an immersion blender to purée soup until smooth.

5. Add shrimp, lobster, cream, and sherry to pot. Let stand on Keep Warm until seafood is cooked through, about 10 minutes. Serve hot.

PER SERVING Calories: 525 | Fat: 39g | Protein: 32g | Sodium: 635mg | Fiber: 1g | Carbohydrates: 10g | Sugar: 4g

Clam Chowder

This rich Clam Chowder makes a complete meal with some crusty slices of bread and a glass of white wine. You can also garnish your bowls with chopped fresh parsley for a little color.

INGREDIENTS | SERVES 8

6 tablespoons unsalted butter

1 rib celery, chopped

1 medium carrot, peeled and chopped

1 medium yellow onion, peeled and diced

2 cloves garlic, peeled and minced

½ teaspoon ground white pepper

¼ teaspoon dried thyme leaves

⅓ cup all-purpose flour

4 cups seafood stock

1 bay leaf

4 large russet potatoes, peeled and diced

2 (6.5-ounce) cans chopped clams

2 cups heavy cream

1. Press Sauté on Instant Pot®. Once machine indicates Hot, add butter and melt 30 seconds. Once melted add celery, carrot, and onion and cook until tender, about 5 minutes. Add garlic, pepper, and thyme and cook until fragrant, about 30 seconds.

2. Sprinkle flour over vegetables and mix well, then cook 1 minute until no dry flour remains. Slowly add stock, whisking constantly until smooth, then add bay leaf and potatoes. Press Cancel.

3. Close lid and set steam release to Sealing, then press Manual and adjust cook time to 5 minutes.

4. Once cooking is complete allow pressure to release naturally, about 15 minutes. Open lid and stir in clams and cream. Discard bay leaf and serve immediately.

PER SERVING Calories: 542 | Fat: 32g | Protein: 19g | Sodium: 275mg | Fiber: 3g | Carbohydrates: 44g | Sugar: 4g

CHAPTER 7

Beans and Lentils

Classic Refried Beans

No Tex-Mex meal is complete without a side of refried beans. These beans are excellent served with scrambled eggs, stuffed into burritos, or dropped on cheesy nachos.

INGREDIENTS | SERVES 8

1 pound dry pinto beans, soaked overnight and drained

1 medium yellow onion, peeled and sliced in half

2 cloves garlic, peeled and lightly crushed

8 stems fresh cilantro, tied into a bundle with butcher's twine

1 teaspoon ground cumin

1 teaspoon salt

8 cups water

1 tablespoon olive oil

¼ cup lard

Refried Bean Dip

Transform your regular refried beans into a tasty dip! For every 1 cup of your prepared refried beans, add 2 teaspoons fresh lime juice, ½ teaspoon chili powder, and ½ teaspoon smoked paprika. Stir well and heat over medium-low heat on the stove until it starts to simmer. Serve warm or at room temperature.

1. Add all ingredients except lard to Instant Pot®. Close lid and set steam release to Sealing, then press Manual and adjust cook time to 20 minutes.

2. Once cooking is complete allow pressure to release naturally, about 20 minutes. Press Cancel. Remove lid and discard onion, garlic, and cilantro. Transfer strained beans to food processor and pulse until smooth with some small chunks. If beans are too thick, add cooking water 1 tablespoon at a time.

3. Clean out pot and press Sauté. Once machine indicates Hot, add lard, melting for 30 seconds. Once lard is melted, add bean purée and cook, stirring constantly, until beans have thickened slightly, about 8 minutes. Serve hot.

PER SERVING Calories: 130 | Fat: 9g | Protein: 3g | Sodium: 450mg | Fiber: 3g | Carbohydrates: 10g | Sugar: 1g

Basic Beans

This recipe does not require presoaking, so you can make these beans anytime. You can use most varieties of dry beans, such as pinto beans, black beans, navy beans, or kidney beans.

INGREDIENTS | SERVES 8

1 pound dry beans

1 medium yellow onion, peeled and sliced in half

2 cloves garlic, peeled and lightly crushed

1 teaspoon salt

8 cups water

1 tablespoon olive oil

1. Add all ingredients to Instant Pot®. Close lid and set steam release to Sealing, then press Manual and adjust cook time to 30 minutes.

2. Once cooking is complete allow pressure to release naturally, about 20 minutes. Remove lid and discard onion and garlic. Use immediately, or store in cooking liquid covered in refrigerator up to five days.

PER SERVING Calories: 210 | Fat: 2g | Protein: 12g | Sodium: 308mg | Fiber: 10g | Carbohydrates: 37g | Sugar: 5g

Pinto Bean Soup with Bacon

Pinto bean soup is a popular appetizer and side dish in the American Southwest. Serve it with grilled meat, like steak and chicken fajitas, or alongside a salad with a zippy dressing.

INGREDIENTS | SERVES 6

½ pound smoked bacon, chopped

1 large yellow onion, peeled and chopped

2 cloves garlic, peeled and minced

1 jalapeño, seeded and minced

2 teaspoons ground cumin

1 teaspoon ground coriander

1 teaspoon smoked paprika

1 pound dry pinto beans, soaked overnight and drained

8 stems fresh cilantro, leaves removed, tied into a bundle with butcher's twine

¼ cup roughly chopped fresh cilantro leaves

8 cups water

½ teaspoon salt

1. Press Sauté on Instant Pot®. Once machine indicates Hot, add bacon. Cook, stirring often, until bacon is browned and fat has completely rendered, about 8 minutes. Add onion and cook, stirring often, until tender, about 5 minutes. Add garlic, jalapeño, cumin, coriander, and paprika and cook 2 minutes until garlic and spices are fragrant.

2. Add beans, cilantro stems, and chopped cilantro leaves to pot and toss to coat in onion and spices. Add water, then press Cancel. Close lid, set steam release to Sealing, and press Bean.

3. Once cooking is complete allow pressure to release naturally, about 15 minutes. Remove lid, remove cilantro stems, season with salt, and serve hot.

PER SERVING Calories: 233 | Fat: 15g | Protein: 9g | Sodium: 653mg | Fiber: 4g | Carbohydrates: 15g | Sugar: 2g

White Beans with Ham and Onion

This is a simple yet hearty and comforting bean dish. It is also an excellent place to use up leftover ham from the holidays. If you do not have a ham bone, no worries—you'll still have delicious beans without it!

INGREDIENTS | SERVES 6

1 pound great northern beans, soaked overnight and drained

1 ham bone, meat removed

1 medium yellow onion, peeled and diced

1 clove garlic, peeled and minced

2 tablespoons packed light brown sugar

3 cups diced ham

1 teaspoon salt

½ teaspoon ground black pepper

8 cups water

1 tablespoon olive oil

1. Add all ingredients to Instant Pot®. Close lid and set steam release to Sealing, then press Manual and adjust cook time to 20 minutes.

2. Once cooking is complete allow pressure to release naturally, about 20 minutes. Remove lid and stir well. Serve hot.

PER SERVING Calories: 240 | Fat: 9.5g | Protein: 17g | Sodium: 1,514mg | Fiber: 3.5g | Carbohydrates: 17g | Sugar: 5g

Curried Lentils

Serve these lentils over warm basmati rice or wrapped in warm, buttered naan. If you find these lentils to be a little too thick for you, you can add more cream or a little extra chicken stock.

INGREDIENTS | SERVES 4

2 tablespoons salted butter

1 medium yellow onion, peeled and chopped

1 tablespoon red curry paste

½ teaspoon garam masala

½ teaspoon ground turmeric

½ teaspoon packed light brown sugar

2 cloves garlic, peeled and minced

2 teaspoons grated fresh ginger

3 tablespoons tomato paste

1 cup dry red lentils

2 cups chicken stock

¼ cup heavy cream

1. Press Sauté on Instant Pot®. Once machine indicates Hot, add butter. Melt butter 30 seconds, then add onion and cook until just tender, about 3 minutes. Add curry paste, garam masala, turmeric, brown sugar, garlic, and ginger and cook until fragrant, about 30 seconds. Stir in tomato paste and cook 30 seconds. Press Cancel.

2. Add lentils and chicken stock to pot. Close lid and set steam release to Sealing, then press Manual and adjust cook time to 15 minutes.

3. Once cooking is complete allow pressure to release naturally, about 15 minutes. Remove lid and stir in cream. Serve warm.

PER SERVING Calories: 346 | Fat: 13g | Protein: 16g | Sodium: 326mg | Fiber: 7g | Carbohydrates: 42g | Sugar: 6g

White Beans with Chicken and Sausage

This dish is great to make on Sunday, then box it up for lunches and dinners all week long. The flavor actually improves when made ahead!

INGREDIENTS | SERVES 4

2 tablespoons olive oil

1 pound bone-in, skin-on chicken thighs

2 ribs celery, chopped

1 medium carrot, peeled and chopped

1 medium yellow onion, peeled and chopped

2 cloves garlic, peeled and lightly crushed

½ teaspoon salt

1 pound kielbasa, cut into ½" slices

1 (15-ounce) can diced tomatoes

2 (15-ounce) cans cannellini beans

½ teaspoon dried thyme leaves

¼ teaspoon dried oregano leaves

4 cups chicken stock

1. Press Sauté on Instant Pot®. Once machine indicates Hot, add oil. Heat 30 seconds, then add chicken thighs skin-side down. Cook until skin is browned, about 5 minutes. Turn and brown other side, another 5 minutes. Remove thighs from pot and set aside.

2. Add celery, carrot, and onion to pot. Cook until vegetables are tender, about 5 minutes. Add garlic and cook until fragrant, about 30 seconds. Press Cancel.

3. Add remaining ingredients to pot and top with chicken thighs. Close lid and set steam release to Sealing, then press Manual and adjust cook time to 10 minutes.

4. Once cooking is complete quick-release pressure, open lid, and stir. Serve hot.

PER SERVING Calories: 916 | Fat: 50g | Protein: 64g | Sodium: 1,553mg | Fiber: 12g | Carbohydrates: 50g | Sugar: 10g

Basic Lentils

Plain lentils are a wonderful thing to have handy, as you can add them to soups, toss them into green salads, or simply dress them with olive oil and lemon for a quick meal. They are filling, and a flavorful addition to your meals!

INGREDIENTS | YIELDS 2 CUPS

1 tablespoon olive oil

1 medium yellow onion, peeled and chopped

2 cloves garlic, peeled and minced

1 cup dry lentils, green, red, or brown

½ teaspoon salt

2 cups chicken stock

How to Use Cooked Lentils

Cooked lentils are great in salads and soups, but you can also use them in stuffing, mashed and fried in patties, and as a bulking agent in pasta and chicken salad. Lentil purée also makes an excellent dip with toasted pita chips!

1. Press Sauté on Instant Pot®. Once machine indicates Hot, add oil. Heat oil 30 seconds, then add onion and cook until just tender, about 3 minutes. Add garlic and cook until fragrant, about 30 seconds.

2. Add remaining ingredients to pot. Press Cancel. Close lid and set steam release to Sealing, then press Manual and adjust cook time to 15 minutes.

3. Once cooking is complete allow pressure to release naturally, about 15 minutes. Remove lid and stir. Serve warm, or store in refrigerator until ready to use.

PER SERVING (1 cup) Calories: 510 | Fat: 10g | Protein: 30g | Sodium: 933mg | Fiber: 11g | Carbohydrates: 75g | Sugar: 8g

Green Lentil Stew

When the weather is chilly and you need something to warm you up, this is the stew for you! You can use any hearty winter vegetables here, so play around with the ingredients!

INGREDIENTS | SERVES 6

2 tablespoons olive oil

1 medium yellow onion, peeled and chopped

1 medium carrot, peeled and chopped

2 cloves garlic, peeled and minced

½ teaspoon salt

2 cups dry green lentils

1 medium sweet potato, peeled and diced

6 cups chicken stock

1. Press Sauté on Instant Pot®. Once machine indicates Hot, add oil. Heat oil 30 seconds, then add onion and carrot and cook until just tender, about 3 minutes. Add garlic and salt and cook until fragrant, about 30 seconds. Press Cancel.

2. Add remaining ingredients to pot. Close lid and set steam release to Sealing, then press Manual and adjust cook time to 25 minutes.

3. Once cooking is complete allow pressure to release naturally, about 15 minutes. Remove lid and stir. Serve warm.

PER SERVING Calories: 335 | Fat: 6.5g | Protein: 21g | Sodium: 289mg | Fiber: 8g | Carbohydrates: 50g | Sugar: 3g

Lentil Pâté

Experiment with the cooking time on this dish: some cooks find the lentils take slightly less time to cook than the time provided.

INGREDIENTS | SERVES 8

2 tablespoons olive oil, divided

1 cup peeled diced yellow onion

3 cloves garlic, peeled and minced

1 teaspoon red wine vinegar

2 cups dry green lentils

4 cups water

1 teaspoon salt

¼ teaspoon ground black pepper

1. Press Sauté on Instant Pot®. Once machine indicates Hot, add 1 tablespoon oil. Heat oil 30 seconds, then add onion and cook 3 minutes until translucent. Add garlic and vinegar and cook additional 30 seconds.

2. Add lentils, water, remaining oil, and salt to pot and stir to combine. Press Cancel. Close lid, set steam release to Sealing, and press Bean.

3. Once cooking is complete allow pressure to release naturally 10 minutes. Quick-release any remaining pressure, then open lid.

4. Transfer lentil mixture to a food processor or blender and blend until smooth. Season with pepper and serve warm.

PER SERVING Calories: 208 | Fat: 4g | Protein: 12g | Sodium: 298mg | Fiber: 5g | Carbohydrates: 32g | Sugar: 2g

Red Beans and Rice

If you are able to find authentic andouille sausage, which is firmer and usually found in specialty markets in rings or links, and not the mushy andouille found at most supermarkets, try using it in place of the smoked sausage in this recipe.

INGREDIENTS | SERVES 6

2 tablespoons unsalted butter

1 pound smoked sausage, diced

2 ribs celery, chopped

1 medium yellow onion, peeled and chopped

1 medium green bell pepper, seeded and chopped

3 cloves garlic, peeled and minced

1 teaspoon Cajun seasoning

1 teaspoon dried basil leaves

2 bay leaves

½ teaspoon salt

1 pound dry red beans

4 cups water

1 teaspoon hot sauce

3 cups cooked long-grain white rice

Homemade Cajun Seasoning

Try making your own Cajun seasoning! Mix ¼ cup each paprika and salt; 2 tablespoons each pepper, garlic powder, and onion powder; and 1 teaspoon each thyme and cayenne pepper. Mix well and use anywhere Cajun seasoning is called for.

1. Press Sauté on Instant Pot®. Once machine indicates Hot, add butter and let heat 30 seconds, then add sausage and cook 5 minutes until beginning to brown. Transfer sausage to a large bowl.

2. Add celery, onion, and bell pepper to pot and cook until tender, about 5 minutes. Add garlic, Cajun seasoning, dry basil, bay leaves, and salt and cook 30 seconds until fragrant. Press Cancel.

3. Add sausage and remaining ingredients except hot sauce and rice to pot. Close lid and set steam release to Sealing, then press Manual and adjust cook time to 35 minutes.

4. Once cooking is complete allow pressure to release naturally, about 15 minutes. Remove lid and stir. Discard bay leaves.

5. Remove 2 cups beans from pot and mash in a medium bowl until smooth, then stir back into pot. Season with hot sauce, then serve warm divided onto six plates with cooked rice.

PER SERVING Calories: 598 | Fat: 18g | Protein: 30g | Sodium: 701mg | Fiber: 15g | Carbohydrates: 78g | Sugar: 7g

Basic Chickpeas

Chickpeas can be added to salads, soups, and stews and also mashed into hummus. When you cook your own dry chickpeas, they have a fresher flavor than chickpeas out of a can.

INGREDIENTS | SERVES 5

2 cups dry chickpeas

½ teaspoon salt

6 cups water

Presoaking Chickpeas

This recipe is for cooking unsoaked chickpeas, but you can speed up the cooking process if you presoak. Soak your chickpeas for at least 4 hours (overnight is best). Then, when you are ready to use them, drain off the soaking liquid and cook per this recipe, but for 20 minutes instead of 40.

1. Add chickpeas, salt, and water to Instant Pot®. Close lid and set steam release to Sealing, then press Manual and adjust cook time to 40 minutes.

2. Once cooking is complete allow pressure to release naturally 10 minutes, then quick-release remaining pressure. Remove lid and drain cooked chickpeas. Use immediately, or cool and store covered in refrigerator until ready to use.

PER SERVING Calories: 302 | Fat: 4g | Protein: 16g | Sodium: 260mg | Fiber: 9g | Carbohydrates: 50g | Sugar: 8g

Lentils with Spinach and Ham

You can add diced potato or sweet potato to this dish to make it heartier and more filling. You can also change out the ham for diced chicken breast.

INGREDIENTS | SERVES 6

2 tablespoons unsalted butter

2 ribs celery, chopped

1 medium yellow onion, peeled and chopped

1 medium carrot, peeled and chopped

2 cloves garlic, peeled and minced

½ teaspoon dried thyme leaves

½ teaspoon salt

2 cups dry red lentils

6 cups chicken stock

3 cups baby spinach

2 cups cubed ham

1. Press Sauté on Instant Pot®. Once machine indicates Hot, add butter and let heat 30 seconds, then add celery, onion, and carrot and cook 3 minutes until just tender. Add garlic, thyme, and salt and cook until fragrant, about 30 seconds. Press Cancel.

2. Add remaining ingredients to pot. Close lid and set steam release to Sealing, then press Manual and adjust cook time to 15 minutes.

3. Once cooking is complete allow pressure to release naturally, about 15 minutes. Remove lid and stir. Serve warm.

PER SERVING Calories: 389 | Fat: 10g | Protein: 29g | Sodium: 886mg | Fiber: 7g | Carbohydrates: 48g | Sugar: 3g

White Beans with Garlic and Fresh Tomato

Cherry or Roma tomatoes work best for this recipe, but any variety will do in a pinch. At the risk of breaking the romantic spell that makes them so popular, we'll let you in on a not-so-secret fact: nearly all Roma tomatoes sold in the US trace back to a tomato developed in Maryland in the 1950s.

INGREDIENTS | SERVES 4

1 cup dried cannellini beans

4 cups vegetable broth

1 tablespoon vegetable oil

1 teaspoon salt

2 cloves garlic, peeled and minced

½ cup diced tomatoes

½ teaspoon dried sage

½ teaspoon ground black pepper

1. Add beans, broth, oil, and salt to Instant Pot® and stir. Close lid and set steam release to Sealing, then press Manual and adjust cook time to 30 minutes.

2. Once cooking is complete quick-release pressure, open lid, and stir. Press Cancel.

3. Press Sauté, then press Adjust and set to Less. Add remaining ingredients and simmer uncovered 10 minutes until thickened.

PER SERVING Calories: 202 | Fat: 4g | Protein: 11g | Sodium: 1,143mg | Fiber: 11g | Carbohydrates: 31g | Sugar: 3g

Lentils with Cilantro and Lime

This lentil dish is a perfect companion to grilled fish, chicken, or tofu, and it makes for an interesting change from the typical sides of rice or beans.

INGREDIENTS | YIELDS 2 CUPS

2 tablespoons olive oil

1 medium yellow onion, peeled and chopped

1 medium carrot, peeled and chopped

¼ cup chopped fresh cilantro

½ teaspoon ground cumin

½ teaspoon salt

2 cups dry green lentils

4 cups chicken stock

2 tablespoons freshly squeezed lime juice

1. Press Sauté on Instant Pot®. Once machine indicates Hot, add oil. Heat oil 30 seconds, then add onion and carrot and cook until just tender, about 3 minutes. Add cilantro, cumin, and salt and cook until fragrant, about 30 seconds. Press Cancel.

2. Add lentils and chicken stock to pot. Close lid and set steam release to Sealing, then press Manual and adjust cook time to 15 minutes.

3. Once cooking is complete allow pressure to release naturally, about 15 minutes. Remove lid and stir in lime juice. Serve warm.

PER SERVING (1 cup) Calories: 454 | Fat: 9g | Protein: 28g | Sodium: 381mg | Fiber: 11g | Carbohydrates: 67g | Sugar: 4g

Chickpea Curry

Dry chickpeas can be rehydrated by soaking them overnight in cool water in the refrigerator or by boiling them for one minute and then letting them soak in the hot water for an hour.

INGREDIENTS | SERVES 6

2 tablespoons vegetable oil

1 medium yellow onion, peeled and chopped

2 cloves garlic, peeled and minced

1 tablespoon grated fresh ginger

2 teaspoons ground coriander

2 teaspoons ground cumin

1 teaspoon garam masala

1 teaspoon ground turmeric

1 teaspoon paprika

1 teaspoon salt

½ teaspoon cayenne pepper

1 pound boneless, skinless chicken thighs, cut into 1" pieces

1 (15-ounce) can diced tomatoes, drained

1 pound dry chickpeas, soaked 4 hours

1 cup water

¼ cup chopped fresh cilantro

1. Press Sauté on Instant Pot®. Once machine indicates Hot, add oil and let heat 30 seconds, then add onion and sauté until it starts to soften, about 3 minutes. Add garlic, ginger, coriander, cumin, garam masala, turmeric, paprika, salt, and cayenne pepper and cook 1 minute until very fragrant.

2. Add chicken to pot and turn to coat with onion and spices. Add tomatoes, chickpeas, and water and mix well. Press Cancel, close lid, and set steam release to sealing. Press Manual and adjust cook time to 35 minutes.

3. Once cooking is complete allow pressure to release naturally, about 15 minutes. Remove lid and stir well. If curry looks thin, press Cancel and then you can set pot to Sauté and reduce until it reaches your desired thickness. Serve hot with cilantro for garnish.

PER SERVING Calories: 442 | Fat: 12g | Protein: 31g | Sodium: 561mg | Fiber: 11g | Carbohydrates: 52g | Sugar: 10g

Wasabi Barbecue Chickpeas

Barbecue sauce pairs surprisingly well with hot wasabi, and here they are combined with nutty chickpeas for a dish everyone will enjoy. You can use your favorite prepared barbecue sauce here, or even a spicy ketchup.

INGREDIENTS | SERVES 4

2 tablespoons vegetable oil, divided

½ cup peeled diced yellow onion

1 tablespoon wasabi powder

1 tablespoon plus 4 cups water, divided

1 cup dried chickpeas

1 cup barbecue sauce

1. Press Sauté on Instant Pot®. Once machine indicates Hot, add 1 tablespoon oil and let heat 30 seconds. Add onion and cook until translucent, about 5 minutes.

2. Mix wasabi in a small bowl with 1 tablespoon water, then add to sautéed onion. Remove mixture from pot and set aside.

3. Add chickpeas, remaining water, and 1 tablespoon oil to pot and stir to combine. Press Cancel, close lid, and set steam release to Sealing. Press Manual and adjust cook time to 30 minutes at high pressure.

4. Once cooking is complete let pressure release naturally 10 minutes. Quick-release any remaining pressure and remove lid. Add onion mixture and barbecue sauce and stir to combine. Serve warm or at room temperature.

PER SERVING Calories: 378 | Fat: 10g | Protein: 11g | Sodium: 718mg | Fiber: 7g | Carbohydrates: 61g | Sugar: 28g

CHAPTER 8

Meatless Main Dishes

Three-Cheese Lasagna Bake

If you want to make this lasagna vegan, you can substitute the ricotta with gently crumbled soft tofu, the mozzarella with vegan cheese shreds, and the Parmesan with nutritional yeast.

INGREDIENTS | SERVES 6

2 tablespoons olive oil, divided

1 medium yellow onion, peeled and chopped

1 medium red bell pepper, seeded and chopped

1 medium zucchini, sliced into ¼" pieces

1 cup water

1 cup whole-milk ricotta cheese

1 large egg

1 teaspoon Italian seasoning

1 (24-ounce) jar marinara sauce

2 no-boil lasagna sheets, broken into 3" pieces

1 cup shredded mozzarella cheese

½ cup Parmesan cheese

What Are No-Boil Lasagna Sheets?

No-boil lasagna sheets are thin, parcooked dried pasta sheets that can be used in a recipe like lasagna without any additional cooking. The moisture in the sauce and cheese will rehydrate the noodles as they cook. These sheets are available in most grocery stores in the pasta section.

1. Press Sauté on Instant Pot®. Once machine indicates Hot, add 1 tablespoon oil and let heat 30 seconds, then add onion and bell pepper and cook 8 minutes until vegetables are softened. Transfer to a large bowl and set aside.

2. Add remaining oil to pot and heat 30 seconds. Once hot add zucchini and cook until tender, about 6 minutes. Press Cancel. Transfer to bowl with onions and peppers. Set aside.

3. Clean out pot, then place rack inside pot and add water. Fold a long piece of aluminum foil in half. Lay foil over rack to form a sling.

4. In a medium bowl combine ricotta cheese, egg, and Italian seasoning and mix well. Set aside.

5. Spray an 8" × 8" baking dish with nonstick cooking spray. Spread ⅓ marinara sauce in bottom of dish. Layer lasagna noodle pieces on sauce. Next add ⅓ ricotta cheese mixture and spread evenly, then add ⅓ vegetable mixture and spread evenly. Top with ⅓ mozzarella cheese. Repeat with remaining ingredients, then top with Parmesan cheese.

6. Cover dish tightly with aluminum foil and place on rack in pot. Close lid and set steam release to Sealing, then press Manual and adjust cook time to 25 minutes.

7. Once cooking is complete quick-release pressure. Press Cancel and open lid. Let dish stand 10 minutes before carefully removing from pot with sling. Remove foil and serve. If you would like to brown lasagna cheese, place dish under broiler on high 4 minutes.

PER SERVING Calories: 328 | Fat: 19g | Protein: 16g | Sodium: 782mg | Fiber: 3g | Carbohydrates: 21g | Sugar: 9g

Ratatouille

Originally from Nice, France, ratatouille literally means "to stir up." If you want to make this more authentic to its French roots, substitute herbes de Provence in place of Italian seasoning.

INGREDIENTS | SERVES 8

1 medium eggplant, cut into 1" cubes

2 teaspoons salt, divided

⅓ cup olive oil, divided

1 medium white onion, peeled and chopped

1 medium green bell pepper, seeded and chopped

1 medium red bell pepper, seeded and chopped

1 medium zucchini, chopped

1 medium yellow squash, chopped

4 cloves garlic, peeled and minced

4 large tomatoes, cut into 1" pieces

2 teaspoons Italian seasoning

¼ teaspoon crushed red pepper flakes

6 fresh basil leaves, thinly sliced

Salting Eggplant

Many people do not like eggplant because it tastes bitter. You can reduce or even eliminate that bitter flavor by salting your eggplant prior to cooking. Salting draws out the bitter liquid in eggplants, making it easy to rinse away. Younger, firm eggplants are less likely to be bitter, but if you want to be sure, it is best to salt.

1. Add eggplant to a colander and sprinkle evenly with salt. Let stand 30 minutes, then rinse and dry eggplant. Set aside.

2. Press Sauté on Instant Pot®. Once machine indicates Hot, add 1 tablespoon oil and let heat 30 seconds, then add onion and bell pepper. Cook, stirring often, until vegetables are just tender, about 5 minutes. Transfer to a large bowl and set aside.

3. Add 1 tablespoon oil to pot and heat for 30 seconds, then add zucchini and squash. Cook, stirring constantly, until vegetables are tender, about 5 minutes. Add garlic and cook until fragrant, about 30 seconds. Transfer to bowl with onions and peppers.

4. Add 1 tablespoon oil to pot and heat for 30 seconds. Add eggplant and cook, stirring constantly, until eggplant is golden brown, about 8 minutes. Add tomato and cook until tomato is tender and releasing juice, about 4 minutes.

5. Add back reserved vegetables, Italian seasoning, and red pepper flakes. Press Cancel. Close lid and set steam release to Sealing, then press Manual and adjust cook time to 5 minutes.

6. Once cooking is complete quick-release pressure. Press Cancel, open lid, and stir well. Serve topped with basil and remaining olive oil.

PER SERVING Calories: 101 | Fat: 5.5g | Protein: 2.5g | Sodium: 591mg | Fiber: 4.5g | Carbohydrates: 12g | Sugar: 7.5g

Meatless Taco Bake

This recipe calls for meatless soy crumbles, which can usually be found in the freezer section of your market. If you can't find these or don't like them, you can substitute crumbled firm tofu seasoned with 1 teaspoon of smoked paprika and a tablespoon of liquid aminos.

INGREDIENTS | SERVES 8

2 tablespoons olive oil, divided

1 medium yellow onion, peeled and chopped

1 clove garlic, peeled and minced

1 (15-ounce) can whole kernel corn, drained and rinsed

1 (15-ounce) can black beans, drained and rinsed

1 (12-ounce) bag meatless soy crumbles

1 (1.25-ounce) packet taco seasoning

1½ cups water, divided

8 (6") corn tortillas

2 cups shredded Mexican-style cheese

1. Press Sauté on Instant Pot®. Once machine indicates Hot, add 1 tablespoon oil and let heat 30 seconds, then add onion and cook 5 minutes until tender. Add garlic and cook until fragrant, about 30 seconds. Add corn, black beans, soy crumbles, and taco seasoning and stir well. Add ½ cup water and cook, stirring often, until mixture thickens, about 5 minutes. Press Cancel and transfer vegetable mixture to a large bowl.

2. Clean out pot, then place rack inside pot and add remaining water. Fold a long piece of aluminum foil in half. Lay foil over rack to form a sling.

3. Spray an 8" × 8" baking dish with nonstick cooking spray. Place 2 tortillas into bottom of dish, cover with ¼ vegetable mixture, and top with ¼ cheese. Repeat until all ingredients are used, then place dish on rack and cover with another piece of aluminum foil. Close lid and set steam release to Sealing, then press Manual and adjust cook time to 20 minutes.

4. Once cooking is complete quick-release pressure. Press Cancel and open lid. Let dish stand 10 minutes before carefully removing from pot with sling. Serve warm.

PER SERVING Calories: 393 | Fat: 18g | Protein: 19g | Sodium: 704mg | Fiber: 7g | Carbohydrates: 39g | Sugar: 4g

Wild Mushroom Pilaf

Most produce departments carry a variety of wild or exotic mushrooms, but if you can't find any wild mushrooms, you can substitute a mix of sliced button and cremini mushrooms in this recipe.

INGREDIENTS | SERVES 8

2 tablespoons olive oil

1 medium yellow onion, peeled and chopped

3 cloves garlic, peeled and minced

1 pound mixed wild mushrooms, chopped

½ teaspoon salt

½ teaspoon ground black pepper

½ teaspoon dried thyme leaves

½ teaspoon dried oregano leaves

¼ teaspoon crushed red pepper flakes

¼ cup white wine

2 cups uncooked brown rice

2 cups vegetable broth

1. Press Sauté on Instant Pot®. Once machine indicates Hot, add oil and let heat 30 seconds, then add onion and cook 3 minutes until just starting to soften. Add garlic and mushrooms and cook until mushrooms are tender, about 10 minutes. Add salt, pepper, thyme, oregano, and red pepper flakes and cook 1 minute until fragrant.

2. Add wine and scrape bottom of pot. Cook until wine is almost evaporated, about 3 minutes, then add rice and mix to coat. Cook 3 minutes to toast rice. Press Cancel.

3. Stir in broth. Close lid and set steam release to Sealing, then press Manual and adjust cook time to 22 minutes.

4. Once cooking is complete allow pressure to release naturally, about 10 minutes. Open lid and stir. Serve warm.

PER SERVING Calories: 231 | Fat: 5g | Protein: 5.5g | Sodium: 288mg | Fiber: 2.5g | Carbohydrates: 40g | Sugar: 2g

Butternut Squash and Sweet Potato Casserole

You can often find peeled and diced butternut squash in your market's produce section that you can use if you don't feel like breaking down a whole squash. It is better to use fresh butternut squash to retain more of its texture after cooking: frozen butternut squash tends to get a little mushy.

INGREDIENTS | SERVES 8

2 tablespoons olive oil

1 medium yellow onion, peeled and chopped

2 ribs celery, chopped

2 medium carrots, peeled and chopped

2 cloves garlic, peeled and minced

2 tablespoons tomato paste

1 medium tomato, peeled and chopped

2 cups vegetable broth

8 cups peeled chopped butternut squash, cut in 1" cubes

2 medium sweet potatoes, peeled and cut into 1" cubes

1 teaspoon dried thyme leaves

½ teaspoon dried rosemary leaves

½ teaspoon salt

½ teaspoon ground black pepper

1 bay leaf

1. Press Sauté on Instant Pot®. Once machine indicates Hot, add oil and let heat 30 seconds, then add onion, celery, and carrot. Cook 5 minutes until tender. Add garlic and cook 30 seconds, then add tomato paste and stir to coat vegetables.

2. Add tomatoes and vegetable broth and scrape bottom of pot to release any browned bits. Add remaining ingredients and mix well. Press Cancel and close lid. Set steam release to Sealing, press Manual, and adjust cook time to 3 minutes.

3. Once cooking is complete quick-release pressure. Press Cancel and open lid. Discard bay leaf and serve hot.

PER SERVING Calories: 145 | Fat: 3.5g | Protein: 3g | Sodium: 359mg | Fiber: 5g | Carbohydrates: 28g | Sugar: 7g

Reaction to Butternut Squash

Some people have a reaction when handling butternut squash that leaves their hands feeling itchy and red and makes their skin feel tight. This reaction is not harmful and should go away within a day or two. If you are sensitive to butternut squash, it is a good idea to wear gloves when peeling and chopping or buy your squash already peeled and sliced.

Creole Jambalaya

Jambalaya is a quintessentially New World dish, with roots in Provence and eastern Spain that have marinated for centuries in the flavors of Louisiana. Try adding sliced sausage to add depth of savory flavor to this classic bayou-country dish.

INGREDIENTS | SERVES 8

½ cup olive oil

1 medium white onion, peeled and chopped

1 medium green bell pepper, seeded and chopped

2 ribs celery, chopped

3 cloves garlic, peeled and minced

3 cups vegetable broth

1 cup water

1 cup tomato sauce

2 cups cooked long-grain white rice

2 bay leaves

2 teaspoons dried thyme leaves

2 teaspoons cayenne pepper

2 teaspoons Cajun seasoning

¼ teaspoon salt

1. Press Sauté on Instant Pot®. Once machine indicates Hot, add oil and let heat 30 seconds, then add onion, bell pepper, celery, and garlic and cook 10 minutes until soft.

2. Add broth, water, tomato sauce, rice, bay leaves, thyme, cayenne pepper, and Cajun seasoning to pot and stir to combine. Press Cancel. Close lid and set steam release to Sealing, then press Manual and adjust cook time to 6 minutes.

3. Once cooking is complete allow pressure to release naturally, then remove lid. Discard bay leaves. Season with salt and serve warm.

PER SERVING Calories: 204 | Fat: 13g | Protein: 2g | Sodium: 426mg | Fiber: 1g | Carbohydrates: 18g | Sugar: 2g

Cranberry Pecan Pilaf

This pilaf calls to mind a crisp autumn afternoon, but it makes for a great light dish any time of year. Try sprinkling in ground ginger or cloves to add more flavor. To make this dish heartier, just add meatless crumbles.

INGREDIENTS | SERVES 4

1 cup uncooked long-grain white rice

2 cups vegetable broth

⅔ cup dried cranberries

1 teaspoon dried thyme leaves

1 bay leaf

1 cup raw pecan pieces

2 tablespoons olive oil

¼ teaspoon salt

¼ teaspoon ground black pepper

1. Add rice, broth, cranberries, thyme, and bay leaf to Instant Pot®. Close lid, set steam release to Sealing, and press Rice.

2. Once cooking is complete allow pressure to release naturally, then remove lid. Discard bay leaf and stir in pecans, olive oil, salt, and pepper. Serve warm.

PER SERVING Calories: 378 | Fat: 26g | Protein: 3.5g | Sodium: 421mg | Fiber: 4g | Carbohydrates: 35g | Sugar: 15g

Eggplant Olive Ratatouille

The somewhat plain eggplant and zucchini take on the incredible Mediterranean flavors of the basil and garlic of this dish. The olives lend a salty touch to round out this recipe.

INGREDIENTS | SERVES 4

1 tablespoon coconut oil

1 medium Vidalia onion, peeled and chopped

1 medium yellow bell pepper, seeded and chopped

1 medium eggplant, peeled and diced into 1" cubes

3 cloves garlic, peeled and minced

1 (28-ounce) can diced tomatoes, including juice

¼ cup sliced green olives

1 medium zucchini, cut into 1" cubes

½ teaspoon salt

½ teaspoon ground black pepper

¼ cup chopped fresh basil

2 tablespoons chopped fresh Italian flat-leaf parsley

1. Press Sauté on Instant Pot®. Once machine indicates Hot, add coconut oil and let heat 30 seconds, then add onion and bell pepper and cook 4 minutes until onions are translucent. Add eggplant and garlic and cook until fragrant, about 1 minute.

2. Add diced tomatoes including juice to pot and scrape sides and bottom of pot. Add olives, zucchini, salt, pepper, and basil. Press Cancel. Close lid and set steam release to Sealing, then press Manual and adjust cook time to 2 minutes.

3. Once cooking is complete quick-release pressure and open lid. Garnish with parsley and serve warm.

PER SERVING Calories: 135 | Fat: 5g | Protein: 4g | Sodium: 588mg | Fiber: 9g | Carbohydrates: 21g | Sugar: 12g

Steamed Spring Rolls

Serve with a spicy peanut sauce or sweet and sour dipping sauce to bring out the traditional Southeast Asian essence of these rolls. You'll rarely find a fresher, more straight-from-the-garden quality to spring rolls than in this easy Instant Pot® dish.

INGREDIENTS | SERVES 12

1 cup shredded Napa cabbage

1 cup sliced bamboo shoots

¼ cup chopped fresh cilantro

2 cloves garlic, peeled and minced

5 shiitake mushrooms, sliced

2 medium carrots, peeled and grated

1 teaspoon soy sauce

1 teaspoon rice wine vinegar

12 wheat spring roll wrappers

2 cups water

Spring Roll Wrappers

The term *spring roll* is used to describe a number of fresh and fried rolls, and the wrappers for each type are different. For rolls that are cooked (either fried or steamed), use the thin, fresh wheat wrappers. For uncooked spring rolls—also called *summer rolls* or *fresh rolls*—use a hard, circular rice wrapper that is briefly soaked in water before filling and serving.

1. Combine cabbage, bamboo shoots, cilantro, garlic, mushrooms, carrot, soy sauce, and vinegar in a medium bowl. Stir until just combined.

2. Place spring roll wrappers on a flat surface. Divide filling among wrappers, placing filling in a line ⅓ of the way down each wrapper. Roll bottom of wrapper up, tuck in sides, and roll the rest of the way, dotting top corner of wrapper with water to help it seal. Place rolls side by side in steamer basket.

3. Add water to Instant Pot® and insert steamer basket. Close lid and set steam release to Sealing, then press Steam and adjust cook time to 3 minutes.

4. Once cooking is complete allow pressure to release naturally, about 15 minutes, then open lid. Remove rolls from pot and serve warm.

PER SERVING Calories: 113 | Fat: 0g | Protein: 2.5g | Sodium: 85mg | Fiber: 1g | Carbohydrates: 24g | Sugar: 1g

Yeasty Tofu and Vegetables

Nutritional yeast has a cheesy flavor that is an excellent substitute for dairy cheese if you don't eat dairy. This is one of the quickest start-to-finish meals you'll prepare with your Instant Pot®.

INGREDIENTS | SERVES 4

1 (16-ounce) package extra-firm tofu, drained

2 tablespoons vegetable oil, divided

2 tablespoons soy sauce, divided

1 cup water

½ medium red onion, peeled and chopped

1 cup chopped fresh broccoli, blanched

½ medium green bell pepper, seeded and chopped

½ medium zucchini, chopped

½ cup chopped yellow squash

¼ cup nutritional yeast

1. Wrap tofu in paper towels and place a heavy plate on top; let sit 5 minutes. Remove paper towels and cut tofu into ½" cubes.

2. Press Sauté on Instant Pot®. Once machine indicates Hot, add 1 tablespoon oil and let heat 30 seconds, then add tofu and cook 7 minutes until light brown on all sides. Add 1 tablespoon soy sauce and cook 10 seconds. Remove tofu from pot and set aside.

3. Add remaining oil, water, onion, broccoli, bell pepper, zucchini, and squash to pot. Cook, stirring often until tender, about 8 minutes. Add tofu and remaining soy sauce and cook 1 minute. Sprinkle nutritional yeast on top and serve.

PER SERVING Calories: 182 | Fat: 9g | Protein: 14g | Sodium: 1,054mg | Fiber: 3g | Carbohydrates: 10g | Sugar: 3.5g

Barley Risotto

You can make this dish vegan friendly by substituting an extra tablespoon of olive oil for the butter, and replacing the dairy cheese with vegan cheese. Vegan cheeses are available in most dairy sections or in the produce department with the vegetarian meat substitutes.

INGREDIENTS | SERVES 4

1 tablespoon unsalted butter

1 tablespoon olive oil

1 medium yellow onion, peeled and chopped

1 clove garlic, peeled and minced

1 rib celery, finely minced

1½ cups pearl barley, well rinsed

⅓ cup dried cremini mushrooms

4 cups vegetable broth

2¼ cups water

1 cup Parmesan cheese

2 tablespoons minced fresh Italian flat-leaf parsley

¼ teaspoon salt

1. Press Sauté on Instant Pot®. Once machine indicates Hot, add butter and oil and let heat 30 seconds. Once butter melts, add onion and cook 3 minutes until just soft. Add garlic and cook 30 seconds. Stir in celery and barley until barley is coated with oil.

2. Add mushrooms, broth, and water to pot. Press Cancel. Close lid and set steam release to Sealing, then press Manual and adjust cook time to 18 minutes.

3. Once cooking is complete quick-release pressure and remove lid. Drain excess liquid, leaving just enough to leave risotto slightly soupy.

4. Press Cancel, then press Sauté and adjust setting to Low. When risotto has thickened, about 6 minutes, stir in cheese and parsley. Add salt and serve.

PER SERVING Calories: 454 | Fat: 14g | Protein: 18g | Sodium: 1,094mg | Fiber: 12g | Carbohydrates: 65g | Sugar: 4g

Mediterranean Sweet Potato Salad

Serve this salad at room temperature or refrigerate it for a few hours and serve chilled. Note: "Room temperature" is within the range of a living or dining room in a climate-controlled building. If the temperature in your room is above 73 degrees, by all means chill this salad!

INGREDIENTS | SERVES 6

¼ cup olive oil

1 medium yellow onion, peeled and chopped

2 cloves garlic, peeled and minced

1 teaspoon ground cumin

1 teaspoon paprika

¼ cup freshly squeezed lemon juice

1 cup water

3 cups peeled and cubed sweet potatoes

¼ cup chopped green olives

3 tablespoons chopped fresh Italian flat-leaf parsley

¼ teaspoon salt

¼ teaspoon ground black pepper

1. Press Sauté on Instant Pot®. Once machine indicates Hot, add olive oil and let heat 30 seconds, then add onion and cook 10 minutes until just beginning to turn golden brown. Add garlic, cumin, paprika, and lemon juice and cook until very fragrant, about 2 minutes. Transfer mixture to a large bowl and set aside.

2. Add water and sweet potatoes to pot. Press Cancel. Close lid and set steam release to Sealing, then press Manual and adjust cook time to 10 minutes.

3. Once cooking is complete allow pressure to release naturally, about 10 minutes, and remove lid. Drain potatoes in a colander, then toss in bowl with onion mixture. Add olives, parsley, salt, and pepper and serve.

PER SERVING Calories: 155 | Fat: 10g | Protein: 2g | Sodium: 178mg | Fiber: 3g | Carbohydrates: 16g | Sugar: 3.5g

Irish Soda Bread (Chapter 16)

Lobster Rolls (Chapter 13)

Three-Cheese Lasagna Bake (Chapter 8)

White Chocolate Oreo Cheesecake (Chapter 17)

Vietnamese Caramel Pork (Chapter 11)

Shrimp and Lobster Bisque (Chapter 6)

Shredded Barbecue Beef Brisket (Chapter 10)

Green Chicken Chili (Chapter 6)

Instant Pot® Elotes (Chapter 15)

Cranberry-Stuffed Pork Roast (Chapter 11)

Japanese-Style Potato Salad (Chapter 15)

Decadent Drinking Chocolate (Chapter 18)

White Beans with Ham and Onion (Chapter 7)

Ropa Vieja (Chapter 10)

Cinnamon Apple Oats (Chapter 2)

Chicken in Satay Sauce (Chapter 12)

Buffalo Chicken Meatballs (Chapter 5)

Shrimp Scampi (Chapter 13)

Giant Blueberry Pancake with Blueberry Maple Syrup (Chapters 3 and 4)

Sausage with Cauliflower Mash (Chapter 9)

Quick and Easy Mac and Cheese (Chapter 14)

Chocolate Pot de Crème (Chapter 17)

Stuffed Chicken Breasts (Chapter 12)

Quinoa with Corn and Black Beans (Chapter 14)

Spinach and Portobello Benedict

This vegan version of the traditional breakfast classic is made with savory mushrooms, a creamy tofu-based hollandaise sauce, and sautéed spinach. You can also add a few strips of vegetarian bacon.

INGREDIENTS | SERVES 2

½ cup silken tofu

1 tablespoon freshly squeezed lemon juice

1 teaspoon Dijon mustard

⅛ teaspoon cayenne pepper

⅛ teaspoon ground turmeric

1 tablespoon vegetable oil

¼ teaspoon salt

1 tablespoon olive oil

4 small portobello mushroom caps

2 cups fresh spinach leaves

2 English muffins, toasted

Check the Ingredients

If serving this recipe to vegans, you need to verify that the English muffins do not contain any animal by-products such as whey, eggs, or butter. Most grocery store bread sections stock vegan-friendly breads, so if you are unable to find a vegan English muffin, simply cut rounds of your favorite vegan bread or substitute a bagel instead.

1. Add tofu to a food processor and purée until smooth. Add lemon juice, mustard, cayenne pepper, and turmeric. Blend until well combined. With food processor still running, slowly add vegetable oil and blend until combined. Season with salt, then pour sauce into a small saucepan and heat on stovetop on low until ready to serve.

2. Press Sauté on Instant Pot®. Once machine indicates Hot, add olive oil and let heat 30 seconds, then add mushroom caps and spinach and stir 3 minutes until coated with oil and slightly softened. Press Cancel. Close lid and set steam release to Sealing, then press Manual and adjust cook time to 9 minutes.

3. Once cooking is complete allow pressure to release naturally, about 10 minutes, and remove lid.

4. Place one English muffin open-faced on each plate and top each half with one portobello cap and divided sautéed spinach. Drizzle each half with hollandaise mixture and serve.

PER SERVING Calories: 370 | Fat: 18g | Protein: 16g | Sodium: 662mg | Fiber: 4.5g | Carbohydrates: 36g | Sugar: 5g

Olive and Pepper Couscous Salad

Black Kalamata olives add a deep, savory flavor to this Olive and Pepper Couscous Salad. For a similar flavor with a bit less olive in every bite, try the larger-pitted Nicoise olive.

INGREDIENTS | SERVES 4

1 cup couscous

2 cups water

½ cup Kalamata olives, pitted and chopped

1 medium red bell pepper, seeded and diced

1 clove garlic, peeled and minced

1 teaspoon olive oil

1 teaspoon red wine vinegar

1 teaspoon salt

1. Stir together couscous and water in Instant Pot®. Close lid and set steam release to Sealing, then press Manual and adjust cook time to 7 minutes.

2. Once cooking is complete allow pressure to release naturally, about 10 minutes, and remove lid. Fluff couscous with a fork. Add remaining ingredients and stir until combined. Refrigerate covered 2 hours before serving.

PER SERVING Calories: 202 | Fat: 3g | Protein: 6g | Sodium: 714mg | Fiber: 3g | Carbohydrates: 36g | Sugar: 1g

Quick Single-Serve Paella

While the rest of the world tends to consider paella Spain's national dish, the cooks of Valencia take special pride in this nineteenth-century creation, and their fellow Spaniards respect its Valencian origin. Turmeric is a budget-friendly alternative to saffron here—just increase the portion to 1 tablespoon.

INGREDIENTS | SERVES 4

3 tablespoons olive oil

1 medium Vidalia onion, peeled and chopped

1 cup peeled and grated carrot

1 medium red bell pepper, seeded and chopped

1 cup fresh or frozen green peas

1 clove garlic, peeled and minced

1 cup uncooked basmati rice

1½ teaspoons ground turmeric

2 cups vegetable broth

¼ cup chopped fresh Italian flat-leaf parsley

¼ teaspoon salt

¼ teaspoon ground black pepper

1. Press Sauté on Instant Pot®. Once machine indicates Hot, add oil and let heat 30 seconds, then add onion, carrot, bell pepper, and peas and cook 5 minutes until they begin to soften. Add garlic, rice, and turmeric and stir until well coated.

2. Add broth and parsley to pot. Press Cancel. Close lid and set steam release to Sealing, then press Manual and adjust cook time to 9 minutes.

3. Once cooking is complete allow pressure to release naturally, about 10 minutes, and remove lid. Season with salt and pepper before serving.

PER SERVING Calories: 223 | Fat: 10g | Protein: 4g | Sodium: 447mg | Fiber: 4g | Carbohydrates: 28g | Sugar: 7g

Stuffed Grape Leaves

A medium (5-ounce) lemon yields about 2 teaspoons of lemon zest and 3 tablespoons of lemon juice. For this recipe, make sure to start with at least a dozen lemons if you're squeezing the juice yourself.

INGREDIENTS | SERVES 16

⅓ cup olive oil

4 green onions, chopped

⅓ cup minced fresh mint

⅓ cup minced fresh Italian flat-leaf parsley

3 cloves garlic, peeled and minced

1 cup uncooked long-grain white rice

2 cups vegetable broth

1 teaspoon salt

¼ teaspoon ground black pepper

½ teaspoon lemon zest

1 (16-ounce) jar grape leaves, drained and rinsed, thick ribs removed

2 cups water

½ cup freshly squeezed lemon juice

1. Press Sauté on Instant Pot®. Once machine indicates Hot, add oil and let heat 30 seconds, then add green onion, mint, and parsley and cook 2 minutes until green onions are soft. Add garlic and cook 30 seconds. Add rice and stir-fry 1 minute.

2. Add broth, salt, pepper, and lemon zest to pot and stir well to mix. Press Cancel. Close lid and set steam release to Sealing, then press Manual and adjust cook time to 8 minutes.

3. Once cooking is complete quick-release pressure and open lid. Press Cancel. Transfer rice mixture to a medium bowl.

4. Arrange grape leaves rib-side up on a work surface. Spoon 2 teaspoons rice mixture onto each leaf. Fold sides of each leaf over filling, then roll leaves from bottom to top. Arrange stuffed leaves (seam-side down) in a single layer in steamer basket.

5. Pour water in pot. Set steamer basket in pot and pour lemon juice over stuffed grape leaves. Close lid, set steam release to Sealing, and press Steam.

6. Once cooking is complete quick-release pressure and remove lid. Lift steamer basket out of pot and let stuffed leaves rest 5 minutes. Serve hot or cold.

PER SERVING Calories: 241 | Fat: 9g | Protein: 10g | Sodium: 1,005mg | Fiber: 15g | Carbohydrates: 30g | Sugar: 0.5g

CHAPTER 9

Low-Carb Main Meals

Italian Spaghetti Squash

This dish is similar to spaghetti pie but without the high-carb noodles. If you need instructions on how to prepare a spaghetti squash in your Instant Pot®, see the Basic Spaghetti Squash recipe in Chapter 15.

INGREDIENTS | SERVES 4

4 boneless, skinless chicken thighs, about 2 pounds

¼ teaspoon salt

¼ teaspoon ground black pepper

2 tablespoons avocado oil

3 cups cooked spaghetti squash

1 teaspoon Italian seasoning

1 cup marinara sauce

1 cup shredded mozzarella cheese

1. Season chicken thighs with salt and pepper. Set aside.

2. Press Sauté on Instant Pot®. Once machine indicates Hot, add oil and let heat 30 seconds, then add chicken thighs and brown 5 minutes on each side. Remove thighs from pot.

3. Add spaghetti squash to pot and toss with chicken drippings. Add Italian seasoning and marinara sauce and toss to coat. Nestle chicken thighs into squash. Press Cancel.

4. Close lid and set steam release to Sealing, then press Manual and adjust cook time to 5 minutes.

5. Once cooking is complete quick-release pressure and open lid. Top with cheese and close lid. Let stand 10 minutes to melt. Serve hot.

PER SERVING Calories: 456 | Fat: 22g | Protein: 45g | Sodium: 667mg | Fiber: 5g | Carbohydrates: 16g | Sugar: 7g

Cheesy Meatball Bake

You can use homemade meatballs here if you prefer, but frozen meatballs make this dish an easy weeknight favorite. Be sure to check the ingredients of your ready-cooked meatballs and avoid those with bread or starch fillers to keep the carb count low.

INGREDIENTS | SERVES 4

1 (16-ounce) bag precooked frozen Italian-style beef meatballs

1¼ cups low-sugar marinara sauce

½ teaspoon Italian seasoning

½ teaspoon salt

¼ teaspoon crushed red pepper flakes

¼ teaspoon ground fennel

1 cup shredded mozzarella cheese

1. Add meatballs, marinara sauce, Italian seasoning, salt, red pepper flakes, and fennel to Instant Pot®. Mix to evenly coat meatballs in sauce.

2. Close lid and set steam release to Sealing, then press Manual and adjust cook time to 3 minutes.

3. Once cooking is complete quick-release pressure and open lid. Top with cheese and close lid. Let stand 10 minutes to melt. Serve hot.

PER SERVING Calories: 410 | Fat: 31g | Protein: 22g | Sodium: 1,235mg | Fiber: 3g | Carbohydrates: 10g | Sugar: 4g

Cauliflower and Cheese

Traditional macaroni and cheese is loaded with carbohydrates because of the pasta. This dish ditches the pasta and replaces it with cauliflower. For the best texture be sure to cut the florets into ½" pieces or smaller.

INGREDIENTS | SERVES 8

5 cups fresh or frozen cauliflower florets

½ cup water

1 cup heavy cream

1 tablespoon unsalted butter

1 (8-ounce) package cream cheese

2 cups shredded Cheddar cheese

½ teaspoon salt

½ teaspoon ground black pepper

1. Place cauliflower and water in Instant Pot®. Close lid and set steam release to Sealing, then press Manual and adjust cook time to 3 minutes.

2. Once cooking is complete quick-release pressure. Press Cancel. Strain cauliflower and transfer to a large bowl.

3. Press Sauté on Instant Pot® and add cream and butter. Once cream simmers and butter has melted, about 30 seconds, add cream cheese. Whisk until cream cheese melts and sauce comes to a boil. Press Cancel. Once sauce has stopped bubbling, about 1 minute, stir in Cheddar cheese, salt, and pepper. Fold in cauliflower. Serve hot.

PER SERVING Calories: 316 | Fat: 28g | Protein: 10g | Sodium: 442mg | Fiber: 2g | Carbohydrates: 5g | Sugar: 2.5g

Sour Cream Chicken Enchilada Bowls

If you want something to make ahead and take to work all week, this recipe is for you! You can serve this with a light side, such as cauliflower rice or shredded cabbage, or on Fried Cheese Taco Shells!

INGREDIENTS | SERVES 8

1 tablespoon olive oil

1 pound boneless, skinless chicken thighs

½ medium yellow onion, peeled and chopped

1 (4.5-ounce) can diced green chilies

1 clove garlic, peeled and minced

1 teaspoon ground cumin

½ teaspoon ground coriander

1 tablespoon chopped chipotle in adobo sauce

⅓ cup chicken broth

1 cup sour cream, divided

1 cup Monterey jack cheese, divided

¼ cup chopped fresh cilantro

1 medium plum tomato, seeded and chopped

1 medium avocado, diced

Fried Cheese Taco Shells

A quick and easy low-carb tortilla swap is a fried cheese shell. In a large pan over medium heat, melt ¼ cup of a smooth melting cheese, such as Cheddar or mozzarella. Once the bottom is starting to brown, flip and cook until the second side is browned. Transfer to a plate, top, and devour!

1. Press Sauté on Instant Pot®. Once machine indicates Hot, add oil and let heat 30 seconds, then add chicken and brown 5 minutes on each side. Remove from pot and set aside.

2. Add onion to pot and cook until just tender, about 3 minutes, then add chilies, garlic, cumin, and coriander and cook until spices and garlic are fragrant, about 1 minute. Press Cancel.

3. Add chipotle to pot and mix well, then stir in chicken broth. Top with browned chicken. Close lid and set steam release to Sealing, then press Manual and adjust cook time to 5 minutes.

4. Once cooking is complete quick-release pressure. Press Cancel and open lid. Transfer chicken to a large plate and let rest until cool enough to handle, then shred.

5. Stir sauce. If sauce seems thin, press Sauté, adjust to Low, and simmer until desired thickness is reached. Add ½ cup sour cream and ½ cup shredded cheese. Mix well. Stir shredded chicken back into pot.

6. Divide mixture into eight bowls and serve topped with remaining sour cream and cheese, cilantro, tomato, and avocado.

PER SERVING Calories: 227 | Fat: 15g | Protein: 16g | Sodium: 172mg | Fiber: 2g | Carbohydrates: 5g | Sugar: 2g

Loaded Cauliflower Soup

If you miss rich, creamy potato soup on a low-carb diet, you won't want to miss this recipe! Cauliflower takes the place of the carb-heavy potato, and when it is dressed up with green onion, bacon, and cheese it is almost better than the traditional version!

INGREDIENTS | SERVES 6

6 strips thick-cut bacon, chopped

½ medium yellow onion, peeled and chopped

1 rib celery, chopped

1 medium carrot, peeled and chopped

½ teaspoon dried thyme leaves

4 cups fresh or frozen cauliflower florets

2 cups chicken stock

1 cup heavy cream

1 (8-ounce) package cream cheese

1½ cups shredded Cheddar cheese, divided

¼ cup chopped green onion tops

1. Press Sauté on Instant Pot®. Once machine indicates Hot, about 3 minutes, add bacon and cook until fat has rendered and bacon is crisp, about 8 minutes. Remove from pot, leaving fat behind.

2. Add onion, celery, and carrot to pot. Cook, stirring often, 3 minutes. Add thyme, cauliflower, and stock. Press Cancel. Close lid and set steam release to Sealing, then press Manual and adjust cook time to 5 minutes.

3. Once cooking is complete allow pressure to release naturally, about 15 minutes. Remove lid.

4. Use a blender to purée soup until smooth, about 2 minutes. Stir in cream and cream cheese. Process until cream cheese is thoroughly incorporated. Stir in 1 cup Cheddar cheese and mix until melted. Serve immediately with additional cheese, cooked bacon, and green onions for garnish.

PER SERVING Calories: 441 | Fat: 39g | Protein: 13g | Sodium: 561mg | Fiber: 2g | Carbohydrates: 9g | Sugar: 4g

Lemon Chicken

This is not Chinese takeout–style lemon chicken, but rather browned chicken cooked with fresh lemons, butter, garlic, and spices. You can serve this dish with fresh vegetables or slice it into strips and use it for topping a green salad.

INGREDIENTS | SERVES 8

1 pound boneless, skinless chicken thighs

½ teaspoon salt

½ teaspoon ground black pepper

¼ teaspoon smoked paprika

1 tablespoon olive oil

¼ cup unsalted butter

½ medium yellow onion, peeled and chopped

3 cloves garlic, peeled and minced

1 medium lemon, sliced

¼ cup chicken broth

2 tablespoons freshly squeezed lemon juice

3 tablespoons heavy cream

1 tablespoon chopped fresh chives

1. Press Sauté on Instant Pot®. While machine heats, season chicken with salt, pepper, and paprika. Once machine indicates Hot, add oil and let heat 30 seconds, then add chicken and brown 5 minutes on each side. Remove chicken from pot and reserve.

2. Add butter to pot and melt 30 seconds. Once melted add onion and cook until just tender, about 2 minutes. Add garlic and cook until fragrant, about 30 seconds. Press Cancel.

3. Add cooked chicken to pot. Top with lemon slices, then pour in broth and lemon juice. Close lid and set steam release to Sealing, then press Manual and adjust cook time to 5 minutes.

4. Once cooking is complete quick-release pressure. Press Cancel and open lid. Stir in cream. Spoon sauce over chicken and serve hot garnished with chives.

PER SERVING Calories: 162 | Fat: 12g | Protein: 12g | Sodium: 204mg | Fiber: 0.5g | Carbohydrates: 2g | Sugar: 0g

Sausage with Cauliflower Mash

Beer-braised bratwursts and creamy, cheesy mashed cauliflower are a match made in heaven. Fresh bratwursts can be found in your grocer's meat market either fresh or frozen. Check the ingredients to avoid added sugar.

INGREDIENTS | SERVES 4

1 cup water

1 head cauliflower, leaves and stem removed

2 tablespoons salted butter

¼ cup sour cream

⅓ cup shredded Cheddar cheese

½ teaspoon salt

¼ teaspoon ground white pepper

2 tablespoons olive oil

4 uncooked sausages

1 cup light lager beer

Choosing Low-Carb Sausage

Be sure to read ingredients carefully on commercially prepared sausage. Many are loaded with starchy fillers, sugar, and high fructose corn syrup. Locally produced sausage is often a better bet, but it may be a little more expensive. Look for sausages with a slightly higher fat content, as they will be more flavorful and less likely to be dry.

1. Add water to Instant Pot®, place rack in pot, and place cauliflower on rack. Close lid and set steam release to Sealing, then press Steam and adjust cook time to 15 minutes.

2. Once cooking is complete quick-release steam, remove lid, press Cancel, and let stand 15 minutes.

3. Carefully move cauliflower to medium bowl and add butter, then mash with potato masher. Stir in sour cream, cheese, salt, and pepper. Cover with aluminum foil and set aside.

4. Clean out pot. Press Sauté and add oil. Once hot, about 30 seconds, add sausages. Brown sausages 3 minutes on each side.

5. Add beer. Press Cancel. Close lid and set steam release to Sealing, then press Manual and adjust cook time to 3 minutes.

6. Once cooking is complete quick-release pressure. Press Cancel and open lid. Remove sausages from pot and serve with mashed cauliflower.

PER SERVING Calories: 281 | Fat: 24g | Protein: 10g | Sodium: 637mg | Fiber: 3g | Carbohydrates: 8g | Sugar: 3g

Beefy Taco Pie

Grass-fed beef is the best option here because it has a higher level of healthy omega-3 fatty acids and heart-healthy fats. Serve this taco pie with some fresh-made guacamole, sour cream, and spicy salsa!

INGREDIENTS | SERVES 8

1 pound ground beef

½ medium onion, peeled and finely chopped

2 cloves garlic, peeled and minced

1 (1.25-ounce) packet taco seasoning

1 cup water

6 large eggs

¼ teaspoon salt

¼ teaspoon ground black pepper

1 cup shredded Mexican-style cheese

Lower-Fat Alternatives

Diets lower in carbs are usually higher in fats, so most low-carb meals avoid lower-fat meat alternatives like chicken or turkey. However, if you are watching your fat intake, you can easily substitute lean ground beef, ground turkey, or lean ground chicken for the higher-fat beef. Just add 2 teaspoons of olive oil to the pot before browning the meat to help prevent sticking.

1. Spray an 8" × 8" baking dish with nonstick cooking spray.

2. Press Sauté on Instant Pot®. Once machine indicates Hot, add beef. Cook, crumbling beef with a wooden spoon, until browned, about 8 minutes. Add onion and garlic and cook 2 minutes. Add taco seasoning and cook 2 minutes until spices are well mixed into meat and are fragrant. Press Cancel.

3. Transfer meat mixture to prepared dish and clean out pot.

4. Place rack in Instant Pot® and add water. Fold a long piece of aluminum foil in half. Lay foil over rack to form a sling.

5. In a small bowl mix eggs with salt and pepper. Spread cheese evenly over meat, then pour eggs on top of cheese. Place dish on rack and cover with another piece of aluminum foil, tightly crimping edges. Close lid and set steam release to Sealing, then press Manual and adjust cook time to 7 minutes.

6. Once cooking is complete quick-release pressure. Press Cancel and open lid. Let dish stand 10 minutes before carefully removing from pot with sling and serving.

PER SERVING Calories: 237 | Fat: 14g | Protein: 20g | Sodium: 585mg | Fiber: 1g | Carbohydrates: 4g | Sugar: 1g

Italian Chicken with Bacon

Wrapping chicken in bacon adds flavor and helps keep the chicken extra moist. This chicken is fine alone, but it is even better when paired with some grilled squash or zucchini or over spaghetti squash.

INGREDIENTS | SERVES 4

4 boneless, skinless chicken thighs, about 2 pounds

1 teaspoon Italian seasoning

½ teaspoon salt

¼ teaspoon ground black pepper

8 strips smoked bacon

2 cups tomato sauce

¼ cup Parmesan cheese

2 tablespoons chopped fresh Italian flat-leaf parsley

1. Season both sides chicken thighs with Italian seasoning, salt, and pepper. Roll chicken thighs closed. Wrap each thigh with 2 bacon strips.

2. Press Sauté on Instant Pot® and once machine indicates Hot, about 3 minutes, add chicken thighs with bacon seam-side down. Let sear 4 minutes on each side until well browned. Remove from pot.

3. Add tomato sauce to pot and stir in bacon drippings. Press Cancel and lay chicken thighs on sauce. Close lid and set steam release to Sealing, then press Manual and adjust cook time to 5 minutes.

4. Once cooking is complete quick-release pressure. Press Cancel and open lid. Serve chicken and sauce with cheese and parsley.

PER SERVING Calories: 517 | Fat: 28g | Protein: 52g | Sodium: 1,091mg | Fiber: 2g | Carbohydrates: 7g | Sugar: 5g

Pizza Meatballs

Pizza is delicious, but it is off-limits on a low-carb diet. The starchy crust is a no-no. Well, now you can enjoy all of your favorite pizza flavors mixed with tender meatballs—and none of the carbs!

INGREDIENTS | SERVES 4

1 pound fresh meatballs

½ medium green bell pepper, seeded and chopped

½ medium yellow onion, peeled and chopped

2 cloves garlic, peeled and minced

½ teaspoon dried oregano leaves

½ teaspoon ground fennel

1 cup tomato sauce

½ cup whole-milk ricotta cheese

1 cup shredded mozzarella cheese

½ cup chopped pepperoni

1. Press Sauté on Instant Pot®. Once machine indicates Hot, add meatballs. Brown well, 2 minutes per side and 6 minutes total. Remove from pot and reserve.

2. Add bell pepper and onion to pot. Cook until just tender, about 3 minutes, then add garlic, oregano, and fennel. Cook until fragrant, about 30 seconds. Stir in tomato sauce and mix well. Press Cancel.

3. Add meatballs to pot and mix into sauce. Drop tablespoons of ricotta cheese over top of meatballs, then top with shredded mozzarella cheese and pepperoni. Close lid and set steam release to Sealing, then press Manual and adjust cook time to 3 minutes.

4. Once cooking is complete quick-release pressure. Press Cancel and open lid. Serve hot.

PER SERVING (2 meatballs) Calories: 558 | Fat: 42g | Protein: 29g | Sodium: 1,309mg | Fiber: 4g | Carbohydrates: 16g | Sugar: 7g

Sesame Zoodles

Zucchini zoodles are an excellent substitute for traditional Asian rice or wheat noodles. Their mild flavor complements the zippy sesame sauce, and they cook very quickly. These are filling alone, but you can also enjoy them with stir-fried beef or chicken!

INGREDIENTS | SERVES 4

¼ cup water

4 cups spiralized zucchini (about 3 small zucchini)

¼ cup coconut aminos

2 tablespoons granulated sugar substitute

1 teaspoon sriracha

2 teaspoons sesame oil

1 tablespoon creamy almond butter

¼ cup diced green onions

1 tablespoon toasted sesame seeds

Don't Have a Spiralizer?

If you don't own a spiralizer, your produce department will likely carry a variety of pre-spiralized vegetables. Another option is to use a vegetable peeler to create strips of zucchini and then cut those strips into narrow noodles.

1. Add water to Instant Pot® and insert steamer basket.

2. In a large bowl combine zucchini, coconut aminos, sugar substitute, sriracha, sesame oil, almond butter, and green onion.

3. Place marinated zucchini in steamer basket. Pour any remaining marinade over zucchini. Close lid and set steam release to Sealing, then press Steam and adjust cook time to 10 minutes.

4. Once cooking is complete quick-release pressure and remove lid. Transfer zucchini to a serving bowl. Garnish with toasted sesame seeds. Serve immediately.

PER SERVING Calories: 93 | Fat: 6g | Protein: 4g | Sodium: 361mg | Fiber: 2g | Carbohydrates: 7g | Sugar: 4g

Tex-Mex Chicken and Peppers

When cooking low-carb you want to avoid too much onion and the sweeter peppers, so this recipe uses green bell peppers to keep the carbs lower. If, however, you have room in your diet for orange or red peppers, feel free to sub some in here!

INGREDIENTS | SERVES 6

2 pounds boneless, skinless chicken thighs

1 tablespoon fajita seasoning

2 medium green bell peppers, seeded and cut into strips

1 medium yellow onion, peeled and halved and sliced

2 cloves garlic, peeled and minced

1 cup tomatillo salsa

¼ cup chopped fresh cilantro, divided

1. Season both sides of chicken thighs with fajita seasoning. Cover and refrigerate 2 hours.

2. Place pepper, onion, garlic, salsa, and 2 tablespoons cilantro in Instant Pot®. Place seasoned chicken on top of mixture. Close lid and set steam release to Sealing, then press Manual and adjust cook time to 6 minutes.

3. Once cooking is complete quick-release pressure. Press Cancel and open lid. Serve hot with reserved cilantro for garnish.

PER SERVING Calories: 216 | Fat: 6g | Protein: 30g | Sodium: 585mg | Fiber: 2g | Carbohydrates: 8g | Sugar: 3g

Kimchi Chicken Wings

Kimchi is a popular Korean side dish traditionally eaten with white rice or incorporated into porridges, cakes, and fried rice. Here it is used as a flavoring for wings.

INGREDIENTS | SERVES 3

1½ pounds chicken wings, separated at the joint

½ cup kimchi brine

1 cup water

1 cup kimchi

What Is Kimchi?

Kimchi is fermented spicy cabbage and is a popular Korean side dish. There are various kinds of kimchi with different kinds of spices and chilies. You can find recipes online for making your own homemade kimchi, and it is surprisingly easy to make. Kimchi is wonderful scrambled into eggs or served with grilled meats.

1. Add chicken wings and kimchi brine to a large resealable plastic bag. Seal and shake. Refrigerate in bag 30 minutes up to 2 hours.

2. Add water to Instant Pot® and insert steamer basket. Add chicken wings to basket and pour in extra brine from plastic bag. Close lid and set steam release to Sealing, then press Manual and adjust cook time to 8 minutes.

3. Once cooking is complete quick-release pressure until float valve drops and remove lid. Transfer chicken wings to a large bowl and serve with kimchi.

PER SERVING Calories: 435 | Fat: 29g | Protein: 39g | Sodium: 395mg | Fiber: 0g | Carbohydrates: 2g | Sugar: 1g

Chicken Legs with Satay Sauce

Chicken drumsticks are always popular, and these ones are particularly good, as they are marinated in a creamy peanut satay sauce! If you are watching your carb intake, be sure to use natural, unsweetened peanut butter in your satay sauce.

INGREDIENTS | SERVES 5

½ cup smooth all-natural peanut butter

¼ cup canned unsweetened full-fat coconut milk

¼ cup coconut aminos

⅛ cup freshly squeezed lime juice

1 teaspoon minced fresh ginger

½ teaspoon fish sauce

1 teaspoon granulated sugar substitute

½ teaspoon sea salt

3 pounds chicken drumsticks (about 10 drumsticks)

1 cup water

1. In a medium bowl whisk together peanut butter, coconut milk, coconut aminos, lime juice, ginger, fish sauce, sugar substitute, and salt. Pour into a shallow dish and add drumsticks. Cover and refrigerate overnight.

2. Add water to Instant Pot® and insert rack. Arrange chicken standing up, with meaty side down, on rack. Close lid, set steam release to Sealing, and press Poultry.

3. Once cooking is complete allow pressure to release naturally 5 minutes. Quick-release any remaining pressure and open lid. Check chicken using a meat thermometer to ensure the internal temperature is at least 165°F.

4. Preheat oven to 550°F. Place chicken legs on an ungreased baking sheet and broil 3 minutes on each side to crisp. Transfer chicken to a serving plate and serve warm.

PER SERVING Calories: 615 | Fat: 40g | Protein: 55g | Sodium: 945mg | Fiber: 1.5g | Carbohydrates: 7g | Sugar: 2g

Pork and Cabbage Egg Roll in a Bowl

This dish is also called Crack Slaw because it is addictive! The ingredients are similar to those found inside egg rolls. This version uses ground pork, but you can also substitute ground beef or chicken.

INGREDIENTS | SERVES 6

1 tablespoon avocado oil

1 pound ground pork

½ medium yellow onion, peeled and chopped

1 clove garlic, peeled and minced

2 teaspoons minced fresh ginger

¼ cup chicken broth

2 tablespoons soy sauce

2 (10-ounce) bags shredded cabbage or tricolor slaw mix

1 teaspoon sesame oil

1 teaspoon garlic chili sauce

Make It Fried Cauli Rice

Craving fried rice but avoiding the carbs? Try cauliflower rice. Simply prepare the egg roll as directed, reducing the cabbage to 1 bag. Next, clean out the pot, press Cancel and then Sauté, and add 1 tablespoon oil. Cook 2 cups riced cauliflower 5 minutes until tender and dried out. Add to egg roll mixture. Add 1 more tablespoon oil to the pot and scramble two eggs. Add eggs to bowl and stir to combine.

1. Press Sauté on Instant Pot®. Once machine indicates Hot, add oil and let heat 30 seconds, then add pork and cook until cooked through, about 8 minutes. Add onion, garlic, and ginger and cook until fragrant, about 2 minutes. Stir in chicken broth and soy sauce. Press Cancel.

2. Spread slaw mix over meat, but do not mix. Close lid and set steam release to Sealing, then press Manual and adjust cook time to 0 minutes.

3. Once cooking is complete quick-release pressure and remove lid. Stir in sesame oil and garlic chili sauce. Serve hot.

PER SERVING Calories: 256 | Fat: 19g | Protein: 14g | Sodium: 367mg | Fiber: 2.5g | Carbohydrates: 7g | Sugar: 3g

CHAPTER 10

Beef Main Dishes

Beef Short Ribs

These short ribs are marinated after cooking, which seems backward but actually allows the meat to absorb flavor as it cools and adds a glaze to it. Broiling the meat as indicated is optional but adds extra color and flavor.

INGREDIENTS | SERVES 6

2 pounds bone-in beef shorts ribs

2 teaspoons salt

2 teaspoons ground black pepper

2 tablespoons olive oil

2 cups beef broth

1 cup water

2 medium white onions, peeled and halved

2 ribs celery, halved

3 cloves garlic, peeled and smashed

1 bay leaf

1 teaspoon dried thyme leaves

½ teaspoon crushed red pepper flakes

½ cup honey

½ cup Dijon mustard

1 tablespoon apple cider vinegar

1. Season short ribs on all sides with salt and pepper. Set aside.

2. Press Sauté on Instant Pot®. Once machine indicates Hot, add oil and let heat 30 seconds, then add ½ short ribs and brown 4 minutes on each side. Remove from pot and repeat with remaining short ribs. Press Cancel.

3. Add ribs, beef broth, water, onion, celery, garlic, bay leaf, thyme, and red pepper flakes to pot. Close lid and set steam release to Sealing, then press Manual and adjust cook time to 35 minutes.

4. Once cooking is complete allow pressure to release naturally, about 15 minutes. Remove lid. Discard bay leaf.

5. Combine honey, mustard, and vinegar in a large dish. Place short ribs meat-side down into honey mixture. Coat ribs, cover with aluminum foil, and let rest 20 minutes.

6. Heat broiler on high. Place ribs on a foil-lined baking sheet meat-side up. Broil 6 minutes until ribs are lightly charred and bubbling. Serve hot.

PER SERVING Calories: 421 | Fat: 20g | Protein: 30g | Sodium: 1,295mg | Fiber: 2g | Carbohydrates: 29g | Sugar: 24g

Shredded Barbecue Beef Brisket

Brisket sandwiches are great for a summer picnic, tailgating, or enjoying by the pool. This recipe cuts the cooking time to a fraction of what brisket typically takes but leaves the meat just as tender! If any meat is left over, you can scramble it into eggs for breakfast the next day.

INGREDIENTS | SERVES 6

1 (2-pound) beef brisket, cut into 4 pieces

1 teaspoon salt

1 teaspoon ground black pepper

2 tablespoons vegetable oil

1 cup beef broth

2 cups barbecue sauce, divided

2 medium yellow onions, peeled and halved and sliced into ½" thick strips

2 cloves garlic, peeled and smashed

Brisket Sliders

You can make these into baked sliders by slicing sweet Hawaiian-style dinner rolls in half and placing the bottoms into a baking dish. Place ¼ of a slice of slice Cheddar cheese on each bottom bun. Add ¼ cup brisket to each bun, top with a second ¼ piece of cheese, and top with top buns. Brush buns with melted butter, cover with foil, and bake at 350°F for 25 minutes.

1. Season brisket pieces on all sides with salt and pepper. Set aside.

2. Press Sauté on Instant Pot®. Once machine indicates Hot, add oil and let heat 30 seconds, then add 2 pieces brisket and brown 5 minutes on each side. Remove from pot and repeat with remaining brisket.

3. Press Cancel. Add remaining ingredients and 1 cup barbecue sauce to pot and mix well, then add browned brisket pieces. Close lid and set steam release to Sealing, then press Manual and adjust cook time to 40 minutes.

4. Once cooking is complete allow pressure to release naturally, about 15 minutes. Open lid and carefully remove brisket from pot. Let cool 10 minutes, then shred with two forks. Serve hot with remaining barbecue sauce.

PER SERVING Calories: 352 | Fat: 15g | Protein: 32g | Sodium: 1,082mg | Fiber: 0.5g | Carbohydrates: 18g | Sugar: 15g

Steak House Pot Roast

This pot roast is flavored with traditional steak house flavors like garlic, pepper, and caramelized onion. It is great served with crispy baked potatoes and roasted vegetables!

INGREDIENTS | SERVES 6

1 (2-pound) boneless chuck roast

2 teaspoons steak seasoning

1 tablespoon olive oil

1 medium yellow onion, peeled and chopped

2 ribs celery, chopped

1 tablespoon tomato paste

4 cloves garlic, peeled and minced

2 cups beef broth

1 bay leaf

Quick and Easy Gravy

Once the pressure has released, press Cancel, remove lid, transfer roast to a serving platter, and strain cooking liquid, then set the vegetables aside. Add 2 tablespoons butter to the pot and Press Sauté. Once butter melts, about 30 seconds, add 2 tablespoons all-purpose flour. Cook 1 minute, then slowly whisk in the cooking liquid. Bring to a boil, whisking constantly, until thickened to your liking. Serve hot.

1. Season roast on all sides with steak seasoning. Set aside.

2. Press Sauté on Instant Pot®. Once machine indicates Hot, add oil and let heat 30 seconds, then add roast and brown 5 minutes on each side. Remove roast from pot and reserve.

3. Add onion and celery to pot. Cook until just tender, about 3 minutes, then add tomato paste and cook 1 minute. Add garlic and cook 30 seconds, then stir in broth, making sure to scrape the bottom of pot to release any browned bits. Press Cancel.

4. Add bay leaf and roast to pot. Close lid and set steam release to Sealing, then press Manual and adjust cook time to 60 minutes.

5. Once cooking is complete allow pressure to release naturally. Open lid, discard bay leaf, and carefully remove roast from pot. Carve or pull into pieces. Serve hot.

PER SERVING Calories: 273 | Fat: 11g | Protein: 39g | Sodium: 439mg | Fiber: 0g | Carbohydrates: 1.5g | Sugar: 0.5g

Guinness Stew

The dream of achieving the long-simmered flavor of Guinness Stew without babysitting a pot on the stove for hours becomes a reality with this easy recipe! While this calls for beef, you can make it with lamb if you prefer the more traditional version.

INGREDIENTS | SERVES 8

2 pounds boneless beef chuck steak, trimmed, cut into 2" cubes

2 tablespoons all-purpose flour

¼ teaspoon cayenne pepper

¼ teaspoon salt

¼ teaspoon ground black pepper

1½ tablespoons vegetable oil, divided

1 medium yellow onion, peeled and chopped

1 clove garlic, peeled and minced

¼ teaspoon dried thyme leaves

1 cup Guinness Draught beer

1 cup beef stock

1 bay leaf

2 large carrots, peeled and cut into 1" pieces

2 medium russet potatoes, scrubbed clean and cut into 1" pieces

¼ cup chopped fresh Italian flat-leaf parsley

1. In a medium bowl toss beef with flour, cayenne pepper, salt, and pepper until thoroughly coated. Set aside.

2. Press Sauté on Instant Pot®. Once machine indicates Hot, add ½ oil and let heat 30 seconds, then add ½ beef and brown well on all sides, about 2 minutes per side. Transfer beef to a large bowl and repeat with remaining oil and beef. Once browned, transfer remaining beef to bowl.

3. Add onion, garlic, and thyme to pot and cook until onions are tender, about 5 minutes. Add ½ cup Guinness and scrape off all browned bits from bottom of pot. Add remaining Guinness, beef stock, bay leaf, carrot, potatoes, and browned beef including juices. Press Cancel.

4. Close lid and set steam release to Sealing, then press Stew and adjust cook time to 40 minutes.

5. Once cooking is complete quick-release steam, open lid, and stir well. Discard bay leaf, and serve hot with fresh parsley as a garnish.

PER SERVING Calories: 284 | Fat: 9g | Protein: 31g | Sodium: 231mg | Fiber: 1.5g | Carbohydrates: 15g | Sugar: 2g

Italian Beef for Sandwiches

Don't toss the liquid used for cooking the beef. You can use it to store the sliced beef in while serving to keep it tender and juicy. It can also be used for dunking crusty sandwich rolls for those who like their sandwiches served wet!

INGREDIENTS | SERVES 10

1 (3-pound) boneless rump roast

1 teaspoon salt

1 teaspoon ground black pepper

1 teaspoon garlic powder

1 tablespoon Italian seasoning

½ teaspoon onion powder

2 tablespoons vegetable oil

3 cups water

2 beef bouillon cubes

1 medium yellow onion, peeled and chopped

4 cloves garlic, peeled and chopped

Italian Beef Sandwiches

Although no one really knows the exact origins, it is thought that Italian beef sandwiches were created by Italian immigrants working at the Union Stock Yard in Chicago. They would take home tough cuts of beef that were more difficult to sell. To tenderize the meat, they would slow cook it, then cut it across the grain and make it into sandwiches with crusty Italian bread.

1. Season roast on all sides with salt, pepper, garlic powder, Italian seasoning, and onion powder. Set aside.

2. Press Sauté on Instant Pot®. Once machine indicates Hot, about 3 minutes, add oil and heat for 30 seconds. Add roast and brown 7 minutes on each side. Remove and set aside.

3. Add water and bouillon cubes to pot, making sure to scrape any brown bits from bottom of pot. Add onion and garlic, then return roast to pot. Press Cancel.

4. Close lid and set steam release to Sealing, then press Manual and adjust cook time to 60 minutes.

5. Once cooking is complete allow pressure to release naturally, about 20 minutes. Open lid and carefully remove roast. Let rest, tented with aluminum foil, 20 minutes, then slice into thin strips. Place sliced beef back into cooking liquid until ready to serve.

PER SERVING Calories: 273 | Fat: 8g | Protein: 44g | Sodium: 495mg | Fiber: 0g | Carbohydrates: 2g | Sugar: 0g

Ropa Vieja

This Cuban dish roughly translates to "old clothes." The traditional version takes hours to become tender enough to shred, but this version can be ready in about an hour!

INGREDIENTS | SERVES 6

2½ pounds boneless chuck roast or brisket, cut into 4" pieces

1 teaspoon salt

1 teaspoon ground black pepper

1 tablespoon olive oil

2 medium yellow onions, peeled and chopped

2 medium red bell peppers, chopped

6 cloves garlic, peeled and minced

2 teaspoons dried oregano leaves

2 teaspoons ground cumin

2 teaspoons smoked paprika

½ teaspoon cayenne pepper

½ cup white wine

1 (15-ounce) can diced tomatoes

1 bay leaf

½ cup Spanish olives, halved

2 teaspoons distilled white vinegar

Flank Steak

Traditionally ropa vieja is made with flank steak. The long fibers of the meat shred into long rope-like strands, but it can be a little tough even after long cooking. This recipe calls for fattier meat to improve the texture, but if you want to be completely authentic, use flank steak and add an extra tablespoon or two of oil to compensate for the leaner meat.

1. Season meat with salt and pepper on all sides. Set aside.

2. Press Sauté on Instant Pot®. Once machine indicates Hot, add oil and let heat 30 seconds. Brown meat in batches until well browned, about 7 minutes on each side. Transfer browned meat to a platter and set aside.

3. Add onion and bell pepper to pot. Cook until vegetables are just tender, about 5 minutes. Add garlic, oregano, cumin, paprika, and cayenne pepper. Cook 1 minute until fragrant. Add wine and cook until liquid is reduced by half, about 2 minutes. Add tomatoes, bay leaf, and meat back to pot. Press Cancel.

4. Close lid and set steam release to Sealing, then press Manual and adjust cook time to 40 minutes.

5. Once cooking is complete quick-release pressure. Press Cancel. Open lid and discard bay leaf. Stir in olives and vinegar, then shred meat with two forks. Serve hot.

PER SERVING Calories: 399 | Fat: 14g | Protein: 49g | Sodium: 693mg | Fiber: 4g | Carbohydrates: 11g | Sugar: 5g

Nana's Sunday Pot Roast

Simply seasoned, this pot roast will take you back to Sunday dinners with your family. This is a complete meal, but you can add some fresh-baked biscuits or a loaf of crusty bread with plenty of butter!

INGREDIENTS | SERVES 6

1 (3-pound) boneless pot roast

1 teaspoon sea salt

1 teaspoon ground black pepper

2 tablespoons olive oil

2 cups beef broth

2 large carrots, peeled and cut into 1" sections

3 medium russet potatoes, scrubbed well and quartered

1 large yellow onion, peeled, halved, and sliced

1 (8-ounce) container whole button mushrooms, stems trimmed

1 tablespoon fresh thyme leaves

1. Pat roast dry with paper towels. Season with salt and pepper, then set aside.

2. Press Sauté on Instant Pot®. Once machine indicates Hot, add oil and let heat 30 seconds. Add meat and brown 5 minutes on each side. Press Cancel. Remove meat and set aside.

3. Add broth and scrape bottom and sides to loosen any browned bits. Add remaining ingredients. Return roast to pot. Close lid and set steam release to Sealing, then press Manual and adjust cook time to 60 minutes.

4. Once cooking is complete allow pressure to release naturally and open lid. Transfer meat and vegetables to a serving platter. Let rest 5 minutes. Slice roast and serve warm.

PER SERVING Calories: 645 | Fat: 26g | Protein: 73g | Sodium: 849mg | Fiber: 3.5g | Carbohydrates: 26g | Sugar: 3.5g

Chuck Roast with Carrots and Onions

Oh, the humble chuck roast. It is usually overlooked because of toughness of the connective tissue that takes hours of low and slow cooking to dissolve. The high pressure and steam of the Instant Pot® takes care of this so much faster. Succulent and delicious, chuck roast is sure to be a new weekday favorite!

INGREDIENTS | SERVES 6

1 (3-pound) boneless chuck roast

2 tablespoons horseradish mustard

1 teaspoon salt

½ teaspoon ground black pepper

2 tablespoons avocado oil

2 cups beef broth

2 teaspoons Worcestershire sauce

1 medium yellow onion, peeled and diced

5 large carrots, peeled and cut into 1" sections

Chuck

The chuck is a large primal cut that comes largely from the shoulder section of the steer. It can weigh as much as 100 pounds and is composed of various muscles. In your Instant Pot® chuck roast takes about 20 minutes per pound to cook under high pressure instead of the one hour per pound it typically takes with traditional cooking methods.

1. Pat roast dry with paper towels. Massage mustard into roast. Season with salt and pepper and set aside.

2. Press Sauté on Instant Pot®. Once machine indicates Hot, add oil and let heat 30 seconds, then add meat and brown 5 minutes on each side. Remove meat and set aside.

3. Add broth to pot and scrape any brown pits from bottom and sides of pot. Stir in Worcestershire sauce. Add onion and carrot. Place roast on top of vegetables. Press Cancel.

4. Close lid and set steam release to Sealing, then press Manual and adjust cook time to 60 minutes.

5. Once cooking is complete allow pressure to release naturally and remove lid. Transfer meat and vegetables to a serving platter. Let rest 5 minutes. Slice roast. Reserve some pot juices if you'd like to serve with au jus. Serve warm.

PER SERVING Calories: 442 | Fat: 17g | Protein: 59g | Sodium: 930mg | Fiber: 2.5g | Carbohydrates: 8.5g | Sugar: 4g

Oxtails with Tomato and Herbs

Oxtails are the tails of all cattle, not just oxen. While you often see oxtails used for making soups due to the high amount of collagen in the meat, here the oxtail is the star of the show!

INGREDIENTS | SERVES 6

3 pounds oxtail

1 teaspoon salt

1 teaspoon ground black pepper

2 tablespoons olive oil

2 medium yellow onions, peeled and chopped

2 ribs celery, chopped

3 cloves garlic, peeled and minced

1 teaspoon dried oregano leaves

½ teaspoon dried rosemary leaves

½ teaspoon ground fennel

2 tablespoons tomato paste

1 (28-ounce) can whole peeled tomatoes

1. Season oxtails on all sides with salt and pepper. Set aside.

2. Press Sauté on Instant Pot®. Once machine indicates Hot, add oil and let heat 30 seconds, then add oxtails in batches and brown 5 minutes on each side. Transfer browned oxtails to platter and reserve.

3. Add onion and celery to pot. Cook until just tender, about 3 minutes, then add garlic, oregano, rosemary, and fennel. Cook until fragrant, about 30 seconds. Stir in tomato paste and whole tomatoes, and top with browned oxtails. Press Cancel.

4. Close lid and set steam release to Sealing, then press Manual and adjust cook time to 50 minutes.

5. Once cooking is complete quick-release pressure. Press Cancel and open lid. Remove oxtails to platter and cover with aluminum foil. Press Sauté on pot and reduce sauce by half, about 20 minutes. Place oxtails back into sauce to reheat for 5 minutes. Serve hot.

PER SERVING Calories: 536 | Fat: 23g | Protein: 68g | Sodium: 741mg | Fiber: 3.5g | Carbohydrates: 10g | Sugar: 5.5g

Sweet-N-Spicy Beef Brisket

The Instant Pot® is a great way to dress up a cheaper cut of meat. With a few fabulous spices, this brisket is a five-star delight. Placing the brisket fat-side down helps render some of that fat cap. Also, the maple syrup in the wet rub creates a layer of caramelization for added flavor!

INGREDIENTS | SERVES 6

2 tablespoons pure maple syrup

2 tablespoons coconut aminos

1 tablespoon adobo paste

1 tablespoon yellow mustard

½ teaspoon garlic salt

1 tablespoon Italian seasoning

1 (3-pound) beef brisket

2 tablespoons coconut oil

1 cup water

1 large yellow onion, peeled and roughly diced

Coconut Aminos

Coconut aminos are made from coconut sap. The aminos have a rich and salty flavor, are gluten-free, and work as a replacement for soy sauce in recipes. The flavor is similar to light soy sauce, which is not as salty as traditional soy sauce. If you have a soy or gluten allergy, or are avoiding soy in your diet for health reasons, consider coconut aminos.

1. In a small bowl whisk together syrup, coconut aminos, adobo paste, mustard, garlic salt, and Italian seasoning. Massage over beef brisket. Set meat aside.

2. Press Sauté on Instant Pot® and add coconut oil. Adjust temperature to Less. Place brisket in pot fat-side down. Cook 6 minutes to render fat. Press Cancel.

3. Add water and scatter onions around brisket. Close lid and set steam release to Sealing, then press Manual and adjust cook time to 60 minutes.

4. Once cooking is complete allow pressure to release naturally, then open lid. Transfer meat to a serving platter. Let rest 10 minutes. Slice and serve warm.

PER SERVING Calories: 419 | Fat: 20g | Protein: 48g | Sodium: 545mg | Fiber: 1g | Carbohydrates: 7.5g | Sugar: 5g

Tender Flank Steak with Mushrooms and Onions

Steak and mushrooms are a classic combination. The savory beef drippings add flavor to the mushrooms, while the umami flavor of the mushrooms complements the meat.

INGREDIENTS | SERVES 4

1 (2-pound) flank steak

1 teaspoon sea salt

½ teaspoon ground black pepper

2 tablespoons avocado oil, divided

1 slice bacon, diced

1 medium yellow onion, peeled and diced

2 cups whole button mushrooms

1½ cups beef broth

What Is Umami?

Everyone knows the sweet, salty, sour, and bitter flavors, but can you define *umami*? This fifth taste is used to describe savory foods, such as those high in glutamates such as the following: mushrooms, fermented foods, meat and bone broths, shellfish, and condiments like soy sauce. The flavor of umami is described as "meaty" or "rich."

1. Pat steak dry with paper towels. Season with salt and pepper and set aside.

2. Press Sauté on Instant Pot®. Once machine indicates Hot, heat 1 tablespoon oil 30 seconds. Sear meat 5 minutes on each side. Remove meat and set aside.

3. Add remaining oil to pot, then add bacon, onion, and mushrooms. Cook 5 minutes until onions are translucent. Add beef broth and scrape the bottom and sides of pot to loosen any browned bits. Place meat on top of onions. Press Cancel.

4. Close lid and set steam release to Sealing, then press Meat and adjust cook time to 35 minutes.

5. Once cooking is complete allow pressure to release naturally and open lid. Transfer meat to a serving platter. Let rest 5 minutes. Thinly slice meat against the grain. Serve immediately with divided mushrooms, onions, and a few tablespoons of liquid from pot.

PER SERVING Calories: 476 | Fat: 26g | Protein: 51g | Sodium: 1,086mg | Fiber: 2g | Carbohydrates: 7g | Sugar: 3g

Korean Beef Short Ribs

There are two types of short ribs cuts: flanken and English cut. For this recipe, flanken is preferred for authenticity and texture. Your butcher can help achieve this if there are no prepackaged options. Otherwise, the sauce in this recipe will work to flavor any cut of meat you prefer.

INGREDIENTS | SERVES 4

¼ cup soy sauce

¼ cup pure maple syrup

1 teaspoon fish sauce

1 tablespoon apple cider vinegar

1 tablespoon sesame oil

1 teaspoon ground white pepper

½ teaspoon ground ginger

½ teaspoon garlic powder

½ teaspoon sea salt

3 pounds beef short ribs

1 cup beef broth

2 green onions, peeled and sliced

1 tablespoon toasted sesame seeds

1. In a medium bowl whisk together soy sauce, maple syrup, fish sauce, vinegar, sesame oil, pepper, ginger, garlic powder, and sea salt. Add ribs and toss to coat. Refrigerate covered at least 60 minutes or up to overnight.

2. Add beef broth to Instant Pot® and insert rack. Arrange ribs standing upright with meaty side facing outward. Close lid and set steam release to Sealing, then press Meat and adjust cook time to 25 minutes.

3. Once cooking is complete allow pressure to release naturally and open lid. Transfer ribs to a serving platter and garnish with green onions and sesame seeds. Serve warm.

PER SERVING Calories: 683 | Fat: 37g | Protein: 66g | Sodium: 1,515mg | Fiber: 0.5g | Carbohydrates: 15g | Sugar: 12g

Sloppy Joes

Make this beefy sandwich filling on Sunday, and you will have speedy and tasty lunches or dinners on hand all week! You can substitute the beef with ground bison if you want to reduce the fat and add more omega-3 fatty acids to your diet.

INGREDIENTS | SERVES 4

1 tablespoon vegetable oil

1 pound ground beef

1 medium yellow onion, peeled and diced

1 small green bell pepper, seeded and diced

1 rib celery, finely chopped

2 teaspoons Worcestershire sauce

2 cups tomato sauce

2 tablespoons tomato paste

1 tablespoon pure maple syrup

1 teaspoon sea salt

1 teaspoon ground black pepper

4 hamburger buns, toasted

1. Press Sauté on Instant Pot®. Once machine indicates Hot, add oil and let heat 30 seconds. Add beef, onion, bell pepper, and celery. Cook 4 minutes until onions are tender and beef is mostly browned.

2. Add remaining ingredients to pot. Press Cancel. Close lid, press Manual, and adjust cook time to 0 minutes.

3. Once cooking is complete quick-release pressure and open lid. Transfer mixture to toasted buns and serve warm.

PER SERVING Calories: 375 | Fat: 16g | Protein: 27g | Sodium: 1,479mg | Fiber: 3.5g | Carbohydrates: 30g | Sugar: 12g

Meatloaf and Gravy

Meatloaf is a worldwide tradition. It seems that every country in the world has a variation of this simple dish. As long as you have some form of ground meat, vegetables, and a binding agent, meatloaf can be made. This quick and easy meatloaf is the perfect weeknight staple, especially when served with potatoes and vegetables.

INGREDIENTS | SERVES 6

1 pound ground beef

1 pound ground pork

3 large eggs

1 large shallot, peeled and finely diced

½ cup tomato sauce

½ cup bread crumbs

1 tablespoon Italian seasoning

½ teaspoon smoked paprika

½ teaspoon garlic powder

1 teaspoon sea salt

½ teaspoon ground black pepper

1 cup beef broth

1 tablespoon all-purpose flour

2 tablespoons whole milk

1. In a large bowl combine beef, pork, eggs, shallot, tomato sauce, bread crumbs, Italian seasoning, paprika, garlic powder, salt, and pepper. Form mixture into a ball and flatten the top. Place meatloaf in a 7-cup bowl lightly greased with oil or cooking spray.

2. Add beef broth to Instant Pot® and add rack. Fold a long piece of aluminum foil in half. Lay foil over rack to form a sling. Place glass bowl on top. Close lid and set steam release to Sealing, then press Meat and adjust cook time to 35 minutes.

3. Once cooking is complete quick-release pressure and open lid. Remove meatloaf and let cool at room temperature 10 minutes. Tilt glass bowl and pour any liquid/rendered fat back into pot.

4. Press Cancel, then press Sauté. Whisk flour and milk in pot juices until a thick gravy forms. Transfer to a gravy boat. Slice meatloaf and serve with gravy.

PER SERVING Calories: 419 | Fat: 26g | Protein: 33g | Sodium: 828mg | Fiber: 1g | Carbohydrates: 10g | Sugar: 2g

Reuben Meatballs with Russian Dressing

Corned beef and sauerkraut are mixed directly in the ground beef for this recipe. Caraway seeds are added to hit that "rye bread" flavor. And the Russian dressing pulls it all together! Feel free to garnish these savory meatballs with some shredded Swiss cheese.

INGREDIENTS | YIELDS 24 MEATBALLS

½ cup mayonnaise

2 tablespoons ketchup

1 small shallot, peeled and minced

1 tablespoon freshly squeezed lemon juice

1 teaspoon prepared horseradish

½ teaspoon smoked paprika

¾ teaspoon salt, divided

1 pound ground beef

½ pound finely chopped corned beef

½ cup finely chopped sauerkraut, drained

¼ cup bread crumbs

2 tablespoons German mustard

1 tablespoon caraway seeds

1 large egg

¼ teaspoon ground black pepper

2 tablespoons avocado oil, divided

1 cup water

1. In a small bowl combine mayonnaise, ketchup, shallot, lemon juice, horseradish, paprika, and ¼ teaspoon salt. Refrigerate covered until ready to use.

2. In a medium bowl combine beef, corned beef, sauerkraut, bread crumbs, mustard, caraway seeds, egg, remaining salt, and pepper. Form into twenty-four 1½" meatballs. Set aside.

3. Press Sauté on Instant Pot®. Once machine indicates Hot, heat 1 tablespoon oil 30 seconds. Add ½ meatballs around the edges of pot and sear on all sides, about 2 minutes per side, 6 minutes total. Remove and set aside. Add remaining oil and meatballs and repeat searing. Remove meatballs. Press Cancel.

4. Discard extra juice and oil from pot. Add water to pot and insert steamer basket. Place meatballs evenly in steamer basket. Close lid and set steam release to Sealing, then press Manual and adjust cook time to 3 minutes.

5. Once cooking is complete quick-release pressure and open lid. Transfer meatballs to a tray and serve.

PER SERVING (1 meatball) Calories: 111 | Fat: 8g | Protein: 7g | Sodium: 292mg | Fiber: 0.5g | Carbohydrates: 2g | Sugar: 0.5g

Corned Beef and Cabbage

It just isn't St. Paddy's Day without a little corned beef and cabbage. Let the Instant Pot® do the legwork, allowing you time to do an Irish jig with your friends. The corned beef brisket even comes with its own spice packet, so sit back, sip your black and tan, and wait for dinner to be cooked for you!

INGREDIENTS | SERVES 6

1 (3-pound) corned beef brisket with spice packet

2 tablespoons avocado oil

1 large yellow onion, peeled and quartered

4 large carrots, peeled and cut into 2" sections

1 small cabbage, cut into 6 wedges

3 cloves garlic, peeled, quartered, and smashed

1 cup beef broth

1 cup water

1. Massage contents of spice packet over corned beef brisket. Set aside.

2. Press Sauté on Instant Pot®. Once machine indicates Hot, heat avocado oil 30 seconds. Add brisket and sear 7 minutes on each side. Set meat aside.

3. Add onion to pot and cook 4 minutes until tender. Add remaining ingredients, including brisket, to pot. Press Cancel. Close lid and set steam release to Sealing, then press Meat and adjust cook time to 40 minutes.

4. Once cooking is complete allow pressure to release naturally and open lid. Transfer brisket to a cutting board. When cooled enough to work with, about 30 minutes, slice and transfer to a serving tray. Serve warm.

PER SERVING Calories: 664 | Fat: 38g | Protein: 63g | Sodium: 2,213mg | Fiber: 4g | Carbohydrates: 14g | Sugar: 7g

Chi-Town Italian Beef and Peppers

A giant bowl of beef and peppers will make you think you are in Chicago—ambling along the Navy Pier or shopping the Magnificent Mile! You can easily make this into sandwiches by adding toasted buns.

INGREDIENTS | SERVES 6

2 tablespoons vegetable oil

1 (3-pound) chuck roast, halved

1 large yellow onion, peeled, halved, and sliced

2 medium red bell peppers, seeded and sliced

2 medium green bell peppers, seeded and sliced

1 (16-ounce) jar sliced pepperoncini, including juice

3 cloves garlic, peeled and quartered

1 cup beef broth

1 teaspoon ground black pepper

1. Press Sauté on Instant Pot®. Once machine indicates Hot, heat oil 30 seconds. Add one roast and sear 5 minutes on each side. Remove from pot and repeat with remaining roast. Return first roast to pot.

2. Add onion, bell pepper, pepperoncini, garlic, and beef broth to pot with roasts. Press Cancel. Close lid, press Manual, and adjust cook time to 40 minutes.

3. Once cooking is complete quick-release pressure and open lid. Transfer roast to a cutting board and let rest 10 minutes. Thinly slice, then place in a large bowl. Use a slotted spoon to transfer onions and peppers to bowl, then add 3 tablespoons pot liquid to the bowl. Toss vegetables and liquid with pepper. Serve warm.

PER SERVING Calories: 444 | Fat: 17g | Protein: 59g | Sodium: 317mg | Fiber: 2g | Carbohydrates: 8g | Sugar: 4g

Cottage Pie

The comforting mix of beef, vegetables, and cheese-topped potatoes makes this dish a family favorite. If you have any leftover mashed potatoes from dinner the night before, this is an excellent place to use them up!

INGREDIENTS | SERVES 6

1 tablespoon vegetable oil

1 pound ground beef

1 medium yellow onion, peeled and chopped

1 rib celery, chopped

1 medium carrot, peeled and chopped

2 cloves garlic, peeled and minced

1 cup frozen peas

1 tablespoon Worcestershire sauce

½ teaspoon salt

½ teaspoon ground black pepper

2 tablespoons all-purpose flour

1 cup beef broth

1 cup water

2 cups prepared Simple Mashed Potatoes (see Chapter 15)

½ cup shredded Cheddar cheese

Shepherd's Pie or Cottage Pie?

In North America any mixture of meat cooked with onion, celery, carrot, and sometimes peas and topped with mashed potatoes is called *Shepherd's Pie*. Technically, though, it is Shepherd's Pie only if it is made with lamb. If you make Shepherd's Pie with beef, it becomes Cottage Pie.

1. Spray an 8" × 8" baking dish with nonstick cooking spray.

2. Press Sauté on Instant Pot®. Once machine indicates Hot, add oil and let heat 30 seconds. Add beef and cook, crumbling well, until just browned, about 5 minutes. Add onion, celery, and carrot and cook 5 minutes until vegetables are just tender.

3. Add garlic and cook until fragrant, about 30 seconds. Stir in peas, Worcestershire sauce, salt, pepper, and flour. Mix well, then cook until flour is moistened by meat juices, about 1 minute. Quickly stir in beef broth and cook until mixture thickens slightly, about 30 seconds. Press Cancel. Transfer meat mixture to prepared dish.

4. Place rack in Instant Pot® and add water. Fold a long piece of aluminum foil in half. Lay foil over rack to form a sling.

5. Spread mashed potatoes evenly over meat mixture. Top with cheese, then loosely cover dish with another piece of aluminum foil. Set dish on rack. Close lid and set steam release to Sealing, then press Manual and adjust cook time to 5 minutes.

6. Once cooking is complete quick-release pressure and open lid. Carefully remove dish from pot with sling. Remove foil top and serve hot.

PER SERVING Calories: 296 | Fat: 13g | Protein: 21g | Sodium: 751mg | Fiber: 3g | Carbohydrates: 21g | Sugar: 3g

Pork Main Dishes

Shredded Pork Shoulder

Use this meat for barbecue sandwiches; folded into pasta, macaroni and cheese, or soups and stews; over salads; or stuffed into wraps. It is never a bad thing to have tender shredded pork available to add into recipes all week long!

INGREDIENTS | SERVES 6

1 (3-pound) boneless pork shoulder, cut into 3" cubes

1 teaspoon salt

1 teaspoon ground black pepper

2 tablespoons vegetable oil, divided

1½ cups chicken broth

3 cloves garlic, peeled and smashed

1 medium yellow onion, peeled and quartered

Customize the Flavors

Add any of the following during cooking! For Tex-Mex pork: 1 teaspoon cumin, 1 teaspoon smoked paprika, 2 tablespoons packed light brown sugar, and ½ cup fresh cilantro leaves. For Asian-style pork: ½ cup hoisin sauce in place of ½ cup broth, ¼ cup fresh cilantro leaves, and 2 teaspoons Chinese five-spice powder. For Italian-style pork: 2 tablespoons Italian seasoning and 1 (15-ounce) can diced tomatoes in place of ½ cup broth.

1. Season pork cubes with salt and pepper. Set aside.

2. Press Sauté on Instant Pot®. Once machine indicates Hot, add 1 tablespoon oil and let heat 30 seconds, then add ½ pork and brown 4 minutes on each side. Remove from pot and repeat with remaining oil and pork.

3. Press Cancel. Add remaining ingredients and browned pork to pot. Close lid and set steam release to Sealing, then press Manual and adjust cook time to 60 minutes.

4. Once cooking is complete quick-release pressure. Press Cancel and open lid. Remove pork from pot and shred with two forks. Serve hot or at room temperature.

PER SERVING Calories: 392 | Fat: 21g | Protein: 45g | Sodium: 576mg | Fiber: 0.5g | Carbohydrates: 3g | Sugar: 0.5g

Cranberry-Stuffed Pork Roast

Tired of turkey for the holidays? This could be the dish for you! The tangy orange-soaked cranberries make this unique and zesty. You can also add a pinch of nutmeg or cinnamon to the stuffing if you like.

INGREDIENTS | SERVES 6

½ cup dried cranberries

2 cups orange juice

⅓ cup panko bread crumbs

4 strips bacon, chopped

1 (2-pound) boneless pork loin

1 teaspoon salt

½ teaspoon ground black pepper

2 teaspoons chopped fresh rosemary

1 teaspoon fresh thyme leaves

1 cup chicken broth

1. Place cranberries and orange juice in a medium saucepan. Heat on stove over medium heat until juice simmers, about 4 minutes. Turn off heat and let cranberries stand 30 minutes. Drain and cool cranberries to room temperature, then add bread crumbs and mix well. Discard juice.

2. Press Sauté on Instant Pot®. Once machine indicates Hot, about 3 minutes, add bacon. Cook, stirring frequently, until bacon is browned and fat has rendered, about 4 minutes. Use a slotted spoon to remove bacon and add to cranberry mixture. Leave bacon drippings in pot. Press Cancel.

3. Butterfly pork loin and season with salt and pepper. Season one side of pork with rosemary and thyme, then spread cranberry mixture over pork and roll meat tightly. Tie roast with twine, cover with plastic wrap, and refrigerate 1 hour.

4. Press Sauté on Instant Pot®. Once bacon drippings are hot, about 30 seconds, add pork loin and brown 4 minutes on each side. Remove pork from pot, then press Cancel.

5. Add broth to pot. Place rack in pot, then place roast on rack. Close lid and set steam release to Sealing, then press Manual and adjust cook time to 20 minutes.

6. Once cooking is complete quick-release pressure. Press Cancel and open lid. Remove roast, let rest 5 minutes, then slice and serve.

PER SERVING Calories: 476 | Fat: 27g | Protein: 34g | Sodium: 643mg | Fiber: 1g | Carbohydrates: 23g | Sugar: 14g

Mustard Thyme Pork Chops

The tang of the mustard makes this dish irresistible! For the best flavor use fresh thyme. Dried will work in a pinch, but just reduce the amount used by half, as dried herbs are more pungent.

4 thick-cut, bone-in pork chops (about 2–3 pounds)

¼ cup all-purpose flour

½ teaspoon salt

½ teaspoon ground black pepper

2 tablespoons vegetable oil, divided

¼ cup white wine

½ cup chicken stock

2 teaspoons chopped fresh thyme

2 cloves garlic, peeled and minced

1 medium yellow onion, peeled and sliced ¼" thick

⅓ cup heavy cream

2 tablespoons Dijon mustard

Cooking with Wine

Cook only with wine you would also drink. That doesn't mean the wine needs to be expensive: There are a number of tasty, well-rated wines available for under $10. Avoid bottles labeled "cooking wine," as they are low-quality wine with very little flavor. Wine reduces as you cook it, concentrating the flavor, so you don't want to reduce substandard flavors into your food!

1. Place pork chops in a large resealable bag and add flour, salt, and pepper. Shake until chops are evenly coated. Remove from bag and set aside.

2. Press Sauté on Instant Pot®. Once machine indicates Hot, add 1 tablespoon oil and let heat 30 seconds, then add 2 chops and brown 3 minutes on each side. Remove from pot and repeat with remaining chops.

3. Add wine to pot and scrape any browned bits from bottom of pot. Mix in stock, thyme, garlic, and onion.

4. Add chops back to pot. Press Cancel. Close lid and set steam release to Sealing, then press Manual and adjust cook time to 10 minutes.

5. Once cooking is complete quick-release pressure. Press Cancel and open lid. Transfer chops to a platter and tent with foil to keep warm.

6. Press Sauté on Instant Pot® and simmer until liquid has reduced by half and is slightly thickened, about 5 minutes, whisking occasionally. Add cream and mustard and whisk to combine. Remove foil from chops and pour sauce and onions over top. Serve immediately.

PER SERVING Calories: 352 | Fat: 23g | Protein: 27g | Sodium: 286mg | Fiber: 0.5g | Carbohydrates: 5g | Sugar: 1g

Pork Sausages with Apple Sauerkraut

Juniper berries can be found with the spices in most grocery stores, and they add a sharp, almost citrus, flavor to this sauerkraut. If you are unable to find them, you can add half a sprig of fresh rosemary to the pot to get a similar flavor.

INGREDIENTS | SERVES 6

1 tablespoon vegetable oil

6 (4-ounce) fresh or frozen raw bratwursts

1 medium Granny Smith apple, peeled and thinly sliced

1 medium yellow onion, peeled and sliced

2 teaspoons dried juniper berries

1 clove garlic, peeled and minced

1 (32-ounce) jar refrigerated sauerkraut, drained well

1 (12-ounce) bottle pilsner or bock-style beer

Sauerkraut

Sauerkraut is made from cabbage and salt. The cabbage is finely shredded, then layered with salt and left to stand at room temperature for at least two weeks. You can find sauerkraut stuffed into pierogi, mixed into soups and stews, and as a topping at your favorite hot dog cart!

1. Press Sauté on Instant Pot®. Once machine indicates Hot, add oil and let heat 30 seconds, then add ½ bratwurst to pot. Brown 2 minutes on each side. Remove from pot and repeat with remaining bratwurst. Remove and set aside.

2. Add apple and onion to pot. Cook until onion is just tender, about 3 minutes. Add juniper and garlic and cook 1 minute. Add sauerkraut and mix well. Press Cancel.

3. Add bratwurst back to pot and pour in beer. Close lid and set steam release to Sealing, then press Manual and adjust cook time to 4 minutes.

4. Once cooking is complete quick-release pressure. Press Cancel and open lid. Transfer bratwurst to a serving tray and add sauerkraut, using slotted spoon to drain off liquid. Serve immediately.

PER SERVING Calories: 332 | Fat: 23g | Protein: 15g | Sodium: 1,206mg | Fiber: 4g | Carbohydrates: 9g | Sugar: 3g

Sweet and Sour Pork

This one-pot Sweet and Sour Pork is different from the overly breaded, overly sweet takeout version, and it is wonderful served over rice. You can also make this with chicken if you prefer, or even extra-firm tofu.

INGREDIENTS | SERVES 4

1 cup water, divided

¾ cup pineapple juice

½ cup granulated sugar

2 tablespoons rice wine vinegar

1 tablespoon soy sauce

2 tablespoons ketchup

2 cloves garlic, peeled and minced

1 teaspoon fresh grated ginger

⅓ cup plus 1 tablespoon cornstarch, divided

1 (1-pound) boneless pork tenderloin, cut into 1" cubes

½ teaspoon salt

½ cup vegetable oil

2 medium red bell peppers, cut into ½" pieces

1 medium yellow onion, peeled and cut into ½" chunks

2 cups sliced button mushrooms

1 (15-ounce) can pineapple chunks, drained

1. Press Sauté on Instant Pot® and add ¾ cup water, pineapple juice, sugar, vinegar, soy sauce, ketchup, garlic, and ginger. Bring to a boil and allow sauce to reduce by half, about 5 minutes. Press Cancel and transfer sauce to a medium bowl. Wipe out pot.

2. In a large resealable bag, combine ⅓ cup cornstarch with cubed pork and salt. Seal the bag and shake well to coat.

3. Press Sauté on pot. Once machine indicates Hot, add oil and let heat 30 seconds, then add ½ pork cubes and brown 1 minute on each side. Transfer to a paper towel–lined plate to drain and repeat with remaining pork. Transfer to plate.

4. Add bell pepper, onion, and mushrooms to pot. Cook until vegetables are tender, about 5 minutes. Return pork to pot along with prepared sauce and pineapple and stir until everything is coated. Press Cancel. Close lid and set steam release to Sealing, then press Manual and adjust cook time to 3 minutes.

5. Once cooking is complete quick-release pressure. Press Cancel and open lid.

6. Press Sauté and combine remaining ¼ cup water with reserved cornstarch and stir into pot. Cook until sauce thickens, about 3 minutes. Serve immediately.

PER SERVING Calories: 670 | Fat: 31g | Protein: 27g | Sodium: 656mg | Fiber: 5g | Carbohydrates: 72g | Sugar: 52g

Pineapple Pork Roast

You may be tempted to use fresh pineapple, but resist the urge, as fresh pineapple can make the pork a little mushy in texture.

INGREDIENTS | SERVES 6

¼ cup all-purpose flour

½ teaspoon salt

½ teaspoon ground black pepper

1 (2-pound) boneless pork roast

2 tablespoons vegetable oil

1 medium yellow onion, peeled and sliced

2 cloves garlic, peeled and minced

1 teaspoon fresh grated ginger

1 (16-ounce) can pineapple chunks, with juice

2 tablespoons soy sauce

2 tablespoons mirin

2 cups water

Cooking with Fresh Pineapple

Fresh pineapple may be delicious, but if you are planning to cook the pineapple with meat, you will want to use canned. Pineapple contains bromelain, an enzyme that can tenderize meat by breaking down the collagen and connective tissue. The enzymes are only active in fresh pineapple because they are very heat-sensitive, so they are destroyed during canning.

1. In a small bowl combine flour, salt, and pepper. Pat pork dry with a paper towel, then coat with flour mixture, reserving any remaining mixture. Set aside.

2. Press Sauté on Instant Pot®. Once machine indicates Hot, add oil and let heat 30 seconds, then add roast and brown 5 minutes on each side. Transfer roast to a plate to rest.

3. Add onion to pot and cook until tender, about 3 minutes. Add garlic and ginger and cook until fragrant, about 30 seconds. Add reserved flour and stir to coat onions.

4. Add pineapple chunks with juice, soy sauce, and mirin. Scrape up any browned bits from bottom of pot. Add roast back to pot and pour in water so it comes halfway up the side of roast. Press Cancel.

5. Close lid and set steam release to Sealing, then press Manual and adjust cook time to 20 minutes.

6. Once cooking is complete quick-release pressure. Press Cancel and open lid.

7. Remove roast from pot and allow to rest, tented with foil, 10 minutes, before slicing and arranging on a platter. Pour braising liquid over pork. Serve hot.

PER SERVING Calories: 307 | Fat: 10g | Protein: 35g | Sodium: 561mg | Fiber: 1.5g | Carbohydrates: 18g | Sugar: 11g

Cuban-Style Pork Roast

If you can source sour oranges, you can substitute a full cup of sour orange juice for the orange juice and lime juice mixture used here. This pork is delicious with fried plantain or stuffed into warm corn tortillas!

INGREDIENTS | SERVES 8

¾ cup fresh squeezed orange juice

¼ cup freshly squeezed lime juice

½ cup olive oil

8 cloves garlic, peeled and minced

1 teaspoon salt

½ teaspoon ground black pepper

½ teaspoon dried oregano leaves

½ teaspoon ground cumin

½ teaspoon paprika

1 (4-pound) pork roast, cut into 3 pieces

2 tablespoons vegetable oil

1 medium yellow onion, peeled and sliced

Cuban Cuisine

Influenced by African, Middle Eastern, Asian, and European cultures, Cuban cuisine is unpretentious and hearty. Many popular dishes are slow cooked with plenty of aromatics and spices such as garlic, cumin, oregano, and peppers. Less expensive cuts of meat are often marinated in citrus to help tenderize before cooking low and slow.

1. In a large resealable bag or large container with a lid, add orange juice, lime juice, olive oil, garlic, salt, pepper, oregano, cumin, and paprika and mix well. Add pork pieces, coat in marinade, seal bag or container, and refrigerate 8 hours, or overnight.

2. Press Sauté on Instant Pot®. Once machine indicates Hot, add oil and let heat 30 seconds, then add two pieces pork and brown 4 minutes on each side. Remove from pot and brown remaining pork. Press Cancel.

3. Add browned pork, pork marinade, and onion to pot. Close lid and set steam release to Sealing, then press Manual and adjust cook time to 70 minutes.

4. Once cooking is complete quick-release pressure. Press Cancel and open lid. Remove pork and let rest 10 minutes, then shred and serve.

PER SERVING Calories: 459 | Fat: 24g | Protein: 50g | Sodium: 404mg | Fiber: 0.5g | Carbohydrates: 5g | Sugar: 2.5g

Garlic Chili Pork

This Vietnamese-inspired pork dish pairs perfectly with rice, a fried egg, and quick pickled vegetables such as carrots and cabbage. If rice isn't your thing, you can also serve this with thin Asian egg noodles and fresh vegetables for a tasty stir-fry!

INGREDIENTS | SERVES 6

1 (3-pound) boneless pork butt, cut into 3" cubes

2 cloves garlic, peeled and finely minced

1 stalk lemongrass, white part only, finely minced

¼ cup store-bought garlic chili sauce

¼ cup hoisin sauce

1 tablespoon granulated sugar

1 tablespoon fish sauce

1 teaspoon salt

1 teaspoon ground black pepper

1 teaspoon sesame oil

2 tablespoons vegetable oil

1 cup water

2 medium yellow onions, peeled and sliced

1. Combine all ingredients except vegetable oil, water, and onion in a large bowl and mix well. Cover and let refrigerate overnight.

2. Press Sauté on Instant Pot®. Once machine indicates Hot, add oil and let heat 30 seconds, then add one layer pork and brown 4 minutes on each side. Remove from pot and repeat with remaining pork.

3. Add water to pot and scrape any browned bits from pot. Press Cancel. Add pork marinade, pork, and onion to pot. Close lid and set steam release to Sealing, then press Manual and adjust cook time to 60 minutes.

4. Once cooking is complete allow pressure to release naturally, about 15 minutes. Press Cancel and open lid. Remove pork and pull into large pieces. Serve hot.

PER SERVING Calories: 427 | Fat: 21g | Protein: 44g | Sodium: 954mg | Fiber: 1g | Carbohydrates: 10g | Sugar: 6g

Hoisin Pork Ribs

These ribs are tender and flavorful. While this recipe calls for broiling the ribs after cooking to help set the glaze, you can also place them on a heated grill for a few minutes on each side until browned to add extra flavor.

INGREDIENTS | SERVES 6

2 slabs baby back ribs, about 3 pounds, cut into 4-rib sections

¾ cup hoisin sauce

¼ cup Shaoxing wine or sherry

¼ cup light soy sauce

1 tablespoon minced fresh ginger

3 cloves garlic, peeled and minced

1 teaspoon Chinese five-spice powder

1 (8-ounce) jar char siu sauce, divided

1 cup water

To Grill or Not to Grill

While ribs cooked in the Instant Pot® are perfectly lovely right out of the pot, you can add a special touch by lightly grilling the ribs after cooking. This will help caramelize the outside of the ribs and add a slight smoky flavor. If you want to grill pressure-cooked ribs, reduce the cooking time by about 5 minutes to ensure the ribs are not falling off the bone.

1. In a large resealable bag add ribs, hoisin sauce, Shaoxing wine, soy sauce, ginger, garlic, five-spice powder, and ½ char siu sauce. Seal bag and turn gently until ribs are coated. Refrigerate covered overnight.

2. Add water to Instant Pot® and add rack. Place ribs on rack. Close lid and set steam release to Sealing, then press Manual and adjust cook time to 25 minutes.

3. Once cooking is complete allow pressure to release naturally, about 15 minutes. Press Cancel and open lid. Remove ribs and place on a platter. Glaze both sides with remaining char siu sauce.

4. Heat broiler on high. Broil back of ribs with meat side down 5 minutes, then turn meat over and broil 8 minutes. Cool slightly before serving.

PER SERVING Calories: 536 | Fat: 40g | Protein: 27g | Sodium: 1,181mg | Fiber: 1g | Carbohydrates: 16g | Sugar: 8g

Vietnamese Caramel Pork

In order to get this pork glazed and sticky, you will need to first make a basic caramel in your Instant Pot® before cooking the pork and then let the cooking liquid reduce after the pork has finished cooking. This may seem like a lot of work, but it is actually very easy—and completely worth it!

INGREDIENTS | SERVES 4

2 pounds pork shoulder or pork belly, cut into 1" cubes

½ teaspoon salt

2 tablespoons vegetable oil

⅓ cup packed light brown sugar

1 tablespoon light soy sauce

2 cloves garlic, peeled and minced

1 medium yellow onion, peeled and sliced

¾ cup coconut water

¼ cup sliced green onion tops

2 cups cooked long-grain white rice

1. Press Sauté on Instant Pot®. Season pork with salt. Once machine indicates Hot, add oil and let heat 30 seconds, then add 1 pound pork to pot and brown 4 minutes on each side. Remove and repeat with remaining pork.

2. Add pork back into pot along with sugar, soy sauce, garlic, and onion. Cook until sugar melts and pork is deeply golden in color, about 6 minutes.

3. Add coconut water and scrape bottom and sides of pot to loosen any brown bits. Press Cancel. Close lid and set steam release to Sealing, then press Manual and adjust cook time to 20 minutes.

4. Once cooking is complete quick-release pressure. Press Cancel and open lid. Stir well.

5. Press Sauté and let pork cook, stirring often, until sauce has reduced by ¾, about 10 minutes. Serve hot, garnished with green onion tops, over rice.

PER SERVING Calories: 576 | Fat: 23g | Protein: 46g | Sodium: 686mg | Fiber: 1g | Carbohydrates: 41g | Sugar: 13g

Bacon Meatloaf

Ground bacon not only adds a lot of flavor to this meatloaf, but it also makes it incredibly moist! To make grinding the bacon a little easier, place the bacon pieces in the freezer 10 minutes before processing.

INGREDIENTS | SERVES 8

½ pound smoked bacon, cut into 1" pieces

½ pound ground pork

½ pound ground beef

½ cup panko bread crumbs

1 large egg

1 teaspoon dried oregano leaves

1 teaspoon ground fennel

½ teaspoon smoked paprika

¼ teaspoon salt

¼ teaspoon ground black pepper

1 cup water

1 cup shredded mozzarella cheese

½ cup marinara sauce

1. Add bacon to a food processor and pulse until ground but not a paste, about twenty pulses.

2. Transfer bacon to a large bowl along with pork, beef, bread crumbs, egg, oregano, fennel, paprika, salt, and pepper. Mix well, cover, and refrigerate covered at least 1 hour, up to 4 hours.

3. Place rack in Instant Pot® and add water. Fold a long piece of aluminum foil in half. Lay foil over rack to form a sling.

4. Spray an 8" × 8" baking dish with nonstick cooking spray. Add ½ meatloaf mixture to prepared dish. Form mixture into a circle with a 1" lip around the inside of pan. Fill center with cheese, then top with remaining meat, pressing the sides to seal.

5. Using a spatula, press around edge of dish to form a smooth, round loaf. Brush top with marinara sauce. Close lid and set steam release to Sealing, then press Manual and adjust cook time to 20 minutes.

6. Once cooking is complete quick-release pressure. Press Cancel and open lid. Carefully remove dish with sling and drain off any excess fat.

7. Turn broiler to high heat. Once hot, about 30 seconds, broil meatloaf 4 minutes until top is bubbling and browned. Let rest 10 minutes before slicing and serving.

PER SERVING Calories: 328 | Fat: 24g | Protein: 18g | Sodium: 520mg | Fiber: 1g | Carbohydrates: 7g | Sugar: 2g

Simple Dijon Pork Tenderloin

Pork tenderloin is a go-to for most busy home cooks, but if it is overcooked it can become a disappointment. The steam in the Instant Pot® helps keep the air around the loin moist while it is cooking, keeping the meat moist too. Enjoy this pork sliced into medallions alongside a simple salad or roasted vegetables.

INGREDIENTS | SERVES 8

2 (2-pound) boneless pork loins, each halved

2 tablespoons Dijon mustard

1 teaspoon sea salt

1 teaspoon ground black pepper

1 cup water

3 cloves garlic, peeled and halved

Pork Loin versus Pork Tenderloin

Have you ever wondered if pork loin and pork tenderloin were one and the same? Well, pork loin and pork tenderloin are actually quite different. The tenderloin is small and somewhat thin, whereas the loin is wide and is sometimes sold in chops or steaks in your butcher department. Pork tenderloin benefits from fast cooking, while the pork loin is better suited to longer cooking.

1. Pat pork loins with paper towels. Massage with mustard, then season with salt and pepper.

2. Pour water into Instant Pot®. Add garlic. Place loins in steamer basket and insert in pot. Close lid and set steam release to Sealing, then press Manual and adjust cook time to 20 minutes.

3. Once cooking is complete quick-release pressure and open lid. Transfer pork loins to a serving tray and either slice into medallions or pull apart with two forks. Serve warm.

PER SERVING Calories: 66 | Fat: 1.5g | Protein: 11.5g | Sodium: 363mg | Fiber: 0.3g | Carbohydrates: 1g | Sugar: 0g

Orange Rosemary Pork Tenderloin

Tenderloin has a mild flavor and is great as a canvas for your chosen flavors. Here the citrus from the orange and the piney essence and earthiness from the rosemary infuse the pork and make it irresistible.

INGREDIENTS | SERVES 8

⅓ cup freshly squeezed orange juice (about 1 orange)

1 tablespoon orange zest

1 tablespoon finely chopped fresh rosemary

2 tablespoons honey

1 teaspoon sea salt

½ teaspoon ground black pepper

2 (2-pound) boneless pork loins, each halved

½ cup water

1. In a large bowl combine orange juice, orange zest, rosemary, honey, salt, and pepper. Add pork, toss, and refrigerate covered at least 30 minutes up to overnight.

2. Place loins in Instant Pot® and add remaining pork marinade. Add water. Close lid and set steam release to Sealing, then press Manual and adjust cook time to 20 minutes.

3. Once cooking is complete quick-release pressure and open lid. Transfer pork loins to a serving tray and either slice into medallions or pull apart with two forks. Serve warm.

PER SERVING Calories: 100 | Fat: 2.3g | Protein: 12g | Sodium: 324mg | Fiber: 0.3g | Carbohydrates: 6g | Sugar: 5g

Steamed Dry-Rubbed Spareribs

These ribs are so good they don't even need the sauce! The meat is smooth as butter and is loaded with the flavors of the broad mix of spices used.

INGREDIENTS | SERVES 6

1 teaspoon salt

1 teaspoon ground black pepper

1 teaspoon smoked paprika

1 teaspoon chili powder

1 teaspoon garlic powder

1 teaspoon Italian seasoning

1 (3½-pound) rack pork ribs, cut into 2-rib sections

1 cup water

1. In a large bowl combine salt, pepper, paprika, chili powder, garlic powder, and Italian seasoning. Toss in rib sections to coat. Refrigerate covered at least 30 minutes up to overnight.

2. Add water to Instant Pot® and insert rack. Arrange ribs standing upright with meaty side facing outward. Close lid and set steam release to Sealing, then press Manual and adjust cook time to 30 minutes.

3. Once cooking is complete let pressure release naturally, about 20 minutes, then open lid. Transfer ribs to a platter and serve warm.

PER SERVING Calories: 161 | Fat: 6g | Protein: 23g | Sodium: 476mg | Fiber: 0.5g | Carbohydrates: 1g | Sugar: 0g

Cowgirl Baby Back Pork Ribs

Coffee crystals are the secret star of this recipe. They add a beautiful earthiness to the ribs. If you want a little crispness to the ribs as well, throw them on the grill or under a broiler on high for 2 minutes per side until browned.

INGREDIENTS | SERVES 4

1 teaspoon instant coffee crystals

1 teaspoon sea salt

½ teaspoon chili powder

½ teaspoon ground cumin

½ teaspoon cayenne pepper

½ teaspoon ground mustard

½ teaspoon garlic powder

½ teaspoon onion powder

¼ teaspoon ground coriander

2 (1½-pound) racks baby back pork ribs, cut into 2-rib sections

1 medium yellow onion, peeled and diced

4 cloves garlic, peeled and halved

2 cups water

1. In a large bowl combine coffee, salt, chili powder, cumin, cayenne pepper, mustard, garlic powder, onion powder, and coriander. Toss in rib sections to coat. Refrigerate covered at least 30 minutes up to overnight.

2. Place onion, garlic, and water in Instant Pot® and insert rack. Arrange ribs standing upright with the meaty side facing outward. Close lid and set steam release to Sealing, then press Manual and adjust cook time to 25 minutes.

3. Once cooking is complete let pressure release naturally, about 20 minutes, then open lid. Transfer ribs to a platter and serve warm.

PER SERVING Calories: 475 | Fat: 19g | Protein: 69g | Sodium: 824mg | Fiber: 0.5g | Carbohydrates: 1g | Sugar: 0g

Baby Back Ribs

Baby back ribs, also known as back ribs, Canadian back ribs, and loin ribs, are from the top of the rib cage above the spareribs. The meat of baby back ribs is leaner than spareribs or country-style ribs, as it is closer to the loin meat. Both baby back ribs and spareribs are best when they are allowed to cook low and slow.

Smothered Pork Chops with Mushroom Gravy

This is a classic country-style dish for a reason. It hits all the right comfort buttons, leaving you happy and satisfied. Add some mashed cauliflower to round out this meal.

INGREDIENTS | SERVES 4

4 (1"-thick, 4-ounce) bone-in pork chops
1 teaspoon sea salt
½ teaspoon ground black pepper
2 tablespoons avocado oil
1 cup beef broth
3 cups sliced cremini mushrooms
1 small Vidalia onion, peeled and sliced
2 tablespoons unsweetened almond milk
2 teaspoons Worcestershire sauce
2 tablespoons cornstarch

1. Season pork chops with salt and pepper. Set aside.

2. Press Sauté on Instant Pot®. Once machine indicates Hot, add oil and let heat 30 seconds, then sear chops in batches, about 3 minutes on each side. Set aside.

3. Add broth, mushrooms, and onion to pot. Press Cancel. Insert steamer basket. Arrange pork chops in basket on their sides so as not to overlap. Close lid and set steam release to Sealing, then press Manual and adjust cook time to 15 minutes.

4. Once cooking is complete let pressure release naturally 5 minutes, then quick-release remaining pressure. Open lid. Remove steamer basket.

5. Add milk and Worcestershire sauce to pot with juices and broth. Quickly whisk in cornstarch, 1 teaspoon at a time, until thick gravy forms. Transfer to a gravy boat and serve with pork chops.

PER SERVING Calories: 390 | Fat: 24g | Protein: 32g | Sodium: 932mg | Fiber: 1g | Carbohydrates: 7g | Sugar: 2g

Barbecue Boneless Pork Loin Roast

The boneless loin roast is a center cut of pork. It is not the tenderloin and it is not the shoulder. Be aware of the different cuts, as they will have different cooking times and results. For instance, pork shoulder or butt is perfect for shredding for barbecue dishes and takes longer to prepare. Pork tenderloin is narrower and long and requires a shorter cooking time.

INGREDIENTS | SERVES 6

2 teaspoons sea salt

1 teaspoon ground black pepper

1 teaspoon garlic powder

1 (2½-pound) boneless pork loin roast

2¼ cups water, divided

¾ cup ketchup

½ medium yellow onion, peeled and grated

¼ cup molasses

1 teaspoon garlic powder

1 teaspoon ground cumin

¼ teaspoon cayenne pepper

1 tablespoon yellow mustard

2 teaspoons apple cider vinegar

1. In a small bowl mix together salt, pepper, and garlic powder. Massage into roast.

2. Add 2 cups water to Instant Pot®. Add roast. Close lid and set steam release to Sealing, then press Manual and adjust cook time to 30 minutes.

3. Once cooking is complete, allow pressure to release naturally 10 minutes. Press Cancel. Transfer loin to a large plate.

4. Discard liquid from pot and add remaining ingredients. Press Sauté button. Stir and cook 5 minutes until sauce starts to reduce and thicken. Ladle out ½ cup sauce and set aside.

5. Return pork to pot and cook 6 minutes, turning roast until all sides are covered and sauce is caramelized. Transfer roast to a cutting board and let rest 5 minutes.

6. Thinly slice roast and pour reserved sauce over slices. Serve warm.

PER SERVING Calories: 380 | Fat: 23g | Protein: 37g | Sodium: 900mg | Fiber: 0.5g | Carbohydrates: 2g | Sugar: 0.5g

CHAPTER 12

Chicken and Poultry

Basic Pulled Chicken

Pulled chicken is one of those things that can make meal prep a breeze. With a reserve of pulled chicken on hand you can make barbecue chicken sandwiches, chicken salad, chicken stir-fry or fried rice, soups, or pot pies at a moment's notice.

INGREDIENTS | SERVES 8

4 pounds chicken breasts
1 cup chicken broth
½ teaspoon salt
½ teaspoon ground black pepper
½ teaspoon poultry seasoning

1. Place all ingredients in Instant Pot®. Close lid and set steam release to Sealing, then press Manual and adjust cook time to 15 minutes.

2. Once cooking is complete quick-release pressure. Press Cancel and let chicken stand 20 minutes with lid on.

3. Remove lid, transfer chicken to a large bowl and shred with two forks. Serve warm, or refrigerate covered up to five days.

PER SERVING Calories: 274 | Fat: 6g | Protein: 51g | Sodium: 225mg | Fiber: 0g | Carbohydrates: 0.5g | Sugar: 0g

Avocado Chicken Salad

A fresh and quick meal, this chicken salad is also a great recipe to make on prep day to portion out for the remainder of the week. It is delicious spread on slices of toasted whole-grain bread, stuffed into a wrap, or served over a bed of your favorite salad greens.

INGREDIENTS | SERVES 6

2 pounds boneless, skinless chicken breasts, cut into 1" cubes
1 teaspoon sea salt
1 teaspoon ground black pepper
1 cup water
½ medium red onion, peeled and diced
2 ribs celery, finely chopped
2 Roma tomatoes, seeded and diced
1 medium avocado, peeled and diced
½ cup mayonnaise
1 tablespoon yellow mustard
½ teaspoon dried dill weed
½ teaspoon freshly squeezed lime juice

1. Season chicken pieces with salt and pepper. Set aside.

2. Add water to Instant Pot® and insert steamer basket. Place chicken in steamer basket. Close lid and set steam release to Sealing, then press Manual and adjust cook time to 5 minutes.

3. Once cooking is complete quick-release pressure and open lid. Transfer chicken to a cutting board to cool for 10 minutes, then finely chop. Combine in a medium bowl with onion, celery, tomatoes, avocado, mayonnaise, yellow mustard, dill, and lime juice. Refrigerate covered until ready to serve, up to five days.

PER SERVING Calories: 377 | Fat: 23g | Protein: 35g | Sodium: 603mg | Fiber: 3g | Carbohydrates: 6g | Sugar: 1.5g

Quick Chicken Mole

Moles are a variety of sauces that originate from Mexico. The most commonly known is mole poblano, a rich, dark red-brown sauce served with meat. Most grocery stores carry ready-made mole sauce and Mexican chocolate in their Latin or Mexican food sections.

INGREDIENTS | SERVES 6

1 tablespoon vegetable oil

1 cup prepared mole sauce

1 ounce Mexican chocolate, chopped

1 tablespoon smooth all-natural peanut butter

3 pounds boneless, skinless chicken breasts

How to Serve Mole

Chicken mole has a complex flavor and does not need much more than some white rice and warm corn tortillas to be a complete meal. You can also add shredded chicken mole as a topping for nachos, the filling for enchiladas, or even as stuffing for a baked sweet potato.

1. Press Sauté on Instant Pot®. Once machine indicates Hot, add oil and let heat 30 seconds, then add mole and stir until warm, about 30 seconds. Add chocolate and peanut butter and stir until both are completely melted, about 40 seconds. Press Cancel.

2. Add chicken to pot and turn to coat in sauce. Close lid and set steam release to Sealing, then press Manual and adjust cook time to 8 minutes.

3. Once cooking is complete quick-release pressure. Press Cancel and open lid. Transfer chicken to a platter and shred with two forks. Add chicken back into pot and mix with sauce. Serve warm.

PER SERVING Calories: 315 | Fat: 9g | Protein: 51g | Sodium: 305mg | Fiber: 1g | Carbohydrates: 5g | Sugar: 3g

Chicken in Satay Sauce

Satay is a peanut-based sauce from Thailand that is used as a dipping sauce for meat, a dressing for salad, or a topping for cold rice noodles. Natural, unsweetened peanut butter is best for this recipe, or, if you want an even better flavor, you can use fresh-ground peanut butter from the bulk section of the food market.

INGREDIENTS | SERVES 6

1 cup water

2 pounds boneless, skinless chicken thighs, cut into 2" cubes

1 tablespoon red curry paste

½ cup smooth all-natural peanut butter

¼ cup water

¼ cup canned unsweetened full-fat coconut milk

1 clove garlic, peeled and minced

1 tablespoon packed light brown sugar

1 teaspoon soy sauce

½ teaspoon freshly squeezed lime juice

¼ cup chopped unsalted peanuts

2 tablespoons sliced green onion tops

Satay

Traditional satay consists of skewered meat that is seasoned, grilled, and served with a dipping sauce. It is popular across Southeast Asia and comes in different flavors with different kinds of dipping sauce. To make this dish more authentic you can marinate the chicken in curry paste, skewer, and grill or broil.

1. Place rack inside Instant Pot® and add water. Fold a long piece of aluminum foil in half. Lay foil over rack to form a sling.

2. Spray an 8"× 8" baking dish with nonstick cooking spray. Place chicken in dish. Mix in curry paste until chicken is coated. Set aside.

3. In a blender add peanut butter, water, coconut milk, garlic, brown sugar, soy sauce, and lime juice. Purée until smooth. Pour sauce over chicken and stir well.

4. Cover dish tightly with another piece of aluminum foil. Place dish on rack. Close lid and set steam release to Sealing, then press Manual and adjust cook time to 20 minutes.

5. Once cooking is complete quick-release pressure. Press Cancel and open lid. Carefully remove dish using sling. Remove foil and stir chicken well, then transfer chicken and sauce to a platter. Garnish with chopped peanuts and green onion tops. Serve hot.

PER SERVING Calories: 372 | Fat: 22g | Protein: 36g | Sodium: 285mg | Fiber: 2g | Carbohydrates: 8g | Sugar: 4g

Tandoori-Style Chicken Wings

If you are looking for a change from the classic buffalo wing, give these Indian spiced wings a try! If you want a dipping sauce for these, try a cool Cucumber Raita.

INGREDIENTS | SERVES 6

1 small yellow onion, peeled and diced

2" knob ginger, peeled and minced

4 cloves garlic, peeled and minced

2 tablespoons freshly squeezed lime juice

1 cup canned unsweetened full-fat coconut milk

2 tablespoons avocado oil

1 tablespoon ground cumin

1 tablespoon ground coriander

2 teaspoons sea salt

1 teaspoon ground white pepper

1 teaspoon cayenne pepper

2 tablespoons tomato paste

3 pounds chicken wings, separated at the joint

1 cup chicken broth

¼ cup chopped fresh mint

1. In a large bowl combine onion, ginger, garlic, lime juice, coconut milk, avocado oil, cumin, coriander, salt, white pepper, cayenne pepper, and tomato paste. Add wings to mixture and toss. Refrigerate covered at least 1 hour up to overnight.

2. Add chicken broth to Instant Pot® and insert steamer basket. Add chicken wings, arranging them so they aren't sitting on top of one another. Close lid and set steam release to Sealing, then press Manual and adjust cook time to 10 minutes.

3. Once cooking is complete allow pressure to release naturally 5 minutes. Quick-release any remaining pressure and open lid. Use a slotted spoon to transfer wings to a serving tray. Garnish with chopped mint and serve.

PER SERVING Calories: 570 | Fat: 42g | Protein: 41g | Sodium: 1,027mg | Fiber: 1g | Carbohydrates: 6g | Sugar: 1g

Cucumber Raita

Raita is a yogurt-based sauce flavored with cucumber, garlic, mint, and cumin. In a medium bowl combine 1 peeled and grated medium cucumber, 2 cups whole-milk yogurt, 1 clove peeled and minced garlic, 2 tablespoons chopped fresh mint, and ½ teaspoon ground cumin. Mix and refrigerate covered 30 minutes before serving.

Whole Roasted Chicken with Herbs

You might not think that a pressure cooker would be an effective roaster, but it is! You will want to brown the bird well on all sides before cooking so there is some color to the skin.

INGREDIENTS | SERVES 6

1 tablespoon unsalted butter, at room temperature

1 teaspoon poultry seasoning

1 teaspoon salt, divided

½ teaspoon ground black pepper

1 (4-pound) whole chicken

2 tablespoons vegetable oil

1 medium lemon, halved

5 sprigs fresh thyme

4 sprigs fresh sage

1 branch fresh rosemary, broken in half

1 medium yellow onion, peeled and quartered

1 cup chicken broth

1. In a small bowl combine butter, poultry seasoning, ½ teaspoon salt, and pepper. Separate skin from chicken breast by hand and spread seasoned butter under skin. Season outside of the bird with remaining salt.

2. Press Sauté on Instant Pot®. Once machine indicates Hot, add oil and let heat 30 seconds, then add chicken breast-side down and brown 6 minutes. Flip and brown back of bird 4 minutes. Remove from pot. Press Cancel.

3. Add juice from half of lemon to pot, then place rack in pot. Add thyme, sage, rosemary, ½ juiced lemon rind, and two pieces onion to cavity of chicken. Add remaining lemon half and onion to pot and add broth.

4. Place chicken breast-side up on rack. Close lid and set steam release to Sealing, then press Manual and adjust cook time to 25 minutes.

5. Once cooking is complete allow pressure to release naturally. Press Cancel and open lid. Carefully transfer bird to serving platter. Serve hot.

PER SERVING Calories: 432 | Fat: 16g | Protein: 65g | Sodium: 631mg | Fiber: 1g | Carbohydrates: 4g | Sugar: 1g

Sesame Chicken

This is different from the deep-fried version popular at Chinese take-out restaurants. The chicken here is browned and then cooked in a sesame glaze, so you get a cleaner flavor and a more healthful dinner!

INGREDIENTS | SERVES 4

2 tablespoons vegetable oil, divided

2 pounds boneless, skinless chicken thighs, cut into 2" pieces

¼ cup soy sauce

¼ cup packed light brown sugar

¼ cup plus 1 tablespoon water, divided

2 cloves garlic, peeled and minced

¼ teaspoon Chinese five-spice powder

1 tablespoon toasted sesame seeds

1 teaspoon cornstarch

¼ cup sliced green onion tops

Toasting Sesame Seeds

It's best to toast your seeds fresh so they retain their flavor and don't go rancid. Simply place sesame seeds into a dry pan over medium heat. Cook, stirring constantly, for 1–2 minutes or until seeds are just turning golden, then immediately remove from heat. Continue to stir until the pan has cooled a little. Store toasted sesame seeds in an airtight container in refrigerator up to one week.

1. Press Sauté on Instant Pot®. Once machine indicates Hot, add 1 tablespoon oil and let heat 30 seconds, then add ½ chicken pieces and brown 3 minutes on each side. Transfer chicken to plate and repeat with remaining oil and chicken.

2. Add first batch back into pot, then add soy sauce, brown sugar, ¼ cup water, garlic, and five-spice powder and stir well. Make sure to scrape bottom of pot to loosen any brown bits. Press Cancel. Close lid and set steam release to Sealing, then press Manual and adjust cook time to 4 minutes.

3. Once cooking is complete quick-release pressure, then open lid. Stir in sesame seeds.

4. In a small bowl whisk together remaining water and cornstarch. Pour cornstarch slurry into pot and mix. Press Cancel, then press Sauté and cook until sauce thickens, about 4 minutes.

5. Transfer chicken and sauce to serving bowl and garnish with green onion.

PER SERVING Calories: 393 | Fat: 17g | Protein: 45g | Sodium: 1,095mg | Fiber: 0.5g | Carbohydrates: 11g | Sugar: 8g

Fruity Chicken Breasts

This recipe could not get much easier, and it packs a lot of flavor! Use your favorite kind of fruity salsa, or if you prefer to keep it savory, you can substitute regular salsa.

INGREDIENTS | SERVES 4

1 pound boneless, skinless chicken breasts

1 teaspoon fajita seasoning

1 tablespoon vegetable oil

1 (16-ounce) jar peach or mango salsa

1 medium yellow bell pepper, seeded and cut into ½" cubes

1 medium yellow onion, peeled and roughly chopped

¼ cup water

⅓ cup roughly chopped cilantro, divided

1. Season chicken with fajita seasoning on all sides. Let stand 10 minutes at room temperature.

2. Press Sauté on Instant Pot®. Once machine indicates Hot, add oil and let heat 30 seconds, then add chicken and brown 3 minutes on each side. Remove from pot and set aside.

3. Add salsa to pot and scrape any browned bits from bottom of pot. Press Cancel, add remaining ingredients, reserving 2 tablespoons of cilantro, and stir well. Place chicken onto sauce, close lid, and set steam release to Sealing. Press Manual and adjust cook time to 8 minutes.

4. Once cooking is complete allow pressure to release naturally, about 15 minutes. Press Cancel. Open lid and transfer chicken to a platter.

5. Press Sauté on pot and reduce sauce until thick, about 5 minutes. Pour sauce over chicken and serve immediately with remaining cilantro for garnish.

PER SERVING Calories: 265 | Fat: 6.5g | Protein: 26g | Sodium: 203mg | Fiber: 2g | Carbohydrates: 25g | Sugar: 18g

Chicken Thighs with Strawberry Salsa

The sweetness of the strawberries plays nicely in this salsa with the bite of the red onion, the zest of the lime, and the creaminess of the avocado. If you prepare this ahead of time, make sure to toss in the avocado right before serving to avoid browning.

INGREDIENTS | SERVES 8

1 cup diced strawberries, hulled

½ cup freshly squeezed lime juice

1 tablespoon lime zest

2 Roma tomatoes, seeded and diced

¼ cup peeled and finely diced red onion

1 medium avocado, peeled, pitted, and diced

¼ cup chopped fresh cilantro

¼ cup chopped fresh mint

2 teaspoons salt, divided

3 pounds boneless, skinless chicken thighs

½ teaspoon ground black pepper

1 cup water

1. In a large bowl combine strawberries, lime juice, lime zest, tomatoes, onion, avocado, cilantro, mint, and 1 teaspoon salt. Refrigerate salsa covered at least 1 hour up to overnight.

2. Pat chicken dry with a paper towel. Season with remaining salt and pepper.

3. Add water to Instant Pot® and insert steamer basket. Arrange chicken evenly in steamer basket. Close lid and set steam release to Sealing, then press Manual and adjust cook time to 10 minutes.

4. Once cooking is complete quick-release pressure, then open lid. Transfer chicken to eight plates. Garnish with strawberry salsa. Serve.

PER SERVING Calories: 262 | Fat: 10g | Protein: 34g | Sodium: 750mg | Fiber: 3g | Carbohydrates: 7g | Sugar: 2g

Stuffed Chicken Breasts

The ham and cheese stuffing in this recipe is similar to the classic chicken cordon bleu but without the breading. You can also add a few leaves of fresh baby spinach, strips of bell pepper, or sautéed onion along with the other filling ingredients.

INGREDIENTS | SERVES 4

4 (6-ounce) boneless, skinless chicken breasts

8 slices smoked deli ham

4 slices Swiss or Cheddar cheese

½ teaspoon salt

½ teaspoon ground black pepper

2 tablespoons vegetable oil

1 cup water

2 tablespoons unsalted butter, room temperature

¼ teaspoon onion powder

¼ teaspoon garlic powder

¼ teaspoon dried thyme leaves

¼ teaspoon smoked paprika

Other Stuffing Options

Stuffed chicken breasts make a delicious dinner, and you have a lot of stuffing options! Some options include garlic herb cheese and asparagus, sautéed spinach and garlic mixed with cream cheese, left-over corn bread dressing, slices of mozzarella and tomato with fresh basil leaves, pepper jack cheese mixed with corn and black beans, or a blend of shredded cheeses of your choice mixed with cream cheese.

1. Slice a pocket into chicken breast along one side. Place two folded slices ham and one folded slice cheese in pocket. Season chicken on all sides with salt and pepper. Set aside. Repeat with remaining breasts.

2. Press Sauté on Instant Pot®. Once machine indicates Hot, add 1 tablespoon oil and let heat 30 seconds, then add two chicken breasts to pot and brown 3 minutes on each side. Transfer to a plate and repeat with remaining oil and chicken. Press Cancel.

3. Add water to pot, then add rack. Place chicken on rack. Close lid and set steam release to Sealing, then press Manual and adjust cook time to 10 minutes.

4. While chicken cooks, combine butter, onion powder, garlic powder, thyme, and paprika in a small bowl and mix well. Set aside.

5. Once cooking is complete quick-release pressure. Press Cancel and open lid. Transfer chicken to serving platter. Top with seasoned butter. Serve hot.

PER SERVING Calories: 521 | Fat: 31g | Protein: 53g | Sodium: 1,187mg | Fiber: 1g | Carbohydrates: 3g | Sugar: 0g

Chicken with Dressing

Chicken and dressing is classic comfort food, and with your Instant Pot® you save time, energy, and cleanup!

INGREDIENTS | SERVES 4

½ teaspoon ground black pepper

½ teaspoon poultry seasoning

¼ teaspoon salt

2 pounds boneless, skinless chicken breasts

1 cup chicken broth

1 (10.5-ounce) can low-sodium cream of chicken soup

¼ cup sour cream

1 (6-ounce) box corn bread stuffing mix

Customize Your Stuffing

Want to add some extra flavor to your stuffing? Well, you can add all sorts of goodies to ramp up the flavor. Try stirring in ½ cup dry cranberries and ½ cup chopped pecans or ¼ cup each sautéed onion and celery. You can also add 1 cup of cooked crumbled sausage if you like meaty stuffing.

1. Mix pepper, poultry seasoning, and salt in a small bowl. Season all sides of chicken with mixture and set aside.

2. Pour chicken broth in Instant Pot® and add rack. Arrange chicken on rack. Close lid and set steam release to Sealing, then press Manual and adjust cook time to 8 minutes.

3. Once cooking is complete quick-release pressure. Use a meat thermometer to check chicken temperature. It should be at 165°F. Remove and tent with foil on a plate to keep warm.

4. Carefully remove rack from pot. Add soup and sour cream and whisk to combine. Stir in stuffing mix. Replace lid, press Cancel, set steam release to Sealing, press Manual, and adjust cook time to 4 minutes. The machine may not come to pressure, as the moisture will be absorbed by stuffing.

5. Slice chicken into ½" thick slices. Once stuffing is done transfer to serving dish and top with sliced chicken. Serve hot.

PER SERVING Calories: 414 | Fat: 13g | Protein: 55g | Sodium: 716mg | Fiber: 1.5g | Carbohydrates: 16g | Sugar: 2g

Salsa Chicken

Tomatillos have a fruity, slightly tart flavor, and in this dish they add a fresh zing along with the cilantro and lime. If you want to save even more time, you can sub out the salsa ingredients for 2 cups of prepared salsa verde.

INGREDIENTS | SERVES 8

½ pound (about 10–12) tomatillos, husked and stems removed, sliced in half

2 jalapeños, seeded and sliced in half

2 cloves garlic, peeled and minced

⅓ chopped fresh cilantro leaves, divided

½ medium yellow onion, peeled and chopped

2 teaspoons freshly squeezed lime juice

1 teaspoon salt, divided

2 pounds boneless, skinless chicken breasts

1 teaspoon ground cumin

½ teaspoon ground black pepper

½ teaspoon smoked paprika

½ cup queso fresco

1. Heat broiler on high. Line a baking sheet with aluminum foil and spray with nonstick cooking spray.

2. Place tomatillos cut-side down on baking sheet along with jalapeños and garlic. Broil 7 minutes until tomatillos are starting to char and blister. Remove from broiler and carefully remove charred skins.

3. Place tomatillos, jalapeños, garlic, ¼ cup cilantro, onion, lime, and ¼ teaspoon salt in food processor. Pulse six times until salsa is mostly smooth with a few small chunks.

4. Pour salsa into Instant Pot®. Season chicken on all sides with remaining salt, cumin, pepper, and paprika, then place chicken on salsa. Close lid and set steam release to Sealing, then press Manual and adjust cook time to 10 minutes.

5. Once cooking is complete quick-release pressure. Press Cancel and open lid. Carefully transfer chicken to a serving platter, top with salsa, and garnish with remaining chopped cilantro and queso fresco. Serve hot.

PER SERVING Calories: 183 | Fat: 6g | Protein: 27g | Sodium: 396mg | Fiber: 1g | Carbohydrates: 3g | Sugar: 1.5g

Layered Green Chili Chicken Enchiladas

Traditional enchiladas can be time consuming to prepare, making them less than ideal for a busy weeknight—but there is another way! Here you have all the enchilada flavor stacked into an easy and tasty casserole.

INGREDIENTS | SERVES 6

2 tablespoons unsalted butter

½ medium yellow onion, peeled and chopped

2 cloves garlic, peeled and minced

1 teaspoon ground cumin

1 pound boneless, skinless chicken thighs

2 cups tomatillo salsa

½ cup sour cream

2 cups shredded Monterey jack cheese, divided

1 cup water

8 (6") corn tortillas

Oven-Baked Option

Instead of pressure cooking the final casserole you can bake it in the oven. Heat the oven to 350°F, cover the dish with aluminum foil, and bake for 25 minutes. Remove foil and bake for another 10 minutes. You can also opt to broil the casserole for 5 minutes after it comes out of the Instant Pot® so the top will be browned.

1. Press Sauté on Instant Pot®. Once machine indicates Hot, add butter and let heat 30 seconds, then add onion and cook until just tender, about 2 minutes. Add garlic and cumin and cook until fragrant, about 30 seconds. Press Cancel.

2. Add chicken and salsa to pot and stir to combine with onion mixture. Close lid and set steam release to Sealing, then press Manual and adjust cook time to 10 minutes.

3. Once cooking is complete quick-release pressure. Press Cancel and open lid. Transfer chicken to a large bowl and shred with two forks. Add 1 cup of cooking juices and sour cream into chicken, then stir in 1½ cups shredded cheese and mix well.

4. Clean out pot, then place rack in pot and add water. Fold a long piece of aluminum foil in half. Lay foil over rack to form a sling.

5. Spray an 8" × 8" baking dish with nonstick cooking spray. Lay one tortilla into prepared dish, spread ⅕ chicken mixture on tortilla, and repeat, ending with last tortilla. Top with reserved cheese and cover dish with foil.

6. Place dish on rack, close lid and set steam release to Sealing, then press Manual and adjust cook time to 10 minutes.

7. Once cooking is complete allow pressure to release naturally, about 15 minutes. Open lid, carefully remove dish with sling, remove foil, and serve hot.

PER SERVING Calories: 437 | Fat: 26g | Protein: 29g | Sodium: 1,055mg | Fiber: 4g | Carbohydrates: 23g | Sugar: 5g

Chili Lime Chicken Legs

Sweet and tangy, salty and spicy, these Chili Lime Chicken Legs do a little dance on your taste buds.
This is an ideal recipe for outdoor socializing with close friends and a cooler full of ice-cold beer!

INGREDIENTS | SERVES 5

2 tablespoons freshly squeezed lime juice

1 teaspoon lime zest

1 teaspoon chili powder

1 teaspoon sriracha

2 teaspoons honey

4 cloves garlic, peeled and minced

1 teaspoon sea salt

3 pounds chicken legs (about 10 legs)

1 cup water

1. In a medium bowl combine lime juice, lime zest, chili powder, sriracha, honey, garlic, and salt. Toss chicken in marinade. Refrigerate covered at least 1 hour up to overnight.

2. Preheat oven to 550°F.

3. Add water to Instant Pot® and insert rack. Arrange chicken standing up, with meaty side down, on rack. Close lid and set steam release to Sealing, then press Poultry and cook for default time.

4. Once cooking is complete allow pressure to release naturally 5 minutes. Quick-release any remaining pressure and open lid. Check chicken using a meat thermometer to ensure the internal temperature is at least 165°F.

5. Place chicken on an ungreased baking sheet and cook in oven 3 minutes on each side to crisp. Transfer to a serving plate and serve warm.

PER SERVING Calories: 490 | Fat: 35g | Protein: 36g | Sodium: 668mg | Fiber: 0.5g | Carbohydrates: 4g | Sugar: 2.5g

Tuscan Chicken

A taste of Italy can be on your dinner table in less than a half hour. What's more thrilling is that there will be only one cooking pot to wash at the end of the evening. Prosciutto and capers add a unique salty, earthy flavor that tops off this healthy meal.

INGREDIENTS | SERVES 4

1 tablespoon avocado oil

1 medium yellow onion, peeled and roughly diced

½ cup sliced cremini mushrooms

1 (14.5-ounce) can diced tomatoes, including juice

¼ cup chopped fresh basil

¼ teaspoon salt

1 pound boneless, skinless chicken breasts, cut into 1" cubes

1 (4-ounce) package prosciutto, torn into pieces

1 tablespoon capers, drained

1. Press Sauté on Instant Pot®. Once machine indicates Hot, add oil and let heat 30 seconds, then add onion and mushrooms and stir-fry 4 minutes until onions are translucent.

2. Add tomatoes, basil, salt, and chicken to pot. Press Cancel. Close lid and set steam release to Sealing, then press Poultry and cook for the default time.

3. Once cooking is complete allow pressure to release naturally 5 minutes. Quick-release any remaining pressure and open lid. Check chicken using a meat thermometer to ensure the internal temperature is at least 165°F.

4. Evenly distribute chicken mixture and sauce among four serving bowls. Garnish with prosciutto and capers.

PER SERVING Calories: 313 | Fat: 17g | Protein: 32g | Sodium: 893mg | Fiber: 3g | Carbohydrates: 6g | Sugar: 4g

Salsa Verde Chicken Meatballs

Who knew chicken meatballs could be so mouthwatering? The diced onion helps keep the ground chicken moist and the salsa verde is the perfect flavorful mild sauce to accompany this dish.

INGREDIENTS | YIELDS 16 MEATBALLS

1 pound ground chicken

1 large egg

½ cup chopped fresh mint

¼ cup bread crumbs

2 tablespoons peeled and finely diced Vidalia onion

1 teaspoon sea salt

¼ teaspoon ground black pepper

2 tablespoons avocado oil, divided

½ cup water

1½ cups prepared salsa verde

1. In a medium bowl combine chicken, egg, mint, bread crumbs, onion, salt, and pepper. Form into sixteen 1½" meatballs. Set aside.

2. Press Sauté on Instant Pot®. Once machine indicates Hot, add 1 tablespoon oil and let heat 30 seconds, then place ½ meatballs around the edges of pot. Sear meatballs 4 minutes, making sure to sear each side. Remove and set aside. Add remaining oil and meatballs and repeat. Remove meatballs. Discard extra juice and oil from pot. Press Cancel.

3. Add water to pot and insert steamer basket. Place meatballs evenly in steamer basket. Close lid and set steam release to Sealing, then press Manual and adjust cook time to 3 minutes.

4. Once cooking is complete quick-release pressure, press Cancel, and open lid. Remove steamer basket and drain pot.

5. Pour salsa verde into pot. Press Sauté and let simmer 5 minutes, gently tossing meatballs. Transfer meatballs and sauce to a serving bowl and serve warm.

PER SERVING (1 meatball) Calories: 97 | Fat: 7g | Protein: 6g | Sodium: 376mg | Fiber: 1g | Carbohydrates: 3.5g | Sugar: 1g

Taco Chicken Lettuce Wraps with Pico Guacamole

Lettuce wraps are a fun way to change up the usual Taco Tuesday! Of course, you can still use tortillas if you like or pile these ingredients on tortilla chips with plenty of shredded cheese for nachos!

INGREDIENTS | SERVES 4

PICO GUACAMOLE

Juice of 1 small lime
1 medium avocado, peeled and diced
2 cloves garlic, peeled and minced
1 small jalapeño, seeded and diced
¼ cup peeled and diced yellow onion
1 teaspoon sea salt
2 tablespoons chopped fresh cilantro
2 Roma tomatoes, seeded and diced

CHICKEN

2 tablespoons taco seasoning
1 pound boneless, skinless chicken breasts, cut into 1" cubes
2 cups water
8 large iceberg lettuce leaves

Keeping Avocado Green

Avocado tends to turn an unpleasant shade when exposed to air. This is due to an enzyme present in the avocado flesh that changes color when it makes contact with air. The best way to prevent browning is to introduce some acid, such as lime or lemon juice, and reduce the amount of air the flesh comes into contact with using plastic wrap.

1. Place lime and avocado in a medium bowl. Use a fork to smash avocado until desired chunkiness. Add garlic, jalapeño, onion, salt, cilantro, and tomatoes. Cover and refrigerate until ready to serve.

2. In a large bowl add taco seasoning. Toss chicken in seasoning and coat evenly.

3. Add water to Instant Pot® and insert steamer basket. Transfer chicken to steamer basket. Close lid and set steam release to Sealing, then press Poultry and cook for the default time.

4. Once cooking is complete quick-release pressure and open lid. Check chicken using a meat thermometer to ensure the internal temperature is at least 165°F.

5. Transfer chicken to a cutting board and chop. Place in a serving bowl and serve with lettuce leaves and guacamole.

PER SERVING Calories: 250 | Fat: 10g | Protein: 27g | Sodium: 952mg | Fiber: 5g | Carbohydrates: 12g | Sugar: 3g

Cornish Game Hens and Vegetables

Cornish game hens can be a romantic meal for two or a fancy dish for guests. If serving guests, split the cooked hens in half and serve with some extra side dishes. When serving two, you each get a whole bird with tender mushrooms and carrots.

INGREDIENTS | SERVES 2

2 (1½-pound) Cornish game hens

1 teaspoon sea salt

1 teaspoon ground black pepper

1 teaspoon smoked paprika

2 cloves garlic, peeled and halved

1 small Granny Smith apple, cored and quartered

1 pound whole button mushrooms, stems trimmed

3 large carrots, peeled and sliced into ½" sections

1½ cups water

1. Dry Cornish game hens with a paper towel. In a small bowl combine salt, pepper, and paprika. Season Cornish game hens evenly with spice mix. Insert garlic and apple into hen cavities.

2. Place mushrooms, carrot, and water in Instant Pot®. Insert steamer basket. Place hens in steamer basket. Close lid and set steam release to Sealing, then press Meat and adjust cook time to 10 minutes.

3. Once cooking is complete allow pressure to release naturally 5 minutes. Quick-release any remaining pressure and open lid. Check hens using a meat thermometer to ensure the internal temperature is at least 165°F.

4. Set oven to Broil on high.

5. Transfer hens to an ungreased baking sheet. Remove and discard apples and garlic. Broil hens 5 minutes.

6. Transfer hens to a serving platter. Use a slotted spoon to remove mushrooms and carrots from pot and place them around hens. Serve warm.

PER SERVING Calories: 377 | Fat: 9g | Protein: 51g | Sodium: 1,295mg | Fiber: 8g | Carbohydrates: 24g | Sugar: 10g

CHAPTER 13

Fish and Seafood

Shrimp Scampi

This super quick shrimp scampi is rich and buttery. Pressure cooking infuses the buttery sauce into the shrimp, so they are extra decadent! Serve this over your favorite kind of cooked pasta or white rice.

INGREDIENTS | SERVES 4

6 tablespoons unsalted butter

3 cloves garlic, peeled and minced

½ teaspoon salt

½ teaspoon ground black pepper

½ cup white wine

½ cup chicken stock

2 pounds tail-on shrimp (21/25 count)

1 tablespoon freshly squeezed lemon juice

2 tablespoons chopped fresh Italian flat-leaf parsley

Scampi Defined

Have you ever wondered what *scampi* means? Apart from meaning simply "a large shrimp," *scampi* also means "a large shrimp cooked in a garlic butter sauce"— which perfectly defines this delicious dish!

1. Press Sauté on Instant Pot®. Once machine indicates Hot, add butter and let heat 30 seconds, then add garlic, salt, and pepper. Cook 45 seconds until garlic is very fragrant. Add white wine and stock and stir quickly to combine. Press Cancel.

2. Add shrimp to pot and toss to coat in garlic butter. Close lid and set steam release to Sealing, then press Manual and adjust cook time to 1 minute.

3. Once cooking is complete quick-release pressure. Press Cancel and open lid. Add lemon juice and parsley. Serve immediately.

PER SERVING Calories: 377 | Fat: 18g | Protein: 46g | Sodium: 572mg | Fiber: 0g | Carbohydrates: 2.5g | Sugar: 0.5g

Steamed Shrimp with Cocktail Sauce

This is one of the easiest and most-appreciated appetizers. It is a low-calorie alternative to those rich chip and dip temptations that are always present at a group get-together.

INGREDIENTS | SERVES 8

COCKTAIL SAUCE

½ cup ketchup
2 tablespoons prepared horseradish
1 teaspoon freshly squeezed lemon juice
¼ teaspoon Worcestershire sauce
¼ teaspoon sriracha sauce

STEAMED SHRIMP

1 cup water
2 pounds large tail-on shrimp, peeled and deveined

1. Combine cocktail sauce ingredients in a small bowl until well blended. Refrigerate covered until ready to use.

2. Add water to Instant Pot® and insert steamer basket. Place shrimp in the steamer basket. Close lid and set steam release to Sealing, then press Steam and adjust cook time to 0 minutes.

3. Once cooking is complete quick-release pressure and open lid. Serve shrimp, warm or cold, with cocktail sauce.

PER SERVING Calories: 112 | Fat: 1g | Protein: 22g | Sodium: 289mg | Fiber: 0g | Carbohydrates: 4.5g | Sugar: 3.5g

Ginger Tilapia

Simple, clean, and super healthy, this fish is perfect when you want a light meal that does not skimp even a little on flavor. Pair this with rice or steamed vegetables.

INGREDIENTS | SERVES 4

1 cup water
1 tablespoon soy sauce
1 teaspoon sesame oil
4 (4-ounce) tilapia fillets
½ teaspoon ground black pepper
2 tablespoons minced fresh ginger
1 clove garlic, peeled and minced

1. Add water to Instant Pot® and add rack. In a small bowl combine soy sauce and sesame oil. Brush over fish fillets, then season with pepper.

2. In a second small bowl combine ginger and garlic. Divide mixture among fish fillets and spread to coat. Place fillets on rack. Close lid and set steam release to Sealing, then press Steam and adjust cook time to 3 minutes.

3. Once cooking is complete quick-release pressure. Press Cancel and open lid. Serve immediately.

PER SERVING Calories: 94 | Fat: 3g | Protein: 14g | Sodium: 553mg | Fiber: 0g | Carbohydrates: 1g | Sugar: 0g

Shrimp and Grits

This classic Southern comfort dish usually takes multiple pots on the stove and excellent timing. With the Instant Pot® you'll use just one pot and one bowl, and you won't have to watch the timer!

INGREDIENTS | SERVES 6

4 tablespoons unsalted butter

½ medium yellow onion, peeled and chopped

½ medium green bell pepper, seeded and chopped

2 cloves garlic, peeled and minced

¼ cup white wine

¼ cup chicken broth

1 cup diced canned tomatoes, drained

1 tablespoon freshly squeezed lemon juice

½ teaspoon hot sauce

½ cup corn grits

1½ cups water

¼ cup heavy whipping cream, divided

½ teaspoon salt, divided

½ teaspoon ground black pepper, divided

1 pound tail-on jumbo shrimp (21/25 count)

Extra Toppings, Extra Flavor!

A shrimp and grits dinner is lovely alone, but you can also add cheese to the grits. Sharp Cheddar is a wonderful choice that adds some tanginess. To change up the shrimp, you can add chopped fried bacon, diced sausage, sautéed vegetables like zucchini or asparagus tips, roasted corn, or some butter mixed with a little Cajun seasoning.

1. Press Sauté on Instant Pot®. Once machine indicates Hot, add butter and let heat 30 seconds, then add onion and bell pepper. Cook until vegetables are softened, about 3 minutes. Add garlic and cook 10 seconds until fragrant. Press Cancel and add wine, chicken broth, tomatoes, lemon juice, and hot sauce, and stir well. Leave ingredients in pot.

2. Add rack to pot and place heatproof 6" to 7" glass bowl on rack. Add grits and water and stir well. Close lid and set steam release to Sealing, then press Manual and adjust cook time to 10 minutes.

   Once cooking is complete allow pressure to release naturally, about 15 minutes. Remove lid and carefully remove bowl and rack. Stir 2 tablespoons heavy cream, ¼ teaspoon salt, and ¼ teaspoon pepper into grits. Set aside.

3. Add shrimp to pot and stir well. Close lid and allow shrimp to cook on Keep Warm 10 minutes. Once cooking is complete remove lid and stir in remaining cream, salt, and pepper.

4. Divide grits among six plates. Top with shrimp and sauce. Serve immediately.

PER SERVING Calories: 239 | Fat: 12g | Protein: 17g | Sodium: 340mg | Fiber: 1.5g | Carbohydrates: 14g | Sugar: 2g

Sweet and Sour Shrimp

Cornstarch is the key to a perfectly glossy, thick sauce. Once the shrimp and vegetables are cooked, you will transfer them with a slotted spoon to your serving platter and then thicken the sauce. White rice is always a great side dish, but consider stir-fried Chinese egg noodles for a change of pace!

INGREDIENTS | SERVES 4

2 tablespoons vegetable oil

1 medium yellow onion, peeled and cut into ½" pieces

1 medium red bell pepper, cut into ½" pieces

2 cloves garlic, peeled and minced

1 tablespoon fresh minced ginger

½ teaspoon red chili flakes

½ cup ketchup

¼ cup light soy sauce

1 (10-ounce) can pineapple chunks in juice

1 pound tail-on extra-large shrimp (26/30 count)

¼ cup water

2 tablespoons cornstarch

¼ cup sliced green onion tops

Other Thickeners

Cornstarch and roux, a mixture of cooked fat and flour, are the most traditional ways to thicken a sauce, but there are other options available. Gums, such as xanthan gum or guar gum, are available in health food stores and in most natural food sections of the grocery store. Xanthan gum can be added directly to sauces, while guar gum needs to be mixed into a slurry first.

1. Press Sauté on Instant Pot®. Once machine indicates Hot, add oil and let heat 30 seconds, then add onion and bell pepper. Cook until vegetables are starting to become tender, about 3 minutes. Add garlic, ginger, and chili flakes and cook 30 seconds until fragrant. Press Cancel.

2. Add ketchup, soy sauce, and pineapple chunks with juice. Stir well. Add shrimp. Close lid and set steam release to Sealing, then press Manual and adjust cook time to 1 minute.

3. Once cooking is complete quick-release pressure and open lid. Use a slotted spoon to transfer shrimp and vegetables to a large bowl. Set aside.

4. Press Cancel, then press Sauté. Whisk together water and cornstarch in a small bowl. Whisk into pot and cook until sauce is thick, about 2 minutes. Press Cancel and return shrimp and vegetables to pot and stir. Serve immediately with green onion for garnish.

PER SERVING Calories: 286 | Fat: 8g | Protein: 25g | Sodium: 1,325mg | Fiber: 2.5g | Carbohydrates: 30g | Sugar: 20g

Instant Pot® Cioppino

Cioppino is the ultimate one-pot wonder! Originally from San Francisco, traditional cioppino was an American seafood stew with tomatoes and whatever seafood was available from the catch of that day. This recipe uses a delicious blend of mussels, shrimp, clams, and fish.

INGREDIENTS | SERVES 6

3 tablespoons olive oil

1 medium yellow onion, peeled and chopped

1 medium red bell pepper, seeded and chopped

2 cloves garlic, peeled and minced

1 (28-ounce) can diced tomatoes

1 cup tomato juice

1 cup dry red wine

2 cups seafood stock

1 tablespoon freshly squeezed lemon juice

1 bay leaf

¼ cup chopped fresh basil

½ teaspoon salt

½ teaspoon ground black pepper

1 pound mussels, scrubbed and beards removed

1 pound extra-large peeled, tail-off shrimp (26/30 count)

1 pound fresh clams, scrubbed

1 pound firm-fleshed fish, such as halibut, cut into 2" chunks

1. Press Sauté on Instant Pot®. Once machine indicates Hot, add oil and let heat 30 seconds, then add onion and bell pepper. Cook until vegetables are just tender, about 3 minutes. Add garlic and cook 30 seconds until fragrant. Add diced tomatoes, tomato juice, wine, stock, lemon juice, bay leaf, basil, salt, and pepper. Stir well. Press Cancel.

2. Close lid and set steam release to Sealing, then press Manual and adjust cook time to 5 minutes.

3. Once cooking is complete quick-release pressure. Press Cancel and open lid. Discard bay leaf and add mussels, shrimp, clams, and fish.

4. Press Sauté and cook until shrimp are pink and shellfish have opened, about 3 minutes. Serve hot.

PER SERVING Calories: 409 | Fat: 11g | Protein: 52g | Sodium: 1,275mg | Fiber: 3.5g | Carbohydrates: 16g | Sugar: 6g

Selecting Mussels and Clams

When shopping for fresh shellfish, look for shells that are tightly closed or that close immediately when you tap the shell. The shellfish should also smell like the sea. If you smell any sour or off odors, skip them. Shellfish should be in open mesh bags on beds of ice, not in buckets of water or they will die. Always cook your fresh shellfish within 24 hours of purchase, and discard any shellfish that don't open during cooking.

Chili Salmon with Mango Salsa

You can add a diced avocado to the mango salsa or serve this salmon dish with some fresh-made guacamole. The salmon is also perfect paired with the Quinoa with Corn and Black Beans in Chapter 14.

INGREDIENTS | SERVES 4

1 cup ¼" cubes peeled mango (about 1 large mango)

½ medium cucumber, peeled and diced

1 jalapeño, seeded and minced

¼ medium red onion, peeled and minced

2 tablespoons minced fresh cilantro

2 tablespoons freshly squeezed lime juice

1 teaspoon salt, divided

1 teaspoon ground black pepper, divided

1 cup water

4 (4-ounce) skin-on salmon fillets

2 teaspoons avocado oil

1 teaspoon chili powder

½ teaspoon ground cumin

1. In a medium bowl combine mango, cucumber, jalapeño, onion, cilantro, lime juice, ¼ teaspoon salt, and ¼ teaspoon pepper. Mix well, cover, and refrigerate at least 1 hour up to overnight.

2. Add water to Instant Pot® and add rack. Brush salmon with avocado oil, then season with remaining salt and pepper, chili powder, and cumin. Lay salmon on rack. Close lid and set steam release to Sealing, then press Steam and adjust cook time to 3 minutes.

3. Once cooking is complete quick-release pressure. Press Cancel and open lid. Serve salmon immediately, topped with mango salsa.

PER SERVING Calories: 219 | Fat: 9g | Protein: 23g | Sodium: 655mg | Fiber: 1.5g | Carbohydrates: 10g | Sugar: 7g

Simple Guacamole

Good guacamole starts with perfectly ripe avocado. Select avocados with shiny, blemish-free skin. When you press the avocado gently, it should be firm at the widest part without being hard, and the narrowest part should gently yield under pressure. For each avocado mashed, add 1 tablespoon peeled minced onion, 1 tablespoon minced fresh cilantro, and juice from ½ lime. Mix well and serve immediately.

White Fish Stew

Fish stew can be made with just about any bits of white fish you have available, and you can also add shrimp, mussels, or clams if you like. Serve this with thick slices of crusty bread for soaking up all the delicious broth!

INGREDIENTS | SERVES 4

4 tablespoons olive oil

1 medium yellow onion, peeled and finely chopped

2 cloves garlic, peeled and minced

½ teaspoon dried oregano leaves

½ teaspoon ground fennel

¼ teaspoon dried thyme leaves

1 (14-ounce) can diced tomatoes

1 cup seafood stock

½ cup white wine

1 pound white fish fillets, such as halibut or sea bass, cut into 2" pieces

¼ teaspoon salt

¼ teaspoon ground black pepper

½ teaspoon hot sauce

1. Press Sauté on Instant Pot®. Once machine indicates Hot, add oil and let heat 30 seconds, then add onion and cook until onion is soft, about 4 minutes. Add garlic, oregano, fennel, and thyme. Cook 30 seconds, then add tomatoes, seafood stock, and wine. Stir well, then close lid, press Cancel, set steam release to Sealing, press Manual, and adjust cook time to 3 minutes.

2. Once cooking is complete quick-release pressure and open lid. Press Cancel, then press Sauté and add fish. Cook until fish is opaque, about 5 minutes. Season with salt and pepper. Add hot sauce just before serving.

PER SERVING Calories: 274 | Fat: 15g | Protein: 22g | Sodium: 412mg | Fiber: 2.5g | Carbohydrates: 7g | Sugar: 4g

Coconut Curry Fish Stew

This soup is inspired by the flavors of Thailand, and you can play with the ingredients to match your taste. If you want, you can add shrimp or cubes of silken tofu to this stew.

INGREDIENTS | SERVES 4

4 tablespoons vegetable oil

1 medium yellow onion, peeled and finely chopped

2 cloves garlic, peeled and minced

1 tablespoon fresh minced ginger

2 teaspoons freshly squeezed lime juice

1 tablespoon Thai red curry paste

1 (14-ounce) can unsweetened full-fat coconut milk

1 cup seafood stock

2 teaspoons fish sauce

1 pound white fish fillets, such as halibut or sea bass, cut into 2" pieces

¼ cup chopped fresh cilantro

Curry Paste

Curry paste is a smooth, thick mixture of chilies, spices, and aromatic ingredients such as ginger, garlic, onion, cilantro, lemongrass, and citrus. There are different types of curry paste, and they are used for different kinds of dishes. You can find green, red, and yellow varieties in most well-stocked grocery stores, but you can also find a wide variety of curry pastes in Asian markets.

1. Press Sauté on Instant Pot®. Once machine indicates Hot, add oil and let heat 30 seconds, then add onion and cook until onion is soft, about 4 minutes. Add garlic, ginger, lime juice, and curry paste. Cook 1 minute, then add coconut milk, seafood stock, and fish sauce. Stir well, close lid, press Cancel, set steam release to Sealing, press Manual, and adjust cook time to 3 minutes.

2. Once cooking is complete quick-release pressure and open lid. Press Cancel, then press Sauté and add fish. Cook until fish is opaque, 5 minutes. Serve with cilantro for garnish.

PER SERVING Calories: 453 | Fat: 37g | Protein: 25g | Sodium: 225mg | Fiber: 1.5g | Carbohydrates: 8g | Sugar: 1.5g

Lobster Tails with Lemon Butter Sauce

Lobster with butter sauce is a luxurious dish that is perfect for special occasions or dinner parties where you want to really impress! Serve this with steamed asparagus or alongside a piece of grilled steak.

INGREDIENTS | SERVES 4

1 cup chicken stock

2 tablespoons seafood seasoning, such as Old Bay Seasoning

2 pounds fresh cold-water lobster tails

1 cup unsalted butter

½ teaspoon salt

½ teaspoon ground black pepper

1 clove garlic, peeled and minced

Juice of 1 lemon

Frozen Lobster Tails

If you want to cook frozen lobster tails, you do not need to bother with thawing before cooking. The Instant Pot® can easily cook them from frozen, and the meat will have a better texture. All you need to do is increase the cooking time by 1 minute, and also note that frozen lobster tails will take longer to come to full pressure than thawed.

1. Add stock and seafood seasoning to Instant Pot® and add rack. Place lobster tails shell-side down on rack. Close lid and set steam release to Sealing, then press Manual and adjust cook time to 3 minutes.

2. In a small saucepan add butter, salt, pepper, garlic, and lemon juice. Heat over low heat about 30 seconds until butter has melted, then increase heat to medium and cook until butter comes to a simmer, about 1 minute. Turn off heat. Cover to keep warm while lobster finishes cooking.

3. Once cooking is complete quick-release pressure. Press Cancel and open lid. Transfer lobster tails to a large platter. Carefully cut bottom of shell with kitchen shears and pull tail meat out in one piece. Slice into ½" thick pieces. Serve immediately with butter sauce.

PER SERVING Calories: 602 | Fat: 48g | Protein: 39g | Sodium: 1,263mg | Fiber: 0.5g | Carbohydrates: 4g | Sugar: 0.5g

Lobster Rolls

The classic lobster roll is a beach-day favorite! If you can find the traditional New England–style top-cut hot dog buns, you will have a much more authentic-looking roll.

INGREDIENTS | SERVES 6

1 cup chicken stock

2 tablespoons seafood seasoning, such as Old Bay Seasoning

3 pounds cold-water lobster tails

2 tablespoons unsalted butter, melted

6 split rolls

⅓ cup mayonnaise

1 rib celery, finely chopped

1 teaspoon freshly squeezed lemon juice

½ teaspoon ground black pepper

2 tablespoons chopped fresh chives

1. Add stock and seafood seasoning to Instant Pot® and add rack. Place lobster tails on rack shell-side down. Close lid and set steam release to Sealing, then press Manual and adjust cook time to 3 minutes.

2. Heat a medium skillet over medium heat. Add butter. Once hot, about 30 seconds, toast rolls until golden, about 2 minutes on each side. Set aside.

3. In a small bowl combine mayonnaise, celery, lemon juice, and pepper. Mix well and refrigerate covered until ready to use.

4. Once cooking is complete quick-release pressure. Press Cancel and open lid. Transfer lobster tails to a large platter. Carefully cut bottom of shell with kitchen shears and pull tail meat out in one piece. Slice into ¼" chunks.

5. Mix lobster meat with prepared mayonnaise dressing and coat well. Divide dressed lobster meat among toasted rolls and garnish with chives. Serve immediately.

PER SERVING Calories: 358 | Fat: 16g | Protein: 40g | Sodium: 1,113mg | Fiber: 0.5g | Carbohydrates: 10g | Sugar: 1g

Mussels with White Wine and Shallots

Mussels simmered in a wine-flavored broth will be sure to satisfy! Serve these with lots of crusty bread, plenty of salted butter, and spoons for slurping up the cooking liquid.

INGREDIENTS | SERVES 6

6 tablespoons unsalted butter, divided

2 shallots, peeled and minced

2 cloves garlic, peeled and minced

½ teaspoon salt

½ teaspoon ground black pepper

3 cups white wine

3 pounds cultivated mussels, scrubbed and beards removed

¼ cup chopped fresh chives

1 tablespoon chopped fresh tarragon

Getting Mussels Ready to Cook

Transfer mussels to a large bowl so they can breathe. Inspect them, and discard any open or broken mussels. Next, soak mussels in cold water for 20 minutes to reduce the salt they retain. Once soaked, remove the beard by using a dry hand towel to grab the beard and sharply tug it toward the hinge of the shell. Use a brush to scrub the outside of the shells to remove any dirt or sand.

1. Press Sauté on Instant Pot®. Once machine indicates Hot, add 2 tablespoons butter and let heat 30 seconds, then add shallots and cook 1 minute until tender. Add garlic, salt, and pepper and cook until garlic is fragrant, about 30 seconds. Press Cancel.

2. Add white wine and mussels to pot and stir to combine. Close lid and set steam release to Sealing, then press Manual and adjust cook time to 3 minutes.

3. Once cooking is complete quick-release pressure and open lid. Transfer mussels to a serving bowl.

4. Press Cancel, then press Sauté. Bring cooking liquid to a simmer, about 5 minutes, and whisk in remaining butter and herbs. Pour liquid over mussels and serve immediately.

PER SERVING Calories: 400 | Fat: 16g | Protein: 27g | Sodium: 843mg | Fiber: 0.5g | Carbohydrates: 13g | Sugar: 2g

Steamed Chili Crab

Part of the fun of eating whole crabs is the process of cracking, hammering, and pulling to get all of the tasty meat out. A little melted butter will also be nice for dipping!

INGREDIENTS | SERVES 2

2 tablespoons prepared garlic chili sauce

1 tablespoon hoisin sauce

1 tablespoon fresh minced ginger

1 teaspoon fish sauce

2 cloves garlic, peeled and minced

2 bird's eye chilies, minced

2 (2-pound) Dungeness crabs

1 cup water

1. In a medium bowl combine garlic chili sauce, hoisin sauce, ginger, fish sauce, garlic, and chilies. Mix well. Coat crabs in chili mixture.

2. Add water to Instant Pot® and insert steamer basket. Add crabs to basket. Close lid and set steam release to Sealing, then press Manual and adjust cook time to 3 minutes.

3. Once cooking is complete quick-release pressure. Press Cancel and open lid. Transfer crabs to serving platter. Serve hot.

PER SERVING Calories: 191 | Fat: 2g | Protein: 29g | Sodium: 911mg | Fiber: 2g | Carbohydrates: 11g | Sugar: 4g

Salmon with Lemon and Dill

You can add sliced vegetables to the cooking liquid so they poach while the fish steams. Good vegetables to include are asparagus, green beans, spinach, and thin strips of red bell peppers.

INGREDIENTS | SERVES 4

1 cup water

4 (4-ounce) skin-on salmon fillets

½ teaspoon salt

½ teaspoon ground black pepper

3 tablespoons chopped fresh dill

1 medium lemon, thinly sliced

2 tablespoons unsalted butter, at room temperature

1 tablespoon chopped fresh Italian flat-leaf parsley

1. Add water to Instant Pot® and add rack.

2. Season fish fillets with salt and pepper. Top each fillet with fresh dill and 2 slices lemon. Place fillets on rack. Close lid and set steam release to Sealing, then press Steam and adjust cook time to 3 minutes.

3. Once cooking is complete quick-release pressure. Press Cancel and open lid. Place salmon fillets on serving platter and add butter and parsley. Serve immediately.

PER SERVING Calories: 215 | Fat: 12g | Protein: 22g | Sodium: 341mg | Fiber: 0.5g | Carbohydrates: 1.5g | Sugar: 0.5g

Low-Country Seafood Boil

This recipe is a complete meal for a crowd in one pot! You can either serve it in the cooking liquid or drain it and spread it out on a table covered in butcher paper for a more casual and convivial meal.

INGREDIENTS | SERVES 6

1 pound small red potatoes

1 pound smoked sausage, cut into 2" pieces

2 ears corn, cut into thirds

2 tablespoons seafood seasoning, such as Old Bay Seasoning, divided

3 teaspoons Cajun seasoning, divided

2 cups water

1½ pounds large shrimp (31/35 count)

½ cup salted butter, melted

1 lemon, wedged

1. Add potatoes, sausage, corn, 1 tablespoon seafood seasoning, and 1 teaspoon Cajun seasoning to Instant Pot®. Mix well. Add water, close lid, and set steam release to Sealing, then press Manual and adjust cook time to 4 minutes.

2. Combine shrimp with remaining seafood seasoning and Cajun seasoning in a large bowl. Coat well.

3. Once cooking is complete quick-release pressure. Open lid and add shrimp. Close lid and let stand on Keep Warm 5 minutes until shrimp are curled into a "C" shape and are opaque.

4. To serve either pour everything into a large bowl and serve immediately or strain off cooking liquid and pour food directly onto a table covered with butcher paper. Serve with melted butter for dipping and lemon wedges.

PER SERVING Calories: 504 | Fat: 29g | Protein: 37g | Sodium: 750mg | Fiber: 2.5g | Carbohydrates: 23g | Sugar: 2.5g

Cajun Crawfish Boil

Keeping crawfish chilled is important. Make sure to cover your crawfish in ice and keep them moist and cool at all times. It is a good idea to use a cooler filled with ice for transporting the crawfish.

INGREDIENTS | SERVES 6

4 ears corn, halved

1 pound small red potatoes

1 cup water

3 tablespoons liquid Louisiana crawfish boil

4 pounds crawfish

1 tablespoon Cajun seasoning

6 tablespoons salted butter at room temperature

2 cloves garlic, peeled and minced

½ teaspoon seafood seasoning, such as Old Bay Seasoning

½ teaspoon hot sauce

1. Add corn, potatoes, water, and crawfish boil to Instant Pot®. Mix well. Close lid and set steam release to Sealing, then press Manual and adjust cook time to 5 minutes.

2. Combine crawfish with Cajun seasoning in a large bowl. Coat well. In a small bowl combine butter, garlic, seafood seasoning, and hot sauce and mix well.

3. Once cooking is complete quick-release pressure. Open lid and add crawfish. Close lid, press Cancel, and set steam release to Sealing, then press Manual and adjust cook time to 2 minutes. Once cooking is complete quick-release pressure.

4. To serve, drain liquid and pour everything into a large bowl. Toss with seasoned butter. Serve immediately.

PER SERVING Calories: 467 | Fat: 15g | Protein: 52g | Sodium: 483mg | Fiber: 3.5g | Carbohydrates: 31g | Sugar: 4g

Drunken Clams

Drunken clams are clams steamed with beer and wine flavored with onion and garlic. If you are avoiding alcohol, you can cook these clams in a mixture of chicken broth and water.

INGREDIENTS | SERVES 4

¼ cup unsalted butter

3 cloves garlic, peeled and minced

½ medium sweet onion, peeled and minced

2 cups ale or lager beer

1 cup water

½ cup white wine

3 pounds clams, scrubbed

¼ cup chopped fresh Italian flat-leaf parsley

1 lemon, wedged

White Wine Sauce

Want a little rich sauce for your clams or other seafood? Simply melt ½ stick of butter in a saucepan over medium heat. Once melted add 1 shallot and cook for 1 minute. Add 1 clove garlic minced and cook for 30 seconds. Whisk in 1 tablespoon chopped fresh herbs like chives or parsley, then whisk in ⅓ cup white wine and 1 tablespoon lemon juice.

1. Press Sauté on Instant Pot®. Once machine indicates Hot, add butter and let heat 30 seconds, then add garlic and onion and cook 1 minute. Add beer, water, and wine. Bring to a simmer about 5 minutes, then press Cancel.

2. Add clams to steamer basket. Place rack in pot, then add basket. Close lid and set steam release to Sealing, then press Manual and adjust cook time to 3 minutes.

3. Once cooking is complete quick-release pressure. Press Cancel and open lid. Transfer clams to a large bowl, discarding any that did not open during cooking along with cooking liquid. Garnish with parsley and lemon.

PER SERVING Calories: 467 | Fat: 14g | Protein: 50g | Sodium: 2,031mg | Fiber: 0.5g | Carbohydrates: 19g | Sugar: 1g

Rice, Pasta, and Grains

Basic Long-Grain Rice

This recipe works best for jasmine and basmati styles of rice. The end result is a firm yet tender rice, so feel free to adjust the cook time to your personal taste.

INGREDIENTS | SERVES 4

1 cup long-grain rice
1 cup water
¼ teaspoon salt

Reheating Rice

When you have leftover rice, it is easy to reheat it to fluffy perfection in your Instant Pot®. Place cold rice into a glass bowl that fits in your pot. Add 1 cup of water to pot, add rack to pot, and insert glass bowl. Close lid and set steam release to Sealing, then press Steam and adjust cook time to 5 minutes. Once cooking is complete quick-release pressure and remove lid.

1. Add all ingredients to Instant Pot®. Close lid and set steam release to Sealing, then press Manual and adjust cook time to 3 minutes.

2. Once cooking is complete allow pressure to release naturally, about 15 minutes. Quick-release any remaining pressure. Press Cancel, open lid, and transfer rice to serving dish. Serve hot.

PER SERVING Calories: 168 | Fat: 0.5g | Protein: 3g | Sodium: 149mg | Fiber: 0.5g | Carbohydrates: 36g | Sugar: 0g

Basic Short-Grain Rice

Short-grain rice is a bit starchier than its long-grain counterpart. It is used most commonly in Asian cooking, and it is the rice that is used for making sushi.

INGREDIENTS | SERVES 4

1 cup short-grain rice, rinsed well and drained
1 cup water
¼ teaspoon salt

Types of Rice

The main types of rice are long-, medium-, and short-grain. These distinctions measure the length of the grain compared to the width, so short-grain is slightly wider than it is long, while long-grain is up to three times longer than it is wide. The shorter the grain of rice the starchier it is, so long-grain is best for pilaf, while medium-grain is perfect for risotto and short-grain is good for sticky rice dishes.

1. Add all ingredients to Instant Pot®. Close lid and set steam release to Sealing, then press Manual and adjust cook time to 5 minutes.

2. Once cooking is complete allow pressure to release naturally, about 15 minutes. Quick-release any remaining pressure. Press Cancel and open lid and transfer rice to serving dish. Serve hot.

PER SERVING Calories: 179 | Fat: 0g | Protein: 3g | Sodium: 147mg | Fiber: 1.5g | Carbohydrates: 39g | Sugar: 0g

Spiced Quinoa Salad

Baby spinach is added to the warm quinoa to wilt slightly, but you can wait until the quinoa is cool and serve it over the crisp fresh leaves. It is entirely up to you!

INGREDIENTS | SERVES 6

2 tablespoons vegetable oil

1 medium white onion, peeled and chopped

2 cloves garlic, peeled and minced

½ teaspoon ground cumin

½ teaspoon ground coriander

½ teaspoon smoked paprika

½ teaspoon salt

¼ teaspoon ground black pepper

1½ cups quinoa, rinsed and drained

2 cups vegetable broth

1⅓ cups water

2 cups fresh baby spinach leaves

2 plum tomatoes, seeded and chopped

1. Press Sauté on Instant Pot®. Once machine indicates Hot, add oil and let heat 30 seconds, then add onion and cook until tender, about 3 minutes. Add garlic, cumin, coriander, paprika, salt, and pepper and cook 30 seconds until garlic and spices are fragrant.

2. Add quinoa to pot and toss to coat in spice mixture. Cook 2 minutes to lightly toast quinoa. Add broth and water, making sure to scrape bottom and sides of pot to loosen any brown bits. Press Cancel.

3. Close lid and set steam release to Sealing. Press Rice and adjust cook time to 12 minutes.

4. Once cooking is complete allow pressure to release naturally, about 20 minutes. Remove lid, add spinach and tomatoes, and fluff quinoa. Serve warm, at room temperature, or cold.

PER SERVING Calories: 218 | Fat: 7g | Protein: 7g | Sodium: 391mg | Fiber: 4g | Carbohydrates: 31g | Sugar: 2g

Fettuccini Alfredo

You have a head start to a silky Alfredo with the Instant Pot®! The small amount of water left after cooking is complete is loaded with starch, and that starch will keep your sauce smooth and help it coat each strand of pasta.

INGREDIENTS | SERVES 4

2 cups water

8 ounces fettuccini, broken in half

½ teaspoon salt

¼ teaspoon garlic powder

1 tablespoon unsalted butter

1 cup heavy cream

1 cup Parmesan cheese

½ teaspoon ground black pepper

1. Add water, fettuccini, salt, garlic powder, and butter to Instant Pot®. Seal lid, set steam release to Sealing, press Manual, and adjust cook time to 5 minutes at high pressure.

2. Once cooking is complete quick-release pressure. Remove lid and add cream. Stir until cream starts to thicken, about 3 minutes, then add cheese and pepper and mix until smooth. Serve immediately.

PER SERVING Calories: 551 | Fat: 33g | Protein: 18g | Sodium: 702mg | Fiber: 2g | Carbohydrates: 44g | Sugar: 3g

Quinoa Salad with Chicken, Chickpeas, and Spinach

*Chickpeas and chicken pack this salad with protein, so it will help fill you up
and give you plenty of energy to tackle the second half of your workday. Make
this salad on Sunday and use it for grab-and-go lunches all week!*

INGREDIENTS | SERVES 6

2 tablespoons vegetable oil

1 medium yellow onion, peeled and chopped

2 cloves garlic, peeled and minced

4 cups fresh baby spinach leaves

½ teaspoon salt

¼ teaspoon ground black pepper

1½ cups quinoa, rinsed and drained

2 cups vegetable broth

1⅓ cups water

2 tablespoons olive oil

1 tablespoon apple cider vinegar

1 (15-ounce) can chickpeas, drained and rinsed

2 cups Basic Pulled Chicken (see Chapter 12)

Chickpeas

Despite the name, chickpeas are actually legumes. You can find them sold either canned or dried. They are also ground into a flour (gram flour), and they are best known as the base for hummus. Rich in nutrients, chickpeas are an excellent source of fiber, protein, iron, and phosphorus for people on vegetarian and vegan diets.

1. Press Sauté on Instant Pot®. Once machine indicates Hot, add vegetable oil and let heat 30 seconds, then add onion and cook until tender, about 3 minutes. Add garlic, spinach, salt, and pepper and cook 3 minutes until spinach has wilted. Transfer spinach to a large bowl. Press Cancel.

2. Add quinoa, broth, and water to pot. Close lid and set steam release to Sealing. Press Rice and adjust cook time to 12 minutes.

3. While quinoa cooks, add olive oil, vinegar, chickpeas, and chicken to spinach mixture and toss to coat. Set aside.

4. Once cooking is complete allow pressure to release naturally, about 20 minutes.

5. Remove lid and fluff quinoa. Press Cancel and let quinoa cool 10 minutes, then transfer to bowl with chicken mixture. Mix well. Serve warm, at room temperature, or cold.

PER SERVING Calories: 361 | Fat: 14g | Protein: 18g | Sodium: 621mg | Fiber: 7g | Carbohydrates: 40g | Sugar: 1.5g

Basic Brown Rice

Brown rice has a lovely nutty flavor and can be used as a more nutritious alternative to white rice in most recipes. Brown rice is especially nice in cold rice salads that use a somewhat tangy dressing where the nuttiness of the rice shines through.

INGREDIENTS | SERVES 4

1 cup long-grain brown rice, rinsed well and drained

1 cup water

¼ teaspoon salt

1. Add all ingredients to Instant Pot®. Close lid and set steam release to Sealing, then press Manual and adjust cook time to 22 minutes.

2. Once cooking is complete allow pressure to release naturally, about 15 minutes. Quick-release any remaining pressure. Press Cancel and open lid and transfer rice to serving dish. Serve hot.

PER SERVING Calories: 171 | Fat: 1g | Protein: 4g | Sodium: 149mg | Fiber: 2g | Carbohydrates: 36g | Sugar: 0g

Spaghetti with Butter and Parmesan

This dish is an Instant Pot® version of the Italian classic cacio e pepe. The beauty of this dish is how simple it is. Grate some extra cheese to sprinkle over the pasta just before serving.

INGREDIENTS | SERVES 6

1 (16-ounce) package spaghetti pasta, broken in half

3½ cups water

2 tablespoons unsalted butter

½ teaspoon salt

1 cup Parmesan cheese

½ cup fresh grated Pecorino cheese

2 teaspoons ground black pepper

1. Place pasta, water, butter, and salt in Instant Pot®. Close lid and set steam release to Sealing, then press Manual and adjust cook time to 5 minutes.

2. Once cooking is complete quick-release pressure and open lid. Stir pasta. There should be a little starchy liquid in pot, but if it seems dry add 3 tablespoons water. Stir in Parmesan cheese and toss until melted. Top with Pecorino cheese and pepper and toss to mix. Serve immediately.

PER SERVING Calories: 395 | Fat: 10g | Protein: 17g | Sodium: 493mg | Fiber: 2.5g | Carbohydrates: 56g | Sugar: 2g

Cacio e Pepe

The name of this dish literally translates to "cheese and pepper," and for a simple dish it is actually quite complex. When made in a skillet there is a delicate balance between pan liquid and the grated cheese, blending them into a creamy sauce. The dish is often seen as a good test of an Italian chef's skill.

Quinoa with Corn and Black Beans

This recipe is good served warm, but it is also good cold or at room temperature, making it an all-star for potlucks, picnics, and whenever you need a tasty side dish or light main dish!

INGREDIENTS | SERVES 6

1½ cups quinoa, rinsed and drained

2 cups vegetable broth

1⅓ cups water

½ teaspoon smoked paprika

½ teaspoon salt

¼ cup chopped fresh cilantro

1 (15-ounce) can black beans, drained and rinsed

1 (15-ounce) can whole kernel corn, drained and rinsed

2 plum tomatoes, seeded and chopped

1. Place quinoa, broth, water, paprika, and salt in Instant Pot®. Mix well, then stir in cilantro. Close lid and set steam release to Sealing. Press Rice and adjust cook time to 12 minutes.

2. Once cooking is complete allow pressure to release naturally, about 20 minutes. Remove lid, add black beans, corn, and tomatoes and fluff quinoa. Serve warm, at room temperature, or cold.

PER SERVING Calories: 292 | Fat: 3.5g | Protein: 12g | Sodium: 592mg | Fiber: 8g | Carbohydrates: 55g | Sugar: 5g

Tomato, Garlic, and Parsley Quinoa Salad

The Mediterranean combination of tomato, garlic, and parsley goes well with just about any grain, so if you're not in a quinoa mood, try couscous or even rice instead. Just make sure you double back and give this quinoa recipe a try, as the texture here is hard to beat.

INGREDIENTS | SERVES 4

2 tablespoons olive oil

2 cloves garlic, peeled and minced

1 cup diced fresh tomatoes

¼ cup chopped fresh Italian flat-leaf parsley

1 tablespoon freshly squeezed lemon juice

1 cup quinoa

2 cups water

1 teaspoon salt

1. Press Sauté on Instant Pot®. Once machine indicates Hot, add olive oil and heat for 30 seconds. Add garlic and cook 30 seconds, then add tomatoes, parsley, and lemon juice. Cook an additional 1 minute. Transfer mixture to a small bowl. Press Cancel.

2. Press Multigrain on pot and add quinoa and water. Close lid, set steam release to Sealing, and adjust cook time to 20 minutes.

3. Once cooking is complete allow pressure to release naturally, about 20 minutes, then open lid. Fluff with a fork. Stir tomato mixture and salt into cooked quinoa. Serve immediately.

PER SERVING Calories: 228 | Fat: 9g | Protein: 6.5g | Sodium: 592mg | Fiber: 3.5g | Carbohydrates: 30g | Sugar: 1.5g

Creamy Risotto

This risotto comes out creamy, rich, and irresistible—without the standing, stirring, and babysitting that traditional risotto requires. Feel free to add things like sautéed mushrooms, fried pancetta, or peas.

INGREDIENTS | SERVES 4

3 tablespoons unsalted butter

3 tablespoons olive oil

1 medium yellow onion, peeled and chopped

1 clove garlic, peeled and minced

1 teaspoon fresh thyme leaves, chopped

1½ cups Arborio rice

½ cup white wine

4 cups chicken stock

½ teaspoon salt

½ teaspoon ground black pepper

½ cup Parmesan cheese

Arborio Rice

Arborio rice is an Italian variety of short-grain rice most commonly used for risotto, but it is also used in rice pudding. It is prized for its high starch content, which creates a creamy texture when cooked. The name *Arborio* comes from the Italian town of the same name that it was originally grown in.

1. Press Sauté on Instant Pot®. Once machine indicates Hot, add butter and olive oil and heat for 30 seconds. Add onion and cook until tender, about 4 minutes. Add garlic and thyme and cook 30 seconds, then add rice. Cook rice, stirring so each grain is coated in fat, 3 minutes.

2. Add wine to pot and cook, stirring constantly, until wine is almost completely evaporated, about 2 minutes. Add stock and bring to a simmer, stirring constantly, about 3 minutes. Press Cancel.

3. Close lid and set steam release to Sealing, then press Manual and adjust cook time to 6 minutes.

4. Once cooking is complete allow pressure to release naturally 15 minutes, then quick-release remaining pressure and open lid. Stir rice 1 minute, then season with salt and pepper and stir in Parmesan cheese. Serve immediately.

PER SERVING Calories: 564 | Fat: 24g | Protein: 15g | Sodium: 560mg | Fiber: 2.5g | Carbohydrates: 66g | Sugar: 2g

Spaghetti Pie

Spaghetti pie is a nice break from the standard spaghetti and meat sauce. Here, spaghetti is cooked in the Instant Pot®, then layered in a dish with crumbled meat and marinara sauce and cooked again to make a savory dinner pie!

INGREDIENTS | SERVES 6

8 ounces spaghetti pasta, broken in half

1½ cups water

1 tablespoon unsalted butter

½ teaspoon salt, divided

1 large egg, lightly beaten

½ cup whole-milk ricotta cheese

1 teaspoon Italian seasoning

½ teaspoon ground black pepper

8 ounces bulk Italian sausage

1 cup water

1 cup marinara sauce

¼ cup shredded mozzarella cheese

¼ cup Parmesan cheese

1. Place pasta, water, butter, and ¼ teaspoon salt in Instant Pot®. Close lid and set steam release to Sealing, then press Manual and adjust cook time to 5 minutes.

2. Once cooking is complete quick-release pressure and open lid. Stir pasta, drain off any extra liquid, and transfer to a large bowl. Add remaining salt, egg, ricotta cheese, Italian seasoning, and pepper. Mix well, then set aside. Press Cancel.

3. Press Sauté on pot and add sausage. Cook, crumbling into small chunks, until sausage is browned and cooked through, about 8 minutes. Press Cancel. Drain off any excess fat and transfer to a separate large bowl. Wipe out pot.

4. Place rack in pot and add water. Fold a long piece of aluminum foil in half. Lay foil over rack to form a sling.

5. Spray an 8" × 8" baking dish with nonstick cooking spray. Put spaghetti mixture into dish and press to form a firm layer. Top with sausage, marinara, and both cheeses. Cover dish with another piece of aluminum foil and place on rack.

6. Close lid and set steam release to Sealing, then press Manual and adjust cook time to 10 minutes.

7. Once cooking is complete allow pressure to release naturally 10 minutes, then quick-release any remaining pressure. Carefully remove dish from pot with sling, remove foil, and let cool 10 minutes before serving.

PER SERVING Calories: 346 | Fat: 15g | Protein: 17g | Sodium: 748mg | Fiber: 2g | Carbohydrates: 32g | Sugar: 3.5g

Chinese-Style Sticky Rice

This recipe calls for glutinous rice, a variety of rice that produces a lot of starch that makes it very sticky. It is available at most Asian markets, but if you are unable to find it you can use regular short-grain rice; it will just be less sticky.

INGREDIENTS | SERVES 4

1 (8-ounce) container fresh shiitake mushrooms, sliced

1 cup glutinous rice

2 links Chinese sausage, sliced

2 cups chicken broth

2 tablespoons oyster sauce

2 teaspoons soy sauce

1 teaspoon sesame oil

Chinese Sausage

Chinese sausage, otherwise known as *Lap Xuong*, is a dry pork sausage used in Chinese cooking. The sausage is marinated and then smoked, and it is most commonly available in the West with a slightly sweet flavor. You can grill, steam, or boil Chinese sausage whole depending on the recipe, or you can slice the sausages and add them to stir-fry, clay pot dishes, or noodles.

1. Add all ingredients to Instant Pot® and stir well. Close lid and set steam release to Sealing, then press Manual and adjust cook time to 10 minutes.

2. Once cooking is complete allow pressure to release naturally 10 minutes, then quick-release any remaining pressure. Open lid, stir rice, then close lid. Allow any additional moisture to be absorbed on Keep Warm, about 10 minutes. Serve warm.

PER SERVING Calories: 251 | Fat: 5g | Protein: 10g | Sodium: 523mg | Fiber: 2g | Carbohydrates: 42g | Sugar: 1g

Coconut Lime Rice

This rice is perfect with Asian dishes, or served with simple grilled chicken or seafood on top. Don't be tempted to substitute light coconut milk here, as it has a higher water content that will result in a watery texture to the cooked rice.

INGREDIENTS | SERVES 4

3 cups long-grain rice, rinsed well and drained

1 (15-ounce) can unsweetened full-fat coconut milk

1 cup water

1 tablespoon fresh lime zest

¼ teaspoon salt

1. Add all ingredients to Instant Pot®. Close lid and set steam release to Sealing, then press Manual and adjust cook time to 4 minutes.

2. Once cooking is complete allow pressure to release naturally 10 minutes, then quick-release any remaining pressure. Press Cancel and open lid and transfer rice to serving dish. Serve hot.

PER SERVING Calories: 708 | Fat: 25g | Protein: 12g | Sodium: 169mg | Fiber: 2g | Carbohydrates: 115g | Sugar: 0.5g

Toasted Couscous Salad

Pearl couscous is larger than traditional couscous and is made from semolina and wheat flour. The larger texture is perfect for salads, and toasting the couscous lightly before cooking adds an irresistible nutty flavor.

INGREDIENTS | SERVES 6

2 tablespoons unsalted butter

2 cups pearl couscous

1 medium red bell pepper, seeded and diced

1 medium yellow onion, peeled and chopped

1 clove garlic, peeled and minced

½ teaspoon salt

½ teaspoon ground black pepper

2½ cups chicken broth

1. Press Sauté on Instant Pot®. Once machine indicates Hot, add butter and let heat 30 seconds, then add couscous and cook until lightly golden brown, about 4 minutes. Add bell pepper, onion, and garlic and cook 1 minute. Add salt and pepper, then press Cancel and stir in broth.

2. Close lid and set steam release to Sealing, then press Manual and adjust cook time to 6 minutes.

3. Once cooking is complete quick-release pressure. Press Cancel and open lid. Fluff couscous and transfer to a serving bowl. Serve warm or at room temperature.

PER SERVING Calories: 299 | Fat: 5g | Protein: 9g | Sodium: 231mg | Fiber: 11g | Carbohydrates: 56g | Sugar: 2g

Mexican Rice

Mexican rice is the perfect side dish for fajitas and enchiladas or stuffed into burritos.

INGREDIENTS | SERVES 8

1 tablespoon unsalted butter

1 tablespoon vegetable oil

1 medium yellow onion, peeled and chopped

½ teaspoon ground cumin

½ teaspoon salt

1 clove garlic, peeled and minced

2 tablespoons tomato paste

2 cups long-grain rice

3½ cups chicken broth

1. Press Sauté on Instant Pot®. Once machine indicates Hot, add butter and oil. Once butter is melted, about 30 seconds, add onion. Cook, stirring often, 3 minutes.

2. Add cumin and salt to pot and cook until cumin is fragrant, about 30 seconds. Add remaining ingredients and stir well. Press Cancel. Close lid and set steam release to Sealing, then press Manual and adjust cook time to 4 minutes.

3. Once cooking is complete allow pressure to release naturally, about 10 minutes. Remove lid and fluff rice. If there is excess liquid in pot, you can let stand covered for 10 minutes on Keep Warm, then stir again. Serve hot.

PER SERVING Calories: 218 | Fat: 4g | Protein: 5.5g | Sodium: 212mg | Fiber: 1g | Carbohydrates: 39g | Sugar: 1g

Baked Macaroni and Four Cheeses

For the holidays and special occasions a super-rich and creamy baked macaroni and cheese is always a favorite. This recipe saves you time because you don't have to babysit the pasta or make a cream sauce, and you dirty only one pot and one dish.

INGREDIENTS | SERVES 8

4 cups water

1 pound elbow macaroni

1 teaspoon salt

1 teaspoon ground mustard

¼ teaspoon smoked paprika

3 tablespoons unsalted butter

1½ cups heavy cream

1 (8-ounce) package cream cheese

2 cups shredded sharp Cheddar cheese

1½ cups shredded Fontina cheese

1½ cups shredded smoked Gouda cheese

½ cup panko bread crumbs

2 tablespoons unsalted butter, melted

Topping Ideas

Up your mac and cheese topping game! Finely chop 3 strips crisp-cooked bacon and add to cup of panko bread crumbs moistened with 1 tablespoon melted butter. Or, grind 2 cups pork rinds until very fine and season with ¼ teaspoon smoked paprika. As a third option, dress up any bread crumb topping by substituting garlic herb butter and adding a few tablespoons grated Parmesan cheese!

1. Preheat oven to 350°F and spray a 9" x 13" casserole dish with nonstick cooking spray.

2. Add water, macaroni, salt, mustard, paprika, and butter to Instant Pot®. Seal lid, set steam release to Sealing, press Manual, and adjust cook time to 4 minutes at high pressure.

3. Once cooking is complete quick-release pressure. Remove lid, add cream, stir well, and then add cream cheese and stir until melted. Add shredded cheeses a handful at a time, mixing each addition until melted before adding the next.

4. Transfer macaroni mixture to prepared dish. In a small bowl combine bread crumbs with butter until evenly coated, then sprinkle over pasta. Bake 20 minutes until sauce is bubbling and bread crumbs are golden brown. Cool 5 minutes before serving.

PER SERVING Calories: 870 | Fat: 59g | Protein: 33g | Sodium: 1,100mg | Fiber: 2g | Carbohydrates: 50g | Sugar: 4g

Cheesy Couscous

This garlic and cheese couscous is similar in texture to risotto but tastes more like macaroni and cheese! Fontina makes the couscous very creamy, but if you can't find it you can substitute Monterey jack.

INGREDIENTS | SERVES 6

3 tablespoons unsalted butter

2 cups pearl couscous

2 cloves garlic, peeled and minced

½ teaspoon salt

½ teaspoon ground black pepper

2½ cups chicken broth

½ cup heavy cream

½ cup Parmesan cheese

½ cup fresh grated Fontina cheese

1. Press Sauté on Instant Pot®. Once machine indicates Hot, add butter. Once melted, about 30 seconds, add couscous and cook until lightly golden brown, about 4 minutes. Add garlic and cook 1 minute. Add salt and pepper, then press Cancel. Stir in broth.

2. Close lid and set steam release to Sealing, then press Manual and adjust cook time to 6 minutes.

3. Once cooking is complete quick-release pressure. Press Cancel and open lid. Fluff couscous and stir in heavy cream, then stir in cheeses. Transfer to a serving bowl and serve immediately.

PER SERVING Calories: 445 | Fat: 19g | Protein: 15g | Sodium: 495mg | Fiber: 10g | Carbohydrates: 54g | Sugar: 1g

Quick and Easy Mac and Cheese

Skip the box and pass on the frozen stuff: This macaroni and cheese is rich, creamy, and requires very little work aside from some gentle stirring. Feel free to play with the cheeses in this recipe, keeping in mind that smooth melting cheeses work best.

INGREDIENTS | SERVES 6

2 cups water

8 ounces elbow macaroni

½ teaspoon salt

½ teaspoon ground mustard

½ teaspoon hot sauce

1 tablespoon unsalted butter

1 (8-ounce) package cream cheese

½ cup heavy cream

3 cups shredded sharp Cheddar cheese

1. Add water, macaroni, salt, mustard, hot sauce, and butter to Instant Pot®. Seal lid, set steam release to Sealing, press Manual, and adjust cook time to 4 minutes at high pressure.

2. Once cooking is complete quick-release pressure. Remove lid and add cream cheese and cream. Stir until cream cheese is melted, then add Cheddar cheese and mix until smooth. Serve immediately.

PER SERVING Calories: 558 | Fat: 38g | Protein: 22g | Sodium: 704mg | Fiber: 1g | Carbohydrates: 30g | Sugar: 2g

CHAPTER 15

Vegetable Side Dishes

Red, White, and Blue Potato Salad

Most produce departments carry mixed bags of different colors of baby potatoes, but if yours does not, you can use full-sized red, white, and blue potatoes and cut them into smaller cubes, or you can just use red and white baby potatoes. It will still be colorful and delicious!

INGREDIENTS | SERVES 8

2 pounds red, white, and blue mixed baby potatoes, cut in half

4 cups water

1 teaspoon salt, divided

4 slices thick-cut bacon, chopped

1 medium yellow onion, peeled and chopped

1 clove garlic, peeled and minced

½ teaspoon ground black pepper

2 tablespoons apple cider vinegar

1 tablespoon extra-virgin olive oil

1. Add potatoes, water, and ½ teaspoon salt to Instant Pot®. Close lid and set steam release to Sealing, then press Steam and adjust cook time to 8 minutes.

2. Once cooking is complete quick-release pressure. Press Cancel and open lid. Strain potatoes and set aside.

3. Press Sauté on pot. Once machine indicates Hot, add bacon. Cook, stirring often, until bacon is crisp and fat has rendered, about 8 minutes. Remove bacon from pot with a slotted spoon and reserve. Drain off all but 3 tablespoons bacon fat from pot.

4. Add onion to pot and cook until translucent, about 4 minutes. Add garlic, pepper, and remaining salt and cook until fragrant, about 30 seconds. Add vinegar and olive oil and stir briskly to combine. Press Cancel and add potatoes and bacon to pot. Toss gently to coat potatoes in onion mixture. Serve warm.

PER SERVING Calories: 154 | Fat: 6g | Protein: 4g | Sodium: 412mg | Fiber: 2g | Carbohydrates: 21 | Sugar: 1g

Simple Mashed Potatoes

Is there anything better than a big bowl of mashed potatoes? These are simple but perfectly balanced. While this recipe calls for white pepper to preserve the pristine color, feel free to use black pepper if desired.

INGREDIENTS | SERVES 8

3 pounds russet potatoes, peeled and halved

4 cups water

1½ teaspoons salt, divided

½ teaspoon ground white pepper

⅓ cup unsalted butter, room temperature

½ cup half-and-half, warmed

1. Add potatoes, water, and ½ teaspoon salt to Instant Pot®. Close lid and set steam release to Sealing, then press Steam and adjust cook time to 12 minutes.

2. Once cooking is complete quick-release pressure. Press Cancel and open lid. Drain potatoes and return to pot.

3. Add remaining salt, pepper, and butter to pot, then use a potato masher to crush potatoes and incorporate butter. Once potatoes are mashed but still chunky, about eight strokes, add half-and-half and mash to desired consistency.

PER SERVING Calories: 220 | Fat: 9g | Protein: 4g | Sodium: 455mg | Fiber: 2g | Carbohydrates: 31g | Sugar: 1.5g

Creamy Roasted Garlic Mashed Potatoes

Roasting garlic gives this dish a mild, sweet flavor, so you can use more. If you are concerned it will be overpowering, you can start with 1 tablespoon and work your way up to an amount that pleases you.

INGREDIENTS | SERVES 8

3 pounds russet potatoes, peeled and halved

4 cups water

1½ teaspoons salt, divided

½ teaspoon ground white pepper

3 tablespoons mashed roasted garlic

¼ cup unsalted butter, room temperature

1 (8-ounce) package cream cheese, room temperature

⅓ cup half-and-half, warmed

1. Add potatoes, water, and ½ teaspoon salt to Instant Pot®. Close lid and set steam release to Sealing, then press Steam and adjust cook time to 12 minutes.

2. Once cooking is complete quick-release pressure. Press Cancel and open lid. Drain potatoes and return to pot.

3. Add remaining salt, pepper, roasted garlic, butter, and cream cheese to pot, then use a potato masher to crush potatoes and incorporate butter. Once potatoes are mashed but still chunky, about eight strokes, add half-and-half and mash to desired consistency.

PER SERVING Calories: 251 | Fat: 12g | Protein: 5g | Sodium: 506mg | Fiber: 2g | Carbohydrates: 32g | Sugar: 2g

Picnic Potato Salad

You can adjust the mayonnaise after chilling if you feel it is not as dressed as you would like. Wait until after the salad chills to add any additional mayonnaise, as it is hard to determine if there is enough mayonnaise when the salad is still warm.

INGREDIENTS | SERVES 8

2 pounds red, white, and blue baby potatoes, quartered

4 cups water

1 teaspoon salt, divided

½ cup mayonnaise

1 tablespoon yellow mustard

2 teaspoons apple cider vinegar

½ teaspoon ground black pepper

½ medium red onion, peeled and finely chopped

1 rib celery, finely chopped

3 large hard-boiled eggs, chopped

1. Add potatoes, water, and ½ teaspoon salt to Instant Pot®. Close lid and set steam release to Sealing, then press Steam and adjust cook time to 8 minutes.

2. Once cooking is complete quick-release pressure. Press Cancel and open lid. Strain potatoes and run under cool water to cool.

3. In a large bowl combine mayonnaise, mustard, and vinegar and whisk to combine. Add remaining salt and pepper and whisk. Add onion, celery, eggs, and potatoes and fold to combine. Cover with plastic wrap and refrigerate 4 hours or overnight. Serve cold.

PER SERVING Calories: 208 | Fat: 12g | Protein: 4.5g | Sodium: 442mg | Fiber: 3g | Carbohydrates: 19g | Sugar: 1.5g

Japanese-Style Potato Salad

*Potato is actually a very popular side dish in Japan and is often a lunch box
(or bento) staple. The Japanese version often includes cucumbers and carrots,
which may seem odd to some but is quite delicious and refreshing.*

INGREDIENTS | SERVES 8

3 large russet potatoes, peeled and cut into ¼" cubes

1 medium carrot, peeled and cut into ¼" cubes

4 cups water

1 teaspoon salt, divided

½ cup Japanese or regular mayonnaise

1 teaspoon granulated sugar

1 teaspoon rice vinegar

½ teaspoon ground black pepper

½ English cucumber, finely chopped

¼ red onion, peeled and finely chopped

2 large hard-boiled eggs, chopped

Yoshoku

In Japan, dishes from foreign countries are referred to as *Yoshoku*. This translates into "Western Food," and it includes things like potato salad, pasta, and hamburgers, all with a Japanese twist. For example, breaded and deep-fried potato patty cakes (*Korokke*) are considered French croquettes, and hamburger steak covered in a wine and ketchup gravy (*Hambagu*) is a Japanese take on American Salisbury steak.

1. Add potatoes, carrot, water, and ½ teaspoon salt to Instant Pot®. Close lid and set steam release to Sealing, then press Steam and adjust cook time to 8 minutes.

2. Once cooking is complete quick-release pressure. Press Cancel and open lid. Strain potatoes and carrots, then run under cool water to cool.

3. In a large bowl combine mayonnaise, sugar, and rice vinegar and whisk to combine. Add remaining salt and pepper and whisk. Add cucumber, onion, eggs, and potatoes with carrots and fold to combine. Cover with plastic wrap and refrigerate 4 hours or overnight. Serve cold.

PER SERVING Calories: 235 | Fat: 12g | Protein: 5g | Sodium: 403mg | Fiber: 2g | Carbohydrates: 27g | Sugar: 2g

Cinnamon Butter Sweet Potatoes

This simple side dish is perfect with steak, chicken, or a classic holiday meal. If you prefer, you can peel, cube, and then cook the sweet potatoes, then mash with the cinnamon butter mixture!

INGREDIENTS | SERVES 6

1 cup water
3 medium sweet potatoes
1 stick salted butter, room temperature
2 tablespoons packed light brown sugar
½ teaspoon ground cinnamon
½ teaspoon vanilla extract
¼ teaspoon ground allspice
⅛ teaspoon salt

1. Add water to Instant Pot®, then add steamer basket and top with sweet potatoes. Close lid and set steam release to Sealing, then press Manual and adjust cook time to 10 minutes.

2. While potatoes cook, mix remaining ingredients in a small bowl until smooth. Set aside.

3. Once cooking is complete allow pressure to release naturally, about 20 minutes. Press Cancel and open lid. Carefully remove sweet potatoes from pot. Slice each in half lengthwise, gently fluff flesh with a fork, and top with prepared butter. Serve immediately.

PER SERVING Calories: 204 | Fat: 15g | Protein: 1g | Sodium: 208mg | Fiber: 2g | Carbohydrates: 16g | Sugar: 5g

Mashed Honey Orange Sweet Potatoes

Orange and sweet potato are like peanut butter and jelly: They are made for each other! The orange flavor here is mildly tangy and complements the earthy sweetness of the potato. Grilled chicken and salmon are great served with this dish!

INGREDIENTS | SERVES 8

1 cup water

3 pounds sweet potatoes, peeled and halved

⅓ cup unsalted butter, room temperature

⅓ cup pulp-free orange juice

2 tablespoons honey

½ teaspoon salt

¼ teaspoon ground cinnamon

1. Add water to Instant Pot®, then add steamer basket and top with sweet potatoes. Close lid and set steam release to Sealing, then press Steam and adjust cook time to 9 minutes.

2. Once cooking is complete quick-release pressure. Press Cancel and open lid. Transfer potatoes to a large bowl.

3. Add remaining ingredients to bowl, then use a potato masher to crush potatoes and incorporate butter to desired consistency. Serve immediately.

PER SERVING Calories: 233 | Fat: 7g | Protein: 3g | Sodium: 239mg | Fiber: 5g | Carbohydrates: 39g | Sugar: 12g

Corn Pudding

This is not a soft, dessert-style pudding but rather a savory, steamed creamy corn cake that you can slice and serve. It is a wonderful side for holiday dinners, potluck parties, and a big game!

INGREDIENTS | SERVES 8

1 cup water

8 ounces sour cream

4 tablespoons unsalted butter, melted and cooled

2 (10-ounce) bags frozen corn kernels, thawed and drained

1 (15-ounce) can cream-style corn

2 large eggs

1 (8.5-ounce) box corn bread mix

1 cup shredded queso quesadilla cheese

Jazz It Up!

Corn pudding is wonderful as is, but it is also the perfect canvas for extra flavors! Add in ¼ to ½ cup of any of the following: sautéed onion and jalapeño, drained tomatoes with green chilies, chopped crisp bacon, chopped ham, shredded turkey, taco meat, shredded pork, chopped brisket, roasted vegetables, or drained beans like black beans or pinto beans.

1. Place rack in Instant Pot® and add water. Fold a long piece of aluminum foil in half. Lay foil over rack to form a sling.

2. In a large bowl combine sour cream, butter, thawed corn, cream corn, and eggs and mix until well combined. Add corn bread mix and mix until just moistened. Fold in shredded cheese until well mixed and no large lumps of dry ingredients remain.

3. Spray an 8" × 8" baking dish with nonstick cooking spray. Pour corn mixture into prepared dish and cover with another piece of aluminum foil. Place dish on rack, close lid, set steam release to Sealing, press Manual, and adjust cook time to 45 minutes.

4. Once cooking is complete allow pressure to release naturally, about 15 minutes. Remove lid. Let stand 15 minutes before carefully removing dish from pot with sling. Serve warm or at room temperature.

PER SERVING Calories: 348 | Fat: 21g | Protein: 10g | Sodium: 373mg | Fiber: 4g | Carbohydrates: 31g | Sugar: 6g

Corn on the Cob

Summer grilling almost demands buttery corn on the cob! This recipe makes quick work of the cooking so you can get right to the best part: eating!

INGREDIENTS | SERVES 4

1 cup water

4 large ears corn, husk and silks removed

4 tablespoons salted butter

1. Add water to Instant Pot®, add rack, and top with corn. Close lid and set steam release to Sealing, then press Manual and adjust cook time to 2 minutes.

2. Once cooking is complete quick-release pressure. Press Cancel and open lid. Carefully transfer corn to a serving platter and top with butter. Serve immediately.

PER SERVING Calories: 224 | Fat: 12g | Protein: 4g | Sodium: 97mg | Fiber: 3.5g | Carbohydrates: 29g | Sugar: 4.5g

Instant Pot® Elotes

This Mexican street-food classic is a tasty change from plain buttered corn on the cob. You may look askance at the addition of liquid margarine, but rest assured it is traditional and actually very, very good!

INGREDIENTS | SERVES 6

1 cup water

6 large ears corn, husk and silks removed

⅓ cup mayonnaise

¼ cup Mexican sour cream

2 tablespoons liquid margarine

½ cup crumbled cotija cheese or queso fresco

2 tablespoons finely chopped fresh cilantro

1 teaspoon chili powder

1 small lime, cut into wedges

1. Add water to Instant Pot®, add rack, and top with corn. Close lid and set steam release to Sealing, then press Manual and adjust cook time to 4 minutes.

2. While corn cooks, combine mayonnaise, sour cream, and margarine in a medium bowl and mix well. Set aside.

3. Once cooking is complete quick-release pressure. Press Cancel and open lid. Carefully transfer corn to a large platter. Insert wooden skewers into bottom of cobs. Brush each cob with mayonnaise mixture, then top with crumbled cheese, cilantro, and chili powder. Serve immediately with lime wedges for squeezing over corn.

PER SERVING Calories: 271 | Fat: 16g | Protein: 7g | Sodium: 164mg | Fiber: 3.5g | Carbohydrates: 30g | Sugar: 5g

Creamed Corn

This Creamed Corn has a slightly nontraditional addition of grated Parmesan cheese. This adds a savory edge that plays well with the sweet corn kernels. If using fresh corn, reduce the cooking time to 2 minutes.

INGREDIENTS | SERVES 6

1 (32-ounce) bag frozen corn kernels

1 cup whole milk

1 stick unsalted butter

1 (8-ounce) package cream cheese, room temperature

¼ cup Parmesan cheese

2 teaspoons salt

1 teaspoon ground black pepper

1. Place corn, milk, and butter in Instant Pot®. Close lid and set steam release to Sealing, then press Manual and adjust cook time to 3 minutes.

2. Once cooking is complete quick-release pressure and open lid. Stir in cream cheese until smooth, then add Parmesan cheese, salt, and pepper. Stir well, then serve hot.

PER SERVING Calories: 392 | Fat: 25g | Protein: 9g | Sodium: 937mg | Fiber: 4g | Carbohydrates: 38g | Sugar: 8g

Sweet and Spicy Glazed Carrots

If it makes your life easier, or if you simply prefer them, you can substitute baby carrots for the regular carrots called for. You will get the same delicious dish, but baby carrots are a time-saver—and cute to boot!

INGREDIENTS | SERVES 8

2 pounds large carrots, peeled, trimmed, and cut into ½" slices

½ cup water

3 tablespoons unsalted butter

¼ cup packed light brown sugar

½ teaspoon ground cinnamon

¼ teaspoon cayenne pepper

½ teaspoon salt

½ teaspoon ground black pepper

1. Add carrots and water to Instant Pot®. Close lid and set steam release to Sealing, then press Manual and adjust cook time to 2 minutes.

2. Once cooking is complete quick-release pressure and open lid. Drain water from pot and return to machine.

3. Add remaining ingredients to pot and stir until butter is melted, about 2 minutes. Let stand, uncovered, 10 minutes on Keep Warm, stirring occasionally, until carrots are glazed. Serve warm.

PER SERVING Calories: 102 | Fat: 4.5g | Protein: 1g | Sodium: 224mg | Fiber: 3g | Carbohydrates: 15g | Sugar: 9g

Asian-Style Asparagus with Garlic and Chili

Marinating the asparagus for 30 minutes helps infuse each bite with flavor, but you can skip this step if you are in a hurry.

INGREDIENTS | SERVES 4

1 pound fresh asparagus, ends trimmed

3 cloves garlic, peeled and minced

3 tablespoons garlic chili paste

2 tablespoons hoisin sauce

1 cup water

Storing Asparagus

So, you have a beautiful bunch of asparagus from the market and don't want it to go limp before you can cook it. What do you do? Well, you want to first trim the bottoms by about ½", then wrap the cut ends in damp paper towels and place in a storage bag. Refrigerate until ready to use, up to two days.

1. In a large resealable bag add all ingredients except water. Close bag, pushing out excess air, and massage to coat asparagus evenly. Let stand at room temperature 30 minutes.

2. Add water to Instant Pot® and add steamer basket. Add asparagus with marinade to basket. Close lid and set steam release to Sealing, then press Steam and adjust cook time to 2 minutes.

3. Once cooking is complete quick-release pressure. Press Cancel and open lid. Transfer asparagus to serving dish. Enjoy warm.

PER SERVING Calories: 44 | Fat: 0.5g | Protein: 3g | Sodium: 77mg | Fiber: 2.5g | Carbohydrates: 7g | Sugar: 4g

Buttery Parmesan Asparagus

This side is simple, elegant, and perfect for both special occasions and family dinners. If you are using very thin asparagus, reduce the cooking time to 1 minute so they do not overcook.

INGREDIENTS | SERVES 4

1 cup water

1 pound fresh asparagus, ends trimmed

4 tablespoons unsalted butter

1 clove garlic, peeled and minced

¼ cup Parmesan cheese

¼ teaspoon salt

½ teaspoon ground black pepper

Parmigiano-Reggiano

Also known as *Parmesan*, Parmigiano-Reggiano is a hard Italian cheese made in Emelia-Romagna. It is strictly regulated and can be produced only in select regions in order to receive the official classification as Parmigiano-Reggiano under Italian law. While in Italy you can find lesser grades of Parmesan, only the highest grades of cheese are exported for sale overseas.

1. Add water to Instant Pot® and add steamer basket. Add asparagus to basket. Close lid and set steam release to Sealing, then press Steam and adjust cook time to 2 minutes.

2. Once cooking is complete quick-release pressure. Press Cancel and open lid. Transfer asparagus to serving dish. Reserve.

3. Remove steamer basket, drain pot, and dry well. Press Sauté. Once machine indicates Hot, add butter. Once melted, about 30 seconds, add garlic and cook 30 seconds. Press Cancel, add asparagus, and toss to coat in garlic butter. Add cheese, then immediately transfer back to serving dish and season with salt and pepper. Enjoy warm.

PER SERVING Calories: 153 | Fat: 13g | Protein: 5g | Sodium: 245mg | Fiber: 3g | Carbohydrates: 5g | Sugar: 2g

Ginger Carrots

To give these carrots extra ginger flavor you can add a couple of slices of fresh gingerroot to the pot before cooking the carrots so they have ginger flavor from the inside out!

INGREDIENTS | SERVES 8

2 pounds large carrots, peeled, trimmed, and cut into ½" slices

½ cup water

¼ cup unsalted butter

1 tablespoon honey

2 teaspoons fresh grated ginger

½ teaspoon salt

½ teaspoon ground black pepper

1. Add carrots and water to Instant Pot®. Close lid and set steam release to Sealing, then press Manual and adjust cook time to 2 minutes.

2. Once cooking is complete quick-release pressure, press Cancel, and open lid. Strain carrots and set aside.

3. Press Sauté. Once machine indicates Hot, add butter to pot. Once melted, about 30 seconds, add remaining ingredients and cook until very fragrant, about 1 minute. Add carrots and toss until carrots are thoroughly coated in butter mixture. Serve warm.

PER SERVING Calories: 106 | Fat: 6g | Protein: 1g | Sodium: 224mg | Fiber: 3g | Carbohydrates: 13g | Sugar: 7g

Garlicky Green Beans

These green beans are simple, but that is what makes them special. The flavor of the green beans really shines through, accented by the garlic. Serve these with a couple pats of butter melted over the top!

INGREDIENTS | SERVES 4

1 cup water

½ teaspoon salt

¼ teaspoon ground black pepper

2 tablespoons unsalted butter

3 cloves garlic, peeled and minced

2 pounds fresh green beans, trimmed

1. Add water, salt, pepper, butter, and garlic to Instant Pot®. Stir well and add green beans. Close lid and set steam release to Sealing, then press Manual and adjust cook time to 1 minute.

2. Once cooking is complete quick-release pressure, Press Cancel and open lid. Transfer green beans with a slotted spoon to a serving bowl. Serve hot.

PER SERVING Calories: 124 | Fat: 6g | Protein: 4g | Sodium: 307mg | Fiber: 6g | Carbohydrates: 16g | Sugar: 7g

Southern-Style Green Beans

*These bacon-dressed green beans are a traditional accompaniment to
Southern staples such as chicken-fried steak and fried chicken. Of course, you
can also enjoy them with lighter fare such as rotisserie chicken.*

INGREDIENTS | SERVES 8

1 cup water

1 teaspoon salt

2 pounds fresh green beans, trimmed

½ pound bacon, chopped

2 tablespoons unsalted butter

1 medium white onion, peeled and chopped

1 clove garlic, peeled and minced

1 teaspoon packed light brown sugar

½ teaspoon ground mustard

¼ teaspoon smoked paprika

¼ teaspoon ground black pepper

1. Add water, salt, and steamer basket to Instant Pot®. Add green beans to basket. Close lid and set steam release to Sealing, then press Manual and adjust cook time to 1 minute.

2. Once cooking is complete quick-release pressure, Press Cancel and open lid. Transfer green beans to a medium bowl, remove steamer basket, and clean out pot.

3. Press Sauté. Once machine indicates Hot, add bacon to pot. Cook, stirring frequently, until fat has rendered and bacon is crisp, about 5 minutes. Transfer bacon with a slotted spoon to a paper towel lined–plate to drain. Pour off all but 2 tablespoons bacon drippings from pot.

4. Add butter to pot. Once melted, about 30 seconds, add onion and cook 3 minutes until tender, then add garlic, brown sugar, mustard, paprika, and pepper. Cook until sugar has melted and garlic is fragrant, about 30 seconds. Add green beans and bacon to pot and toss to coat. Serve hot.

PER SERVING Calories: 184 | Fat: 14g | Protein: 6g | Sodium: 488mg | Fiber: 3g | Carbohydrates: 10g | Sugar: 5g

Instant Pot® Kale

Tender, perfectly cooked kale in under 5 minutes? Yes, please! Cooked kale is great for weekly meal prep, stirring into soups, and adding to casseroles, eggs, and stir-fry dishes to boost flavor and nutrition!

INGREDIENTS | SERVES 4

2 pounds fresh kale, stems removed and chopped
3 tablespoons olive oil
½ cup vegetable broth
1 tablespoon red wine vinegar
½ teaspoon salt

1. Add kale, olive oil, and broth to Instant Pot®. Close lid and set steam release to Sealing, then press Manual and adjust cook time to 3 minutes.

2. Once cooking is complete quick-release pressure. Press Cancel and open lid. Add vinegar and salt. Serve hot or store covered in refrigerator up to five days.

PER SERVING Calories: 201 | Fat: 12g | Protein: 9g | Sodium: 445mg | Fiber: 8g | Carbohydrates: 19g | Sugar: 5g

Basic Spaghetti Squash

Cooked spaghetti squash keeps well in the refrigerator for about five days, so cooking it in advance makes a healthy dinner attainable any night of the week!

INGREDIENTS | SERVES 4

1 cup water
1 large spaghetti squash, halved lengthwise and seeds removed

Spaghetti Squash Ideas

Sure, you can top your spaghetti squash with marinara and have a yummy meal, but there is so much more you can do. Sauté it in olive oil and garlic, then top with pepper and Parmesan cheese, or use it in place of pasta for macaroni and cheese. You can also use cooked spaghetti squash in place of potatoes for things like hash browns, fritters, and potato cakes.

1. Add water to Instant Pot® and insert rack. Place spaghetti squash on rack. Close lid and set steam release to Sealing, then press Manual and adjust cook time to 7 minutes.

2. Once cooking is complete quick-release pressure. Press Cancel and open lid. Carefully remove squash from pot and let cool 10 minutes, then use a fork to shred flesh into a large bowl. Use in your favorite recipe, or refrigerate up to five days.

PER SERVING Calories: 39 | Fat: 0g | Protein: 1g | Sodium: 5mg | Fiber: 2g | Carbohydrates: 10g | Sugar: 3g

Brussels Sprouts with Bacon

Bacon adds a salty, smoky edge to these Brussels sprouts, but you can also use chopped sausage or ham or skip the meat altogether and enjoy them as they are.

INGREDIENTS | SERVES 8

1 cup water

1 teaspoon salt

1 pound fresh Brussels sprouts, trimmed and sliced in half lengthwise

½ pound bacon, chopped

1 medium yellow onion, peeled and chopped

1 clove garlic, peeled and minced

¼ teaspoon ground black pepper

1. Add water, salt, and steamer basket to Instant Pot®. Add Brussels sprouts to basket. Close lid and set steam release to Sealing, then press Manual and adjust cook time to 1 minute.

2. Once cooking is complete quick-release pressure, Press Cancel and open lid. Transfer Brussels sprouts to a medium bowl, remove steamer basket, and clean out pot.

3. Press Sauté. Once machine indicates Hot, add bacon to pot. Cook, stirring frequently, until fat has rendered and bacon is crisp, about 5 minutes. Add onion and cook until tender, about 3 minutes, then add garlic and pepper and cook 30 seconds until garlic is fragrant. Add Brussels sprouts back to pot and toss to coat. Serve hot.

PER SERVING Calories: 147 | Fat: 11g | Protein: 6g | Sodium: 490mg | Fiber: 2.5g | Carbohydrates: 7g | Sugar: 2g

CHAPTER 16

Breads

No-Knead Bread

One of the tricks that professional bakeries use to get flavorful, crusty bread is a proof box. This is a humidity- and temperature-controlled space where bread can rise at optimal temperature. Here, your Instant Pot® acts as a proof box, giving you bakery-quality bread at home!

INGREDIENTS | SERVES 8

3 cups all-purpose flour
1¾ teaspoons salt
1 teaspoon active dry yeast
1½ cups water

No-Knead Bread

Gluten, the proteins that give bread its structure, is usually formed by kneading the dough either by hand or with a mixer. With no-knead breads, the ingredients are gently mixed into a very wet dough that sits, allowing gluten to slowly form. This process is called *autolyze*, and it is what gives fancy artisan bread its open cell structure.

1. Line inside of Instant Pot® liner with parchment paper and spray well with nonstick cooking spray.

2. In a large bowl whisk together flour, salt, and yeast. Add water and mix until a shaggy ball forms. Transfer mixture to pot, close lid, press Yogurt, and adjust cook time to 4 hours and 30 minutes.

3. Preheat oven to 450°F.

4. Carefully remove parchment and dough from pot. Gently fold dough over itself, then gently form into a ball seam-side down. Put parchment and dough back in pot, press Cancel, close lid, press Yogurt, and adjust cook time to 30 minutes.

5. Once cooking is complete open lid, remove insert from Instant Pot®, and cover tightly with foil, making sure to crimp edges well.

6. Put pot into heated oven and bake 25 minutes, then carefully remove foil and bake 15 minutes more until bread is golden brown and sounds hollow when tapped. Remove bread from pot to a rack to cool for 30 minutes.

PER SERVING Calories: 172 | Fat: 0.5g | Protein: 5g | Sodium: 511mg | Fiber: 2g | Carbohydrates: 35g | Sugar: 0g

Multigrain Bread

Multigrain bread takes longer to rise than white bread because the grains take longer to hydrate and the yeast needs to work harder to rise the bread dough. The Instant Pot® gives the bread a boost by creating the perfect environment for rising!

INGREDIENTS | SERVES 8

2½ teaspoons active dry yeast

¼ cup honey, divided

½ cup water, heated to 110°F

1 cup whole milk

4 tablespoons unsalted butter, melted

1 large egg

½ teaspoon salt

2½ cups bread flour

1 cup whole-wheat pastry flour

½ cup rye flour

2 tablespoons hulled pumpkin seeds

2 tablespoons flax seeds

1. In a small bowl combine yeast, 1 tablespoon honey, and water. Let stand until yeast is foamy, about 10 minutes. Line inside of Instant Pot® liner with parchment paper and spray with nonstick cooking spray.

2. Add yeast mixture and remaining ingredients to a stand mixer fitted with a dough hook. Mix on low speed 3 minutes. Dough should feel tacky but should not stick to your fingers. Add additional bread flour or water, 1 tablespoon at a time, until dough reaches proper consistency.

3. Increase mixer speed to medium 8 minutes. Turn dough out onto a lightly floured work surface and form into a smooth ball. Transfer dough to Instant Pot®. Close, press Yogurt, and adjust cook time to 1 hour.

4. Place a pizza stone or heavy baking sheet in oven and preheat to 350°F.

5. Once cooking is complete turn dough out onto a lightly floured work surface and gently press to release any large gas pockets. Form a smooth ball, return to parchment, and place back in machine. Close lid, press Cancel, press Yogurt, and adjust cook time to 40 minutes.

6. Once cooking is complete transfer bread and parchment to pizza stone or baking sheet. With a sharp knife, cut an "X" into top of bread. Bake 30 minutes until bread is golden brown. Transfer to a wire rack to cool for 1 hour before slicing and serving.

PER SERVING Calories: 368 | Fat: 10g | Protein: 10g | Sodium: 171mg | Fiber: 3g | Carbohydrates: 59g | Sugar: 10g

Beer Cheese Bread

You can control the flavor of this bread by choosing a beer that best suits your taste. If you like light beer, go with a pilsner. Want something more robust? Go with a bock, ale, or IPA. This dense bread is perfect for dipping, so consider cutting it into cubes, toasting, and serving with your favorite beer cheese dip!

INGREDIENTS | SERVES 10

1 (12-ounce) bottle beer

3 tablespoons unsalted butter, melted

3 cups all-purpose flour

3 teaspoons baking powder

¾ teaspoon salt

¾ cup shredded sharp Cheddar cheese

⅓ cup sliced green onion tops

1 cup water

Hot Beer Cheese Dip

Whip up a quick beer cheese dip! Clean out pot, press Sauté, and add 2 tablespoons butter when machine indicates Hot. Melt 30 seconds, then whisk in 2 tablespoons flour. Cook 1 minute, then whisk in ¾ cup milk and 6 ounces of pale beer. When mixture thickens, press Cancel. Stir in ½ teaspoon ground mustard, ¼ teaspoon hot sauce, and 2 cups shredded Cheddar cheese.

1. In a large bowl combine beer and butter. Whisk well. Add remaining ingredients except water and stir to combine until dough is mostly uniform with only a few small lumps remaining.

2. Spray a 6-cup Bundt or tube pan with nonstick cooking spray. Transfer bread mixture to prepared pan. Cover loosely with aluminum foil to protect bread from condensation.

3. Add water to Instant Pot® and place rack in pot. Place pan on rack, close lid, set steam release to Sealing, press Manual, and adjust cooking time to 60 minutes.

4. Once cooking is complete allow pressure to release naturally, about 20 minutes. Press Cancel, open lid, and carefully remove foil. Transfer pan to cooling rack and let stand 20 minutes until sides of bread start to pull away from sides of pan. Turn bread out onto rack to cool completely, about 1 hour, before serving.

PER SERVING Calories: 224 | Fat: 7g | Protein: 6.5g | Sodium: 387mg | Fiber: 1g | Carbohydrates: 30g | Sugar: 0g

Banana Bread

Banana bread is universally loved and for good reason: It is tender, moist, and packed with delicious banana flavor. This recipe takes the typically moist bread to the next level! You can omit the pecans or substitute walnuts if you prefer.

INGREDIENTS | SERVES 8

1 cup water

1 stick unsalted butter, room temperature

½ cup granulated sugar

½ cup packed light brown sugar

2 large eggs, room temperature

1 cup mashed banana (about 3 medium bananas)

1 teaspoon vanilla extract

2 cups all-purpose flour

1¼ teaspoons baking soda

½ teaspoon salt

¼ teaspoon ground cinnamon

1 cup chopped raw pecans

1. Add water to Instant Pot® and place rack in pot.

2. In a stand mixer fitted with the paddle attachment or in a large bowl with a hand mixer, cream butter, sugar, and brown sugar on low speed 2 minutes, then increase speed to medium and beat 2 minutes. Add eggs one at a time, mixing 30 seconds after each addition. Add banana and vanilla and stir to mix.

3. In a separate large bowl combine flour, baking soda, salt, and cinnamon and whisk to mix. Add in butter mixture and fold until just combined, about twelve strokes. Add pecans and fold to evenly distribute, about five strokes.

4. Spray a 6-cup Bundt or tube pan with nonstick cooking spray. Transfer mixture to prepared pan. Cover loosely with aluminum foil and place on rack in pot. Close lid and set steam release to Sealing, then press Manual and adjust cook time to 60 minutes.

5. Once cooking is complete allow pressure to release naturally, about 15 minutes. Press Cancel and open lid. Carefully remove foil, then remove pan from pot. Cool bread completely in pan, about 1 hour, before turning out and serving.

PER SERVING Calories: 437 | Fat: 22g | Protein: 6g | Sodium: 364mg | Fiber: 3g | Carbohydrates: 53g | Sugar: 25g

Chocolate Chip Bread

This bread combines the best flavors from chocolate chip cookies into a tasty bread! Serve this for breakfast with steaming cups of coffee or as an after-school snack for hungry kids!

INGREDIENTS | SERVES 8

1 cup water

1 stick unsalted butter, room temperature

1 cup packed light brown sugar

2 large eggs, room temperature

1 teaspoon vanilla extract

2 cups all-purpose flour

1½ teaspoons baking soda

½ teaspoon salt

¾ cup buttermilk

1 cup semisweet chocolate chips

Simple Glaze

Dress up this bread by adding a glaze! Combine ½ cup confectioners' sugar, 1 tablespoon melted butter, ½ teaspoon vanilla, and 1 tablespoon milk. Whisk to combine, then drizzle over baked bread. If you want to make this glaze chocolate flavored, add 2 tablespoons Dutch-processed cocoa powder and an extra tablespoon of milk.

1. Add water to Instant Pot®, and place rack in pot.

2. In a stand mixer fitted with the paddle attachment or in a large bowl with a hand mixer, cream butter and brown sugar on low speed 2 minutes, then increase speed to medium and beat 2 minutes. Add eggs one at a time, mixing 30 seconds after each addition. Add vanilla and stir to mix.

3. In a separate large bowl combine flour, baking soda, and salt and whisk to mix. Mix flour mixture and buttermilk to butter mixture in three additions, starting and ending with flour. Add chocolate chips and fold to evenly distribute, about five strokes.

4. Spray a 6-cup Bundt or tube pan with nonstick cooking spray. Transfer bread mixture to prepared pan. Cover loosely with aluminum foil and place on rack in pot. Close lid and set steam release to Sealing, then press Manual and adjust cook time to 60 minutes.

5. Once cooking is complete allow pressure to release naturally, about 15 minutes. Press Cancel and open lid. Carefully remove foil, then remove pan from pot. Cool bread completely in pan, about 1 hour, before turning out and serving.

PER SERVING Calories: 421 | Fat: 20g | Protein: 6.5g | Sodium: 452mg | Fiber: 2g | Carbohydrates: 57g | Sugar: 31g

Cinnamon Raisin Bread

Is there anything more satisfying than a slice of freshly toasted cinnamon raisin bread in the morning? You can leave out the raisins if you are not fond of them, or you can trade the raisins for chocolate chips!

INGREDIENTS | SERVES 8

2½ teaspoons active dry yeast

¼ cup granulated sugar, divided

½ cup water, heated to 110°F

1 cup whole milk

4 tablespoons unsalted butter, melted

1 large egg

½ teaspoon salt

3 cups bread flour

1 teaspoon ground cinnamon

½ cup raisins

1. In a small bowl combine yeast, 1 tablespoon sugar, and water. Let stand until yeast is foamy, about 10 minutes. While yeast proofs, line inside of Instant Pot® with parchment paper and spray well with nonstick cooking spray.

2. Add yeast mixture and remaining ingredients to work bowl of a stand mixer fitted with a dough hook. Mix on low speed 3 minutes, then test hydration of dough by pressing with your fingers. It should feel tacky but should not stick to your fingers. Add additional flour or water, 1 tablespoon at a time, until dough reaches proper consistency.

3. Increase mixer speed to medium 8 minutes. Turn dough out onto a lightly floured work surface and form into a smooth ball. Transfer dough to Instant Pot®. Close lid, press Yogurt, and adjust cook time to 1 hour.

4. Preheat oven to 350°F and spray an 8" loaf pan with nonstick cooking spray.

5. Once cooking is complete turn dough out onto a lightly floured work surface and gently press to release any large gas pockets. Form dough into an oblong loaf shape the same dimensions as the pan. Place dough in pan, cover with plastic wrap, and let rise 30 minutes.

6. Bake 30 minutes until bread is golden brown on top and sounds hollow when gently tapped. Transfer bread from pan to a wire rack to cool for at least 30 minutes before slicing and serving.

PER SERVING Calories: 320 | Fat: 8g | Protein: 8g | Sodium: 171mg | Fiber: 2g | Carbohydrates: 53g | Sugar: 13g

Café Mocha Muffins

Either for desserts, breakfast-on-the-go, or just a snack, these delicious muffins are the perfect bite for any coffee and chocolate lover!

INGREDIENTS | SERVES 6

⅔ cup cassava flour

¼ cup unsweetened cocoa powder

2 teaspoons instant espresso powder

2 teaspoons baking powder

½ teaspoon baking soda

⅛ teaspoon sea salt

½ teaspoon vanilla extract

3 tablespoons ghee, melted

2 large eggs

2 tablespoons unsweetened almond milk

⅓ cup pure maple syrup

1 cup water

Additional Supplies for the Instant Pot® Baker

The Internet is your best friend when looking for pans, dishes, and other supplies so you can make the most out of baking (and cooking!) with your Instant Pot®. Online stores have lots of great options that are designed especially for the Instant Pot®. You can find a wide variety of silicone egg/cupcake liners, steamer baskets, baking pans, springform pans, and more.

1. In a large bowl combine flour, cocoa powder, espresso powder, baking powder, baking soda, and sea salt.

2. In a medium bowl combine vanilla, ghee, eggs, almond milk, and syrup.

3. Pour wet ingredients into dry ingredients. Gently combine ingredients. Do not overmix. Divide mixture into six lightly greased silicone cupcake liners.

4. Pour water into Instant Pot® and add rack. Place cupcake liners on top. Close lid and set steam release to Sealing, then press Manual and adjust cook time to 9 minutes.

5. Once cooking is complete quick-release pressure and open lid. Remove muffins from pot and set aside to cool 5 minutes before serving.

PER SERVING Calories: 198 | Fat: 8g | Protein: 3g | Sodium: 344mg | Fiber: 1.5g | Carbohydrates: 29g | Sugar: 11g

Sweet Corn Bread

Hearty, simple, and perfect for almost any occasion, corn bread is a classic for a reason! This version is impossibly moist and light. If you prefer your corn bread even sweeter, add an extra tablespoon or two of sugar.

INGREDIENTS | SERVES 8

1 cup water
⅔ cup all-purpose flour
⅔ cup yellow cornmeal
2 tablespoons granulated sugar
1 teaspoon baking powder
¼ teaspoon baking soda
¼ teaspoon salt
1 large egg
1 cup buttermilk
4 tablespoons unsalted butter, melted and cooled

1. Add water to Instant Pot® and place rack in pot.

2. In a large bowl combine flour, cornmeal, sugar, baking powder, baking soda, and salt. Whisk to combine.

3. In a separate medium bowl combine egg, buttermilk, and butter. Pour wet ingredients into dry ingredients and fold to mix, about twelve strokes.

4. Spray a 6-cup Bundt or tube pan with nonstick cooking spray. Transfer bread mixture to prepared pan. Cover loosely with aluminum foil and place on rack in pot. Close lid and set steam release to Sealing, then press Manual and adjust cook time to 20 minutes.

5. Once cooking is complete allow pressure to release naturally, about 15 minutes. Press Cancel and open lid. Carefully remove foil, then remove pan from pot. Cool bread completely in pan, about 1 hour, before turning out and serving.

PER SERVING Calories: 170 | Fat: 7g | Protein: 4g | Sodium: 241mg | Fiber: 1g | Carbohydrates: 23g | Sugar: 5g

Cheesy Jalapeño Corn Bread

Jalapeño corn bread served with a steaming bowl of chili is perhaps the epitome of comfort food in the South. The jalapeño adds a subtle kick, but it is not overpoweringly spicy. If you like it spicy you can add ¼–½ teaspoon of cayenne pepper.

INGREDIENTS | SERVES 8

1 teaspoon vegetable oil

1 jalapeño, seeded and minced

¼ teaspoon ground cumin

⅛ teaspoon garlic powder

1 cup water

⅔ cup all-purpose flour

⅔ cup yellow cornmeal

1 teaspoon granulated sugar

1 teaspoon baking powder

½ teaspoon smoked paprika

¼ teaspoon baking soda

¼ teaspoon salt

1 large egg

1 cup buttermilk

4 tablespoons unsalted butter, melted and cooled

½ cup shredded sharp Cheddar cheese

Corn Bread

Cornmeal is made by grinding raw dry corn grains. It can be finely milled or coarsely milled, but even when finely milled it is still significantly coarser than flour, so corn bread is usually made with a mix of cornmeal and all-purpose flour.

1. Press Sauté on Instant Pot®. Once machine indicates Hot, add oil and let heat 30 seconds, then add jalapeño and cook 1 minute, then add cumin and garlic powder and cook 30 seconds. Transfer to a medium bowl and set aside. Press Cancel. Clean out pot and return to machine.

2. Add water to pot and place rack in pot.

3. In a large bowl combine flour, cornmeal, sugar, baking powder, paprika, baking soda, and salt. Whisk to combine.

4. In medium bowl with jalapeño mixture add egg, buttermilk, and butter. Combine. Pour wet ingredients into dry ingredients and fold to mix, about ten strokes, then add cheese and fold to mix, about five strokes.

5. Spray a 6-cup Bundt or tube pan with nonstick cooking spray. Transfer bread mixture to prepared pan. Cover loosely with aluminum foil and place on rack in pot. Close lid and set steam release to Sealing, then press Manual and adjust cook time to 20 minutes.

6. Once cooking is complete allow pressure to release naturally, about 15 minutes. Press Cancel and open lid. Carefully remove foil, then remove pan from pot. Cool bread completely in pan, about 1 hour, before turning out and serving.

PER SERVING Calories: 200 | Fat: 10g | Protein: 6g | Sodium: 296mg | Fiber: 1g | Carbohydrates: 20g | Sugar: 2g

Bread Baked in a Can

Bread baked in an Instant Pot® is not crunchy or crusty due to the steamy environment it cooks in. If you want some crunch or crustiness, you can take slices of your bread and toast them in a skillet or put them in a panini press.

INGREDIENTS | SERVES 8

1 cup water
2 cups all-purpose flour
1 teaspoon granulated sugar
½ teaspoon baking soda
½ teaspoon salt
1¼ cups buttermilk
1 teaspoon vegetable oil

1. Add water to Instant Pot® and add steamer basket.

2. In a large bowl combine flour, sugar, baking soda, and salt. Whisk to combine. Stir in buttermilk until a shaggy ball forms. With your hands, gently knead dough in bowl until smooth and flour is incorporated. Form into an oval.

3. Grease the inside of a 4-cup heatproof can or container with vegetable oil. Transfer dough to prepared container.

4. Spray a piece of aluminum foil with nonstick cooking spray and loosely cover opening of container, leaving room for expansion. Cover side of can with a second layer of foil, making sure it wraps around edges of foil on top of can. Place can on rack, close lid, set steam release to Sealing, press Manual, and adjust cook time to 23 minutes.

5. Once cooking is complete allow pressure to release naturally, about 15 minutes. Press Cancel and open lid. Carefully remove can and remove foil. Test bread for doneness by inserting a wood skewer into center. If it comes out clean, bread is ready. If bread leaves a sticky residue, return to rack, close lid, set steam release to Sealing, press Manual, and adjust cook time to 5 minutes, then quick-release steam, open lid, and test again. Slide bread out of container and cool completely on a wire rack, about 1 hour, before serving.

PER SERVING Calories: 136 | Fat: 1g | Protein: 4.5g | Sodium: 297mg | Fiber: 1g | Carbohydrates: 26g | Sugar: 2.5g

Irish Soda Bread

This recipe calls for whole-wheat flour, which can be tricky to find outside of gourmet shops. If you are unable to find it, use 2 cups all-purpose flour, mixed with 1¼ cups whole-wheat pastry flour and ¼ cup wheat germ in its place.

INGREDIENTS | SERVES 8

1 cup water
2 cups all-purpose flour
1½ cups whole-wheat flour
1 tablespoon wheat germ
1 teaspoon baking soda
½ teaspoon cream of tartar
½ teaspoon salt
1 large egg
⅓ cup unsalted butter, melted and cooled
1½ cups buttermilk
2 tablespoons honey
1 tablespoon rolled oats

Quick Bread

Irish soda bread, corn bread, and other kinds of breads leavened with things like baking soda and baking powder are called *quick breads*. They are quick because they do not require a long proof or rise like yeast-raised breads. Most quick breads need some sort of acid, like buttermilk, cream of tartar, or vinegar, to help activate the leavening agent.

1. Add water to Instant Pot® and add rack. Fold a long piece of aluminum foil in half. Lay foil over rack to form a sling.

2. In a large bowl combine both flours, wheat germ, baking soda, cream of tartar, and salt. Whisk to combine.

3. In a separate medium bowl combine egg and butter, then whisk in buttermilk and honey.

4. Pour wet ingredients into dry and mix until dry ingredients are moistened. Turn mixture out onto a board lightly dusted with flour and knead until dough forms a smooth ball.

5. Spray an 8" × 8" baking dish with nonstick cooking spray. Transfer bread to prepared dish, lightly brush with water, and sprinkle oats on top. Spray a piece of aluminum foil with nonstick cooking spray and loosely cover opening of dish, leaving room for expansion.

6. Place dish on rack in pot, close lid, set steam release to Sealing, press Manual, and adjust cook time to 40 minutes.

7. Once cooking is complete allow pressure to release naturally, about 25 minutes. Press Cancel and open lid. Carefully remove dish from pot with sling and remove foil. Cool bread in pan 30 minutes, then turn out onto a wire rack to cool completely, about 1 hour.

PER SERVING Calories: 307 | Fat: 9g | Protein: 8g | Sodium: 401mg | Fiber: 3.5g | Carbohydrates: 47g | Sugar: 6g

Brown Bread

This raisin-studded bread is great for breakfast, served with coffee, or spread with butter for snacking. It is traditionally steamed for hours on the stove. With the Instant Pot® that time is cut to a fraction!

INGREDIENTS | SERVES 8

1 cup water
1 cup all-purpose flour
½ cup rye flour
½ teaspoon baking powder
½ teaspoon baking soda
½ teaspoon salt
¼ teaspoon ground allspice
1 cup buttermilk
½ cup molasses
½ teaspoon vanilla extract
⅓ cup raisins
1 teaspoon vegetable oil

1. Add water to Instant Pot® and add steamer basket.

2. In a large bowl combine both flours, baking powder, baking soda, salt, and allspice. Whisk to combine.

3. In a separate medium bowl whisk together buttermilk, molasses, and vanilla. Pour wet ingredients into dry and mix until a shaggy dough forms. Add raisins and mix until well combined.

4. Grease the inside of a 4-cup heatproof can or container with vegetable oil. Pour dough into prepared container.

5. Spray a piece of aluminum foil with nonstick cooking spray and loosely cover opening of container, leaving room for expansion. Cover side of can with a second layer of foil, making sure it wraps around edges of foil on top of can. Place can on rack, close lid, set steam release to Sealing, press Manual, and adjust cook time to 30 minutes.

6. Once cooking is complete allow pressure to release naturally, about 15 minutes. Press Cancel and open lid. Carefully remove can and remove foil. Test bread for doneness by inserting a wood skewer into center. If it comes out clean, bread is ready. If the bread leaves a residue, return can to rack, close lid, set steam release to Sealing, press Manual, and adjust cook time to 5 minutes, then quick-release steam, remove lid, and test again. Slide bread out of container and cool completely on a wire rack.

PER SERVING Calories: 176 | Fat: 1g | Protein: 3.5g | Sodium: 321mg | Fiber: 1.5g | Carbohydrates: 38g | Sugar: 20g

Pull-Apart Garlic Bread

This savory bread is perfect for a big game, party, or dinner with the family. Kids can get involved by dunking the biscuit pieces into garlic butter, then rolling in the grated Parmesan cheese.

INGREDIENTS | SERVES 8

1 cup water
½ cup unsalted butter
2 cloves garlic, peeled and minced
1 cup grated Parmesan cheese
2 (16.3-ounce) cans large biscuits, quartered

Pizza Pull-Apart Bread

To make this a pizza-flavored pull-apart bread, stir ½ teaspoon of your favorite pizza seasoning into the garlic butter. Mix ¼ cup finely chopped pepperoni into the grated cheese, and as you layer in the coated biscuit pieces, sprinkle in ⅓ cup shredded mozzarella cheese so it is evenly layered throughout.

1. Add water to Instant Pot® and place rack in pot.

2. In a small saucepan combine butter and garlic. Cook over medium heat until butter has melted and garlic is fragrant, about 5 minutes. Remove from heat and cool.

3. Place grated Parmesan into a shallow bowl. Dip biscuit cubes in garlic butter, then roll in cheese. Place into a 6-cup Bundt or tube pan greased with nonstick cooking spray. Pour any remaining butter over biscuits and top with any remaining cheese.

4. Spray a piece of aluminum foil with nonstick cooking spray and loosely cover pan. Place pan on rack in pot. Close lid and set steam release to Sealing, then press Manual and adjust cook time to 20 minutes.

5. Once cooking is complete allow pressure to release naturally, about 15 minutes. Press Cancel, open lid, and carefully remove pan from pot. Remove foil cover and cool biscuits in pan 15 minutes before turning out and serving. Enjoy warm.

PER SERVING Calories: 502 | Fat: 22g | Protein: 15g | Sodium: 750mg | Fiber: 2g | Carbohydrates: 60g | Sugar: 6g

Cinnamon Pecan Pull-Apart Bread

This pull-apart bread makes a wonderful addition to a breakfast or brunch buffet or a tasty snack after school for hungry kiddos! Also consider it as a tasty host or hostess gift. Give a pan of it along with a printed copy of this recipe!

INGREDIENTS | SERVES 8

1 cup water

⅓ cup granulated sugar

1 teaspoon ground cinnamon

½ cup finely chopped raw pecans

½ cup unsalted butter, melted

2 (16.3-ounce) cans large biscuits, quartered

Canned Biscuits

Canned biscuits may get a bad rap from food purists, but when they were first invented in 1931 they were considered a major time-saving revolution. These pressurized tubes of dough could be refrigerated and sold, and all homemakers needed to do was pop open the can, bake, and serve. Today, canned biscuits are used for many different recipes, from pigs in a blanket to doughnuts.

1. Add water to Instant Pot® and place rack in pot. Spray a 6-cup Bundt or tube pan with nonstick cooking spray and set aside.

2. In a small bowl combine sugar and cinnamon and mix well. In two additional small bowls add pecans and butter.

3. Dip biscuit cubes in butter, then roll in pecans, followed by cinnamon sugar. Place into prepared pan. Repeat with remaining bread. Pour any remaining butter over biscuits and top with any remaining cinnamon sugar and pecans.

4. Spray a piece of aluminum foil with nonstick cooking spray and loosely cover pan. Place pan on rack in pot. Close lid and set steam release to Sealing, then press Manual and adjust cook time to 20 minutes.

5. Once cooking is complete allow pressure to release naturally, about 15 minutes. Press Cancel, open lid, and carefully remove pan from pot. Remove foil cover and cool in pan 15 minutes before turning out and serving. Enjoy warm.

PER SERVING Calories: 529 | Fat: 23g | Protein: 12g | Sodium: 524mg | Fiber: 3g | Carbohydrates: 67g | Sugar: 14g

Instant Pot® Brazilian Pão de Queijo

Pão de Queijo is a chewy Brazilian bread made from cassava or tapioca flour. If you have ever been to a Brazilian steak house, it is likely you have enjoyed these little rolls along with the other side dishes.

INGREDIENTS | SERVES 12

1 cup whole milk

½ cup vegetable oil

1¼ teaspoons salt

2 cups tapioca flour

2 large eggs

1 cup grated Parmesan cheese

½ cup queso fresco

1 cup water

Tapioca

Tapioca is a starch that is made from cassava root native to South America. Also known as *yucca*, it is boiled, fried, and mashed in ways similar to potatoes. To make tapioca, the root is peeled, washed, and ground into a pulp to release the starch, then dried. In North America it is most commonly sold as little pearls, which are used for pudding and to thicken pies.

1. Press Sauté on Instant Pot® and add milk, oil, and salt. Once it comes to a boil, about 5 minutes, add tapioca flour and rapidly stir with a wooden spoon. Press Cancel. Transfer mixture to a large mixing bowl to cool 5 minutes. Clean out pot.

2. Once dough has cooled, add eggs one at a time and beat with a hand mixer until well mixed and dough is smooth. Add cheeses and stir well.

3. Spray an 8" × 8" baking dish with nonstick cooking spray. Divide dough into twelve balls and place in dish. Cover dish tightly with aluminum foil.

4. Add water to pot and add rack. Fold a long piece of aluminum foil in half. Lay foil over rack to form a sling. Place dish on rack, close lid, set steam release to Sealing, press Manual, and adjust cook time to 20 minutes.

5. Once cooking is complete quick-release pressure. Press Cancel and open lid. Remove foil and transfer balls to an ungreased baking sheet.

6. Heat broiler on high. Broil rolls 2 minutes until golden. Serve warm.

PER SERVING Calories: 251 | Fat: 14g | Protein: 5g | Sodium: 449mg | Fiber: 1g | Carbohydrates: 24g | Sugar: 2g

Desserts

Classic New York Cheesecake

This classic version of cheesecake is just begging for delicious toppings. Drizzle with caramel, melted chocolate, and pecans for a turtle cheesecake or top with your favorite fruit pie filling and a little whipped cream!

INGREDIENTS | SERVES 8

1 cup water

¾ cup graham cracker crumbs

1 tablespoon plus ½ cup granulated sugar, divided

3 tablespoons unsalted butter, melted

2 (8-ounce) packages cream cheese, room temperature

1 teaspoon cornstarch

2 large eggs, room temperature

½ cup sour cream

2 tablespoons heavy whipping cream

1 teaspoon vanilla extract

Fruit-Infused Cheesecake

Add fruit purée or jam to the filling to make this a fruity-flavored cheesecake! Just sauté or boil your favorite fruit or berries with sugar on the stove. Once fruit is soft, purée until smooth, then pour through a strainer. Measure out ½ cup and add it when you start to beat the cream cheese.

1. Add water to Instant Pot® and add rack. Fold a long piece of aluminum foil in half. Lay foil over rack to form a sling.

2. In a medium bowl combine graham cracker crumbs, sugar, and butter. Spray a 7" springform pan with nonstick cooking spray and pour crust mixture into pan. Place in freezer while you prepare cheesecake filling.

3. In a food processor add cream cheese and sugar. Pulse ten times, then allow machine to process until cream cheese is smooth, about ten 30-second bursts. Add cornstarch and set machine to process continuously. Add eggs one at a time, allowing 15 seconds between each addition. Add sour cream, cream, and vanilla and process 10 seconds. Turn off machine and let mixture stand 5 minutes.

4. Pour filling into prepared crust. Place a layer of paper towel over pan, then top with aluminum foil and tightly seal. Place pan on rack in pot. Close lid and set steam release to Sealing, then press Manual and adjust cook time to 40 minutes.

5. Once cooking is complete allow pressure to release naturally, about 20 minutes. Press Cancel and open lid. Using aluminum foil sling, carefully remove cheesecake from pot. Let stand, covered, 20 minutes.

6. Refrigerate cheesecake covered at least 6 hours, or overnight. Unmold from pan and serve.

PER SERVING Calories: 388 | Fat: 31g | Protein: 6g | Sodium: 306mg | Fiber: 0g | Carbohydrates: 22g | Sugar: 15g

Dark Chocolate Cheesecake

If you love chocolate, then you are sure to love this chocolaty cheesecake! It is smooth and rich and has a bold chocolate flavor. You can also add 1 teaspoon of instant espresso powder to the filling for a mocha cheesecake!

INGREDIENTS | SERVES 8

1 cup water

¾ cup ground chocolate cookie crumbs

1 tablespoon packed light brown sugar

3 tablespoons unsalted butter, melted

2 (8-ounce) packages cream cheese, room temperature

½ cup granulated sugar

2 tablespoons Dutch-processed cocoa powder

1 ounce semisweet chocolate chips, melted

1 teaspoon cornstarch

2 large eggs, room temperature

½ cup sour cream

2 tablespoons heavy whipping cream

1 teaspoon vanilla extract

1. Add water to Instant Pot® and add rack. Fold a long piece of aluminum foil in half. Lay foil over rack to form a sling.

2. In a medium bowl combine cookie crumbs, brown sugar, and butter. Spray a 7" springform with nonstick cooking spray and pour mixture into pan. Place in freezer while you prepare cheesecake filling.

3. In a food processor add cream cheese, sugar, and cocoa powder. Pulse ten times, then allow machine to process until cream cheese is smooth, about ten 30-second bursts. Add melted chocolate and cornstarch and set machine to process continuously. Add eggs one at a time, allowing 15 seconds between each addition. Add sour cream, cream, and vanilla and process 10 seconds. Turn off machine and let mixture stand 5 minutes.

4. Pour filling into prepared crust. Place a layer of paper towel over pan, then top with aluminum foil and tightly seal. Place pan on rack. Close lid and set steam release to Sealing, then press Manual and adjust cook time to 40 minutes.

5. Once cooking is complete allow pressure to release naturally, about 20 minutes. Press Cancel and open lid. Using the aluminum foil sling, carefully remove cheesecake from pot. Let stand, covered, 20 minutes.

6. Refrigerate cheesecake covered at least 6 hours, or overnight.

PER SERVING Calories: 406 | Fat: 31g | Protein: 6g | Sodium: 274mg | Fiber: 1g | Carbohydrates: 26g | Sugar: 21g

White Chocolate Oreo Cheesecake

With little bits of chocolate sandwich cookie studded throughout this cheesecake, it is a cookies and cream dream come true! You can also use any flavor of Oreo you like, so get creative!

INGREDIENTS | SERVES 8

1 cup water

¾ cup ground chocolate Oreo cookie crumbs

1 tablespoon packed light brown sugar

3 tablespoons unsalted butter, melted

2 (8-ounce) packages cream cheese, room temperature

½ cup granulated sugar

2 ounces white chocolate chips, melted

1 teaspoon cornstarch

2 large eggs, room temperature

½ cup sour cream

2 tablespoons heavy whipping cream

1 teaspoon vanilla extract

¾ cup crushed Oreo cookies, divided

1. Add water to Instant Pot® and add rack. Fold a long piece of aluminum foil in half. Lay foil over rack to form a sling.

2. In a medium bowl combine cookie crumbs, brown sugar, and butter. Spray a 7" springform pan with nonstick cooking spray and pour mixture into pan. Place in freezer while you prepare the filling.

3. In a food processor add cream cheese and sugar. Pulse ten times, then allow machine to process until cream cheese is smooth, about ten 30-second bursts. Add melted white chocolate and cornstarch and set machine to process continuously. Add eggs one at a time, allowing 15 seconds between each addition. Add sour cream, cream, and vanilla and process 10 seconds. Turn off machine and let mixture stand 5 minutes. Stir in ½ cup crushed cookies.

4. Pour filling into prepared crust. Place a layer of paper towel over pan, then top with aluminum foil and tightly seal. Place pan on rack in pot. Close lid and set steam release to Sealing, then press Manual and adjust cook time to 40 minutes.

5. Once cooking is complete allow pressure to release naturally, about 20 minutes. Press Cancel and open lid. Using the aluminum foil sling, carefully remove cheesecake from pot. Let stand, covered, 20 minutes.

6. Refrigerate cheesecake covered at least 6 hours, or overnight. Serve with reserved crushed cookies for garnish.

PER SERVING Calories: 354 | Fat: 22g | Protein: 5g | Sodium: 173mg | Fiber: 1g | Carbohydrates: 36g | Sugar: 18g

Japanese-Style Cheesecake

A traditional Japanese cheesecake is a somewhat arduous affair of whipping, folding, and praying that it all comes out to jiggling perfection. This shortcut method reduces the ingredients to only three but produces a cheesecake that tastes just like the more complicated original.

INGREDIENTS | SERVES 8

1 cup water

3 large eggs

4 ounces (about ½ cup) white chocolate chips

1 (8-ounce) package cream cheese, room temperature

1. Add water to Instant Pot® and add rack. Fold a long piece of aluminum foil in half. Lay foil over rack to form a sling.

2. Separate eggs and place whites in covered container in refrigerator. Allow yolks to sit in a small bowl at room temperature to warm up.

3. In a large microwave-safe bowl add white chocolate chips. Melt on 30-second bursts, stirring well after each burst, until melted, about 1½ minutes total. Add cream cheese and mix with a hand mixer until cream cheese and white chocolate are smooth. Add egg yolks and beat well to combine.

4. With clean beaters, whip egg whites until they form soft, glossy peaks. Add ¼ egg whites to cream cheese mixture and fold to combine. Add ½ remaining egg whites and fold to combine, then fold in last portion egg whites.

5. Spray a 6" cake pan with nonstick cooking spray, then line pan with parchment paper on bottom and sides. Carefully transfer cake batter to prepared pan. Place pan on rack in pot, close lid, set steam release to Sealing, press Manual, and adjust cook time to 18 minutes.

6. Once cooking is complete allow pressure to release naturally. Press Cancel and open lid. Use sling to carefully remove pan from pot. Cool 30 minutes at room temperature, then refrigerate covered at least 4 hours or overnight.

PER SERVING Calories: 143 | Fat: 10g | Protein: 4g | Sodium: 81mg | Fiber: 1g | Carbohydrates: 10g | Sugar: 8g

Sticky Toffee Pudding

You can make these a few days ahead of time, then just warm them up when you are ready to serve. They are best served warm, smothered in caramel sauce!

INGREDIENTS | SERVES 4

1 cup water
2 tablespoons half-and-half
3 tablespoons unsalted butter
⅔ cup all-purpose flour
1 teaspoon baking powder
¼ teaspoon salt
¼ teaspoon ground cinnamon
¼ teaspoon ground allspice
⅛ teaspoon ground cloves
½ cup hot water
½ teaspoon baking soda
½ cup chopped fresh dates
1 large egg
¾ cup caramel sauce

1. Add water to Instant Pot® and add rack. Spray four 4-ounce ramekins with nonstick cooking spray.

2. Combine half-and-half and butter in medium microwave-safe bowl. Heat 30 seconds, stir, and heat in 20-second bursts until butter is melted and mixture is hot, about 2 minutes total.

3. In a separate large bowl whisk together flour, baking powder, salt, cinnamon, allspice, and cloves.

4. In a medium bowl combine hot water, baking soda, and dates. Mix well. Add date mixture and half-and-half mixture to dry ingredients. Add egg, then mix until batter is smooth. Divide batter among prepared ramekins and cover each tightly with aluminum foil.

5. Place ramekins on rack in pot, close lid, and set steam release to Sealing. Press Manual and adjust cook time to 25 minutes.

6. Once cooking is complete quick-release pressure. Press Cancel and open lid. Remove ramekins from pot and remove foil. Serve pudding in ramekins or unmold and serve on a plate. Cover with caramel sauce and enjoy warm.

PER SERVING Calories: 296 | Fat: 14g | Protein: 8g | Sodium: 498mg | Fiber: 2g | Carbohydrates: 35g | Sugar: 16g

Pineapple Upside-Down Cake

This Instant Pot® version of the classic dessert is super easy to make (thanks to yellow cake mix) but tastes amazing because of a few fun tricks. It will have your friends and family coming back for more!

INGREDIENTS | SERVES 8

6 tablespoons unsalted butter, cut into thin slices

⅓ cup packed light brown sugar

½ (20-ounce) can pineapple rings in juice

4 maraschino cherries, halved

1 cup water

½ box yellow cake mix

½ cup buttermilk

4 tablespoons unsalted butter, melted

1 large egg

1 egg yolk

1 teaspoon vanilla extract

¼ teaspoon salt

Make It Boozy

You can add a little rum to make this cake an adults-only treat! While cake is still cooling, use a toothpick to gently prick holes over the top. Brush ¼ cup dark spiced rum over cake. Let cool for an extra 5 minutes to allow rum a chance to soak in.

1. Spray a 7" cake pan with nonstick cooking spray. Lay butter slices on bottom of pan, spread brown sugar over top, then add pineapple rings. Place ½ cherry in center of each pineapple ring, smooth-side down. Set aside.

2. Add water to Instant Pot® and add rack. Fold a long piece of aluminum foil in half. Lay foil over rack to form a sling.

3. In a medium bowl combine cake mix, buttermilk, melted butter, egg, egg yolk, vanilla, and salt. Beat until mixture is smooth. Carefully spoon batter over pineapples. Spray a piece of aluminum foil with nonstick cooking spray and cover pan, crimping edges well.

4. Place pan on rack in pot. Close lid and set steam release to Sealing, then press Manual and adjust cook time to 20 minutes.

5. Once cooking is complete allow pressure to release naturally 10 minutes, then quick-release any remaining pressure. Press Cancel and open lid. Carefully use sling to remove pan from pot. Uncover and let stand 10 minutes, then turn cake out onto serving platter to cool completely before serving, about 1 hour.

PER SERVING Calories: 194 | Fat: 15g | Protein: 2g | Sodium: 116mg | Fiber: 0g | Carbohydrates: 12g | Sugar: 12g

Carrot Cake with Cream Cheese Frosting

This carrot cake is rich, a little dense, and oh-so-satisfying! The frosting for this cake is generous, so if you are not that into frosting, feel free to cut the ingredients in half.

INGREDIENTS | SERVES 8

1 cup water

½ cup granulated sugar

¼ cup vegetable oil

¼ cup unsalted butter, melted

¼ cup buttermilk

2 large eggs

1 cup all-purpose flour

1 teaspoon baking powder

1 teaspoon ground cinnamon

¼ teaspoon baking soda

¼ teaspoon ground allspice

¼ teaspoon salt

¾ cup peeled shredded carrot

1 stick salted butter, room temperature

1 (8-ounce) package cream cheese, room temperature

2 cups confectioners' sugar

½ teaspoon vanilla extract

1. Add water to Instant Pot® and add rack. Fold a long piece of aluminum foil in half. Lay foil over rack to form a sling.

2. In a medium bowl combine sugar, oil, melted butter, buttermilk, and eggs. Whisk to combine.

3. In a separate large bowl sift together flour, baking powder, cinnamon, baking soda, allspice, and salt. Pour wet ingredients into dry and stir until just combined, then add carrot and stir.

4. Spray a 7" cake pan with nonstick cooking spray. Pour cake batter into pan. Spray a piece of aluminum foil with nonstick cooking spray. Cover pan with foil and crimp edges well. Add pan to rack in pot, close lid, and set steam release to Sealing. Press Manual and adjust cook time to 20 minutes.

5. Once cooking is complete allow pressure to release naturally 10 minutes, then quick-release remaining pressure. Press Cancel and open lid. Carefully use sling to remove pan from pot. Uncover cake and let cool 10 minutes in pan, then turn out onto a serving platter and cool to room temperature, about 1 hour.

6. In a medium bowl add butter and cream cheese. Beat with a hand mixer until completely combined, about 2 minutes. Add confectioners' sugar and vanilla and beat until smooth, about 1 minute. Once cake is cooled, spread on cream cheese frosting. Refrigerate covered 1 hour before serving.

PER SERVING Calories: 537 | Fat: 23g | Protein: 5g | Sodium: 317mg | Fiber: 1g | Carbohydrates: 78g | Sugar: 64g

Steamed Golden Syrup Cake

This cake is uniquely moist and has a caramel flavor—thanks to the golden syrup used in the bowl. If you can't locate golden syrup, feel free to use honey.

INGREDIENTS | SERVES 6

½ cup golden syrup, divided

1 cup water

1 stick unsalted butter, room temperature

⅓ cup granulated sugar

2 large eggs

1 teaspoon vanilla extract

1⅓ cups all-purpose flour

1½ teaspoons baking powder

¼ teaspoon ground cardamom

½ teaspoon salt

½ cup whole milk, room temperature

Golden Syrup

Golden syrup is a thick golden-brown syrup made during the refining process for granulated sugar. Popular in the United Kingdom, it has a rich, buttery flavor and is wonderful on pancakes and biscuits or stirred into tea. Made without animal products, it is a wonderful vegan alternative to honey. Golden syrup can be found with the honey in most markets.

1. Spray a 4-cup glass bowl with nonstick cooking spray. Pour ¼ cup golden syrup into bowl. Add water to Instant Pot® and add rack. Fold a long piece of aluminum foil in half. Lay foil over rack to form a sling.

2. In a large bowl cream together butter and sugar until slightly lighter in color, about 3 minutes. Add eggs, one at a time, and blend well. Add vanilla and stir to incorporate.

3. In a medium bowl sift together flour, baking powder, cardamom, and salt. Add dry ingredients alternately with milk to creamed butter and sugar, starting and ending with flour. Do not overmix.

4. Pour batter carefully into prepared bowl. Cover bowl with aluminum foil, crimping edges tightly. Add bowl to rack in pot and close lid. Set steam release to Sealing, press Manual, and adjust cook time to 25 minutes.

5. Once cooking is complete allow pressure to release naturally 10 minutes, then quick-release remaining pressure. Press Cancel and open lid. Carefully use sling to remove pan from pot. Uncover bowl and let cool 5 minutes, then turn out onto a serving platter and serve warm with remaining golden syrup as a garnish.

PER SERVING Calories: 392 | Fat: 17g | Protein: 6g | Sodium: 379mg | Fiber: 1g | Carbohydrates: 52g | Sugar: 30g

Steamed Matcha Cake

Matcha is powdered green tea, and it has a pleasant, slightly grassy flavor. While it is used for making tea in iconic Japanese tea ceremonies, you can also find it mixed into cakes, cookies, and ice cream.

INGREDIENTS | SERVES 6

1 cup water

1 stick unsalted butter, room temperature

½ cup granulated sugar

2 large eggs

1½ teaspoons vanilla extract

1⅓ cups cake flour

2 tablespoons matcha powder

1½ teaspoons baking powder

½ teaspoon salt

½ cup whole milk, room temperature

¼ cup confectioners' sugar

1. Spray a 4-cup glass bowl with nonstick cooking spray. Add water to Instant Pot® and add rack. Fold a long piece of aluminum foil in half. Lay foil over rack to form a sling.

2. In a large bowl cream together butter and sugar until slightly lighter in color, about 3 minutes. Add eggs, one at a time, and blend well. Add vanilla and stir to incorporate.

3. In a medium bowl sift together flour, matcha powder, baking powder, and salt. Add dry ingredients alternately with milk to creamed butter and granulated sugar, starting and ending with flour. Do not overmix.

4. Pour batter into prepared bowl and cover with aluminum foil, crimping edges tightly. Add bowl to rack in pot and close lid. Set steam release to Sealing, press Manual, and adjust cook time to 23 minutes.

5. Once cooking is complete allow pressure to release naturally 10 minutes, then quick-release remaining pressure. Press Cancel and open lid. Carefully use sling to remove pan from pot. Uncover bowl and let cool 5 minutes, then turn out onto a serving platter and serve warm or at room temperature with confectioners' sugar sifted over top.

PER SERVING Calories: 392 | Fat: 17g | Protein: 5g | Sodium: 351mg | Fiber: 0.5g | Carbohydrates: 52g | Sugar: 26g

Peach Cobbler

*When fresh peaches are in season, you should definitely take advantage and make
yourself a quick and easy cobbler! If you want this when peaches are out of season,
you can use frozen peaches—just increase the cooking time by 2 minutes.*

INGREDIENTS | SERVES 8

1 cup water

4 large peaches, peeled and sliced

¼ cup granulated sugar

1 tablespoon cornstarch

½ teaspoon ground cinnamon

⅛ teaspoon nutmeg

½ box yellow cake mix

¼ cup unsalted butter, room
temperature

Substituting Frozen Fruit

Sometimes you just need a bit of fruity sun-
shine in the heart of winter, but your favorite fruits aren't in season. What do you do?
Use frozen! Frozen fruit is quick frozen at
the peak of the season, and usually when
they are most ripe and ready to go. When
substituting frozen fruit, thaw it well and
drain off any juices before using.

1. Spray an 8" × 8" baking dish with nonstick cooking
   spray. Add water to Instant Pot® and add rack. Fold a
   long piece of aluminum foil in half. Lay foil over rack
   to form a sling.

2. In a medium bowl combine peaches, sugar,
   cornstarch, cinnamon, and nutmeg. Transfer into the
   prepared dish.

3. In a separate medium bowl add cake mix and butter.
   Using two forks, cut butter into cake mix until mixture
   is crumbly. Sprinkle crumbles over peaches, cover dish
   with aluminum foil, and crimp edges tightly.

4. Add bowl to rack in pot and close lid. Set steam
   release to Sealing, press Manual, and adjust cook time
   to 10 minutes.

5. Once cooking is complete allow pressure to release
   naturally 10 minutes, then quick-release remaining
   pressure. Press Cancel and open lid. Carefully remove
   dish with sling. Remove foil.

6. Heat broiler on high. Broil cobbler until topping is
   golden brown, about 5 minutes. Serve warm or at
   room temperature.

PER SERVING Calories: 234 | Fat: 6g | Protein: 1g |
Sodium: 1mg | Fiber: 1g | Carbohydrates: 37g |
Sugar: 13g

Blueberry Oat Crumble

*You can also make this with fresh diced apples, pears, or a mix
of blueberries, raspberries, and blackberries!*

Blueberries

The majority of the health benefits from blueberries comes from anthocyanin, which is the same compound that gives them their color. This compound is a powerful antioxidant, and research has shown that this antioxidant can help increase bone strength and skin health and may help improve blood pressure and overall heart health.

1. Spray an 8" × 8" baking dish with nonstick cooking spray. Add water to Instant Pot® and add rack. Fold a long piece of aluminum foil in half. Lay foil over rack to form a sling.

2. In a medium bowl combine blueberries, brown sugar, cornstarch, and nutmeg. Transfer mixture to prepared dish.

3. In a separate medium bowl add oats, sugar, flour, and cinnamon. Mix well. Add butter and mix until mixture is crumbly. Sprinkle crumbles over blueberries, cover dish with aluminum foil, and crimp edges tightly.

4. Add bowl to rack in pot and close lid. Set steam release to Sealing, press Manual, and adjust cook time to 10 minutes.

5. Once cooking is complete allow pressure to release naturally 10 minutes, then quick-release remaining pressure. Press Cancel and open lid. Carefully remove dish with sling. Remove foil.

6. Heat broiler on high. Broil cobbler until topping is golden brown, about 5 minutes. Serve warm or at room temperature.

PER SERVING Calories: 169 | Fat: 6g | Protein: 1.5g | Sodium: 3mg | Fiber: 2.5g | Carbohydrates: 28g | Sugar: 18g

Creamy Flan

Also known as crème caramel, flan is a custard baked on top of a caramel sauce. It is silky smooth and very rich. This version takes far less time and effort than the original recipe!

INGREDIENTS | SERVES 8

1 cup water
½ cup granulated sugar
4 large eggs
1 cup whole milk
1 (14-ounce) can sweetened condensed milk
1 teaspoon vanilla extract
⅛ teaspoon salt

1. Add water to Instant Pot® and add rack. Fold a long piece of aluminum foil in half. Lay foil over rack to form a sling.

2. In a small saucepan add sugar. Cook over medium heat until sugar melts and starts to boil, about 3 minutes. Continue to cook until sugar is a deep caramel color, about 12 minutes more. Pour the resulting caramel into bottom of an 8" ungreased baking dish. Turn dish to evenly coat with caramel. Set aside.

3. In a medium bowl add eggs, milk, sweetened condensed milk, vanilla, and salt. Whisk until well combined, then pour into dish with caramel sauce. Cover dish with aluminum foil and crimp edges tightly.

4. Place dish on rack. Close lid and set steam release to Sealing, then press Manual and adjust cook time to 5 minutes.

5. Once cooking is complete allow pressure to release naturally 10 minutes, then quick-release any remaining pressure. Press Cancel and open lid. Use sling to carefully remove dish from pot. Cool 30 minutes at room temperature, then refrigerate 4 hours or overnight. To unmold, run a thin knife or spatula around edge of flan, then turn out onto a serving plate.

PER SERVING Calories: 261 | Fat: 7.5g | Protein: 8g | Sodium: 147mg | Fiber: 0g | Carbohydrates: 40g | Sugar: 40g

Chocolate Pot de Crème

If you or someone you love is a chocoholic, then you will want to try out this recipe. The cups are filled with smooth, creamy, and very rich chocolate custard. These are lovely with sweetened whipped cream on top as a garnish!

INGREDIENTS | SERVES 6

1 cup water

1 cup semisweet chocolate chips

1½ cups heavy cream

½ cup whole milk

6 egg yolks

¼ cup granulated sugar

⅛ teaspoon salt

1 teaspoon vanilla extract

Pot de Crème

Silky, creamy, and rich pot de crème is an invention of the French. Translating to "pot of cream," the dish is a creamy, soft, lightly firm chocolate custard cooked in small cups and served chilled. While tradition calls for the small cups to be cooked in a water bath in the oven, the Instant Pot® makes the cooking easier, and faster, with the same delightful result!

1. Add water to Instant Pot® and add rack.

2. Place chocolate chips in a medium bowl and set aside. In a small saucepan add cream, milk, egg yolks, and sugar. Cook over medium heat until milk simmers, about 5 minutes. Strain milk mixture through a strainer over chocolate. Let stand 30 seconds, then mix until chocolate has melted. Stir in salt and vanilla.

3. Divide mixture among six custard cups or ramekins. Cover each cup with aluminum foil and crimp edges tightly. Place four cups on bottom rack in pot, then place a second rack or steamer basket on cups and arrange remaining cups on top. Close lid and set steam release to Sealing, then press Manual and adjust cook time to 6 minutes.

4. Once cooking is complete allow pressure to release naturally, about 15 minutes, then press Cancel and open lid. Carefully remove cups from pot and remove foil covers. Cool 30 minutes at room temperature, then refrigerate 4 hours or overnight. Serve cold.

PER SERVING Calories: 454 | Fat: 36g | Protein: 6g | Sodium: 91mg | Fiber: 2g | Carbohydrates: 31g | Sugar: 27g

Chocolate Chip Instant Pot® Blondies

If you are a fan of fudgy desserts, then these are sure to please! If you can hold yourself back, let them chill in the refrigerator overnight before serving to help them firm up.

INGREDIENTS | SERVES 8

1 cup water

⅓ cup unsalted butter, melted

¾ cup packed light brown sugar

¼ cup granulated sugar

2 teaspoons vanilla extract

2 large eggs

1½ cups all-purpose flour

½ teaspoon baking powder

¼ teaspoon salt

1 cup semisweet chocolate chips

1. Add water to Instant Pot® and add rack. Fold a long piece of aluminum foil in half. Lay foil over rack to form a sling.

2. In a medium bowl add butter, brown sugar, and granulated sugar. Cream together until smooth, then add vanilla and eggs. Mix until eggs are completely combined. Add flour, baking powder, and salt. Mix until flour is almost completely combined, about twelve strokes. Add chocolate chips and mix to distribute chips evenly.

3. Spray an 8" × 8" baking dish with nonstick cooking spray. Spread batter into pan and cover with aluminum foil, crimping edges tightly. Place dish on rack in pot, close lid, set steam release to Sealing, press Manual, and adjust cook time to 40 minutes.

4. Once cooking is complete allow pressure to release naturally, about 15 minutes. Carefully remove dish with sling, remove foil, and let cool to room temperature. Turn blondies out onto a serving dish and serve.

PER SERVING Calories: 359 | Fat: 15g | Protein: 5g | Sodium: 128mg | Fiber: 2g | Carbohydrates: 52g | Sugar: 32g

Chocolate Banana Mason Jar Cakes

These cakes are gluten-free, so they are perfect for those who are gluten sensitive, but they are so flavorful that they are perfect for everyone else too! They also make a tasty breakfast, so go ahead and have cake to start the day!

INGREDIENTS | SERVES 4

1 cup water
1 cup blanched almond flour
3 tablespoons cocoa powder
1 tablespoon coconut flour
¼ teaspoon salt
4 large eggs
⅓ cup packed light brown sugar
1 large banana, mashed
1 teaspoon vanilla extract
½ cup chopped raw pecans

1. Spray four 8-ounce Mason jars with nonstick cooking spray. Add water to Instant Pot® and add rack.

2. In a medium bowl combine almond flour, cocoa powder, coconut flour, and salt. Mix well.

3. In a separate medium bowl combine eggs, brown sugar, banana, and vanilla. Mix well, then pour wet ingredients into dry and mix well. Stir in pecans.

4. Divide batter among prepared jars. Cover each jar tightly with aluminum foil, then place on rack in pot. Close lid and set steam release to Sealing, then press Manual and adjust cook time to 10 minutes.

5. Once cooking is complete quick-release pressure. Press Cancel and open lid. Carefully remove jars from pot and remove foil tops. Cool to room temperature, about 1 hour, before serving.

PER SERVING Calories: 370 | Fat: 15g | Protein: 12g | Sodium: 221mg | Fiber: 5.5g | Carbohydrates: 49g | Sugar: 16g

Easy Angel Food Cake

This cake has two ingredients, about 2 minutes of hands-on work, and one whole cake pan filled with reward! Save your additional cake mix in the refrigerator to keep it fresh.

INGREDIENTS | SERVES 8

2½ cups water, divided

½ box angel food cake mix

Baking Two Cakes

If you want to make the full box of mix, you will need to make it in two batches, as cake pans can't be stacked in the Instant Pot®. Also, be sure to wait until the first cake has come out of the pot before mixing up more batter; otherwise, it will deflate and will not rise.

1. Add 1 cup water to Instant Pot® and add rack. Fold a long piece of aluminum foil in half. Lay foil over rack to form a sling.

2. In a medium bowl combine cake mix and remaining water. Mix until batter is fluffy. Transfer batter to an ungreased 6-cup Bundt or tube pan. Cover pan and crimp edges well. Add pan to rack in pot and close lid. Set steam release to Sealing, press Manual, and adjust cook time to 10 minutes.

3. Once cooking is complete quick-release pressure. Press Cancel and open lid. Carefully use sling to remove pan from pot. Uncover cake and let cool to room temperature, about 1 hour. Once cool, carefully run a thin spatula around edges of cake, then push bottom up to release. If using a Bundt pan, carefully pull sides of cake away from pan with a thin spatula and turn out onto a plate. Serve at room temperature.

PER SERVING Calories: 120 | Fat: 3g | Protein: 1g | Sodium: 180mg | Fiber: 0.5g | Carbohydrates: 21g | Sugar: 12g

Gooey Chocolate Cake Cups

The key to these cakes is not to let them sit in the pot too long after the cooking time is up. The longer they sit, the more cooked the centers will be, and you will lose the gooey center.

INGREDIENTS | SERVES 4

1 cup water
1 cup chopped bittersweet chocolate
½ cup unsalted butter
4 large eggs
½ cup packed light brown sugar
1 teaspoon vanilla extract
¼ cup all-purpose flour

1. Add water to Instant Pot® and add rack. Spray four ramekins with nonstick cooking spray.

2. Add chocolate and butter to a small microwave-safe bowl. Heat 30 seconds, stir well, then return to the microwave in 20-second bursts until chocolate and butter are melted and smooth, about 1½ minutes total.

3. In a separate medium bowl whisk together eggs and sugar until smooth. Stir in vanilla, then whisk in chocolate mixture. Add flour and stir until flour is combined and no lumps remain.

4. Divide batter among ramekins, making sure to fill them no more than ⅔ full. Place uncovered ramekins on rack in pot and close lid. Set steam release to Sealing, press Manual, and adjust cook time to 8 minutes.

5. Once cooking is complete quick-release pressure. Press Cancel and open lid. Carefully remove ramekins to serving plates. Serve warm.

PER SERVING Calories: 593 | Fat: 41g | Protein: 9g | Sodium: 84mg | Fiber: 3g | Carbohydrates: 53g | Sugar: 42g

Black Cherry Sauce

If you want to sound fancy, you can call this sauce a "compote." It is wonderful spooned over ice cream, cake, or yogurt or served simply with some sweetened whipped cream in a bowl.

INGREDIENTS | SERVES 8

1 (16-ounce) bag frozen black cherries

½ cup granulated sugar

1 tablespoon freshly squeezed lemon juice

2 tablespoons cornstarch

2 tablespoons water

¼ teaspoon vanilla extract

⅛ teaspoon almond extract

Cornstarch in the Instant Pot®

When making any kind of sauce, soup, or liquid that needs to be thickened with cornstarch, wait until the food has completed cooking before thickening. If you add it and then cook the food, the cornstarch will lose its thickening power or will burn on the pot. Instead, mix cornstarch with a little liquid, then add to the cooked liquid and thicken on Sauté.

1. Add cherries, sugar, and lemon juice to Instant Pot®. Close lid and set steam release to Sealing, then press Manual and adjust cook time to 3 minutes.

2. Once cooking is complete quick-release pressure. Press Cancel and open lid. Press Sauté.

3. In a small bowl combine cornstarch and water. Stir into cherry mixture and cook until mixture comes to a boil and thickens, about 4 minutes. Once thickened, press Cancel and stir in vanilla and almond extract. Serve immediately, or refrigerate covered up to two weeks.

PER SERVING Calories: 92 | Fat: 0g | Protein: 0.5g | Sodium: 1mg | Fiber: 1g | Carbohydrates: 23g | Sugar: 19g

Cinnamon Apples

This is a simple dessert, but often the simplest things are the best! While this recipe is lovely alone, it is even better with a scoop of vanilla ice cream on top! Feel free to add ⅓ cup raisins or chopped nuts as well.

INGREDIENTS | SERVES 6

4 large apples (Granny Smith or Pink Lady), peeled, cored, and sliced

½ cup granulated sugar

1 teaspoon ground cinnamon

⅛ cup apple cider

⅛ teaspoon vanilla extract

1 tablespoon unsalted butter

1. Add apples, sugar, cinnamon, and apple cider to Instant Pot®. Close lid and set steam release to Sealing, then press Manual and adjust cook time to 3 minutes.

2. Once cooking is complete quick-release pressure. Press Cancel and open lid. Stir in vanilla, then add butter and stir until melted. Serve immediately.

PER SERVING Calories: 154 | Fat: 2g | Protein: 0.5g | Sodium: 1mg | Fiber: 2g | Carbohydrates: 36g | Sugar: 31g

CHAPTER 18

Cocktails and Drinks

Mulled Wine

When the weather gets chilly, there is nothing better to warm you up than a mug of warm mulled wine. The spices are where you can let your own taste shine, so feel free to play around with them!

INGREDIENTS | SERVES 12

1 large apple (Granny Smith or Pink Lady), peeled, cored, and sliced

1 large orange, peel on, quartered

6 whole cloves

3 cinnamon sticks

2 whole star anise

¼ teaspoon ground nutmeg

2 (25.4-ounce) bottles dry red wine

1. Add all ingredients to Instant Pot®. Close lid and set steam release to Sealing, then press Manual and adjust cook time to 1 minute.

2. Once cooking is complete quick-release pressure. Press Cancel and open lid. Serve immediately. You can let wine stand on Keep Warm up to 1 hour.

PER SERVING Calories: 155 | Fat: 2g | Protein: 1g | Sodium: 43mg | Fiber: 5g | Carbohydrates: 16g | Sugar: 4g

Hot Buttered Rum

With a history that dates back to the Colonial days in America, Hot Buttered Rum is a staple of the holiday season. Feel free to adjust the amounts of water and cider, adding more of one and less of another, to suit your taste.

INGREDIENTS | SERVES 8

1 cup packed light brown sugar

¼ cup salted butter

2 cinnamon sticks

5 whole cloves

1 whole vanilla bean, sliced in half

2 cups water

2 cups apple cider

1 cup dark rum

1. Add all ingredients except rum to Instant Pot®. Close lid and set steam release to Sealing, then press Manual and adjust cook time to 1 minute.

2. Once cooking is complete quick-release pressure. Open lid and stir in rum. Serve warm.

PER SERVING Calories: 259 | Fat: 8g | Protein: 1g | Sodium: 103mg | Fiber: 6g | Carbohydrates: 36g | Sugar: 23g

Pressure Cooking and Cocktails

The Instant Pot® is a great tool for infusing cocktail mixers and even mulling lower-alcohol drinks like wine, but you should never pressure cook hard liquor. Alcohol is highly combustible, and when you put hard liquor in a pressure cooker, it evaporates the alcohol quickly and can cause a very dangerous, even explosive, situation.

Caramel Apple Cider

This version of the winter favorite is sweetened with prepared caramel sauce. Top the mugs with whipped cream, a cinnamon stick, and more caramel as a garnish!

INGREDIENTS | SERVES 8

6 large apples, peeled, cored, and chopped
2 cinnamon sticks
4 whole cloves
3 allspice berries
6 cups water
½ cup caramel sauce

1. Add apples, cinnamon sticks, cloves, and allspice berries to Instant Pot®. Stir in water. Close lid and set steam release to Sealing, then press Manual and adjust cook time to 5 minutes.

2. Once cooking is complete quick-release pressure. Press Cancel and open lid. Stir in caramel sauce, then with a stick blender carefully blend until smooth. Serve warm.

PER SERVING Calories: 137 | Fat: 3g | Protein: 2g | Sodium: 60mg | Fiber: 6g | Carbohydrates: 31g | Sugar: 18g

Classic Apple Cider

This cider is a classic for the holiday season. It has apples, citrus, and plenty of warm spices. If serving for a crowd add in a few fresh apple and orange slices and some whole cranberries for a beautiful pop of color after straining the cider!

INGREDIENTS | SERVES 8

5 large apples, cored and sliced
1 large orange, sliced
3 cinnamon sticks
5 whole cloves
1 whole star anise
8 cups water
⅓ cup packed packed light brown sugar

1. Add all ingredients except sugar to Instant Pot® and stir. Close lid and set steam release to Sealing, then press Manual and adjust cook time to 8 minutes.

2. Once cooking is complete quick-release pressure. Press Cancel and open lid. Discard fruit and spices with a slotted spoon, then stir in sugar until dissolved. Serve warm.

PER SERVING Calories: 146 | Fat: 2.5g | Protein: 1.5g | Sodium: 57mg | Fiber: 8g | Carbohydrates: 37g | Sugar: 22g

Spiced Pear Cider

This twist on traditional apple cider is infused with vanilla and cinnamon and sweetened with light brown sugar!

INGREDIENTS | SERVES 8

5 medium pears, peeled, cored, and sliced

3 cinnamon sticks

2 whole cloves

1 whole vanilla bean, sliced in half

8 cups water

⅓ cup packed light brown sugar

Overripe Pears

This cider is a great place to use pears that have gone a day or two past their prime. Since the pears here are blended into the cider you don't have to worry about the pears retaining their shape or texture, and a soft pear is also a little sweeter, so the finished cider has an excellent flavor.

1. Add all ingredients except sugar to Instant Pot® and stir. Close lid and set steam release to Sealing, then press Manual and adjust cook time to 8 minutes.

2. Once cooking is complete quick-release pressure. Press Cancel and open lid. Discard vanilla bean and whole spices with a slotted spoon. Add sugar, then use a stick blender to carefully purée pears. Serve warm.

PER SERVING Calories: 105 | Fat: 1g | Protein: 1g | Sodium: 29mg | Fiber: 6g | Carbohydrates: 27g | Sugar: 16g

Lemonade

On a hot summer day is there anything more refreshing than a tall, cool glass of Lemonade? This version infuses the water with lemon rinds so you get an extra boost of lemon flavor.

INGREDIENTS | SERVES 8

4 cups water

4 whole lemons, quartered

1 cup freshly squeezed lemon juice

¾ cup granulated sugar

Pink Lemonade

Easily transform this recipe with the addition of 1 cup of fresh raspberries or chopped fresh strawberries. You can even do a mix of the two! Once cooking is complete pour your lemonade through a fine-mesh strainer to remove any seeds from the fruit. Be sure to use the sweetest, ripest berries for the most robust flavor!

1. Add water and lemons to Instant Pot®. Close lid and set steam release to Sealing, then press Manual and adjust cook time to 5 minutes.

2. Once cooking is complete quick-release pressure. Open lid and remove lemon. Stir in lemon juice and sugar until sugar has dissolved. Pour into a pitcher and refrigerate 4 hours. Serve cold.

PER SERVING Calories: 87 | Fat: 0g | Protein: 0.5g | Sodium: 7mg | Fiber: 1g | Carbohydrates: 23g | Sugar: 20g

Lemon Ginger Tea

This simple tea is great for easing stomach upset or as a comforting tonic for someone with a cold. If you prefer, you can serve this tea iced in the summer for a refreshing treat!

INGREDIENTS | SERVES 8

4 cups water
4 whole lemons, quartered
5 slices fresh ginger
½ cup honey

1. Add water to Instant Pot®. Squeeze in juice from lemons, then add rinds, along with ginger, to pot. Close lid and set steam release to Sealing, then press Manual and adjust cook time to 5 minutes.

2. Once cooking is complete quick-release pressure. Open lid and remove lemon rinds and ginger slices. Stir in honey until dissolved. Serve warm, or chill and serve over ice.

PER SERVING Calories: 73 | Fat: 0g | Protein: 0.5g | Sodium: 2mg | Fiber: 1g | Carbohydrates: 20g | Sugar: 18g

Milk Tea

Forget the overpriced bubble tea shops—you can make the exact same thing at home! You can find the large tapioca pearls in most Asian markets, specialty shops, or online. Feel free to use your favorite kind of boba, either black or rainbow, for this recipe.

INGREDIENTS | SERVES 4

1 cup large boba or tapioca pearls, black or rainbow
2 cups water
¼ cup granulated sugar
4 cups strong brewed black or green tea
½ cup sweetened condensed milk
2 cups ice cubes

What Is Boba?

Boba, also known as *pearls* or *bubbles*, are made from tapioca starch, formed into large balls, and added to drinks like tea, coffee, and smoothies. The drink originated from Taiwan in the 1980s, where it was originally made with small tapioca pearls.

1. Add boba, water, and sugar to Instant Pot®. Close lid and set steam release to Sealing, then press Manual and adjust cook time to 2 minutes.

2. Once cooking is complete allow pressure to release naturally 5 minutes, then quick-release any remaining pressure. Press Cancel and open lid. Stir and let stand uncovered 30 minutes.

3. To prepare tea, divide boba among four tall glasses. In a shaker, combine ¼ of the tea, sweetened condensed milk, and ice. Shake well to combine, then pour over boba. Repeat with remaining tea, sweetened condensed milk, and ice. Serve immediately.

PER SERVING Calories: 307 | Fat: 3g | Protein: 3g | Sodium: 52mg | Fiber: 0g | Carbohydrates: 67g | Sugar: 34g

Southern Sweet Iced Tea

Just about any Southerner will tell you: if it isn't sweet tea, it isn't worth drinking. You can adjust the sugar to your taste, adding or subtracting to your preference. You can also add an extra tea bag if you like it extra strong.

INGREDIENTS | SERVES 8

8 cups water

7 sweet tea bags, tags removed

2 cups granulated sugar

4 cups cold water

1. Add water and tea bags to Instant Pot®. Close lid and set steam release to Sealing, then press Manual and adjust cook time to 4 minutes.

2. Once cooking is complete quick-release pressure. Open lid, remove tea bags, and stir in sugar. Once dissolved, press Cancel and transfer to a pitcher. Stir in cold water, then refrigerate 4 hours before serving.

PER SERVING Calories: 197 | Fat: 0g | Protein: 0g | Sodium: 6mg | Fiber: 0g | Carbohydrates: 51g | Sugar: 50g

Fresh Peach Iced Tea

Fresh peaches are infused into the water, then slightly reduced with sugar to make a syrup perfect for sweetening the tea with delicious, peachy flavor!

INGREDIENTS | SERVES 12

6 cups water

5 large peaches, diced

2 cups granulated sugar

Brewed tea, cold

Other Uses for Peach Syrup

A jar of peach syrup can be a powerhouse of flavor for all sorts of dishes. Use it in oatmeal, mix it into cake mix in place of half of the water, drizzle it over ice cream and gelato, or even use it as part of a marinade for meats like chicken for grilling and roasting.

1. Add water and peaches to Instant Pot®. Close lid and set steam release to Sealing, then press Manual and adjust cook time to 4 minutes.

2. Once cooking is complete quick-release pressure. Open lid, add sugar, and stir until sugar is dissolved. Let stand uncovered on Keep Warm 10 minutes. Press Cancel and let stand 10 minutes more. Strain liquid into a storage container for up to one week.

3. To serve, pour brewed tea over ice and stir in peach syrup to taste.

PER SERVING Calories: 158 | Fat: 0g | Protein: 0g | Sodium: 0mg | Fiber: 1g | Carbohydrates: 40g | Sugar: 39g

Strawberry Limeade

Limeade makes a nice change from lemonade, and when you add the flavor of fresh strawberries, you have a drink sure to be a family favorite. Serve with fresh lime wedges and sliced strawberry in the glass!

INGREDIENTS | SERVES 8

4 cups water
4 whole limes, quartered
1 cup sliced fresh strawberries, hulled
1 cup freshly squeezed lime juice
¾ cup granulated sugar

1. Add water, limes, and strawberries to Instant Pot®. Close lid and set steam release to Sealing, then press Manual and adjust cook time to 5 minutes.

2. Once cooking is complete quick-release pressure. Open lid and remove limes and strawberries from pot with a slotted spoon. Stir in lime juice and sugar and stir until sugar has dissolved. Pour into a pitcher and refrigerate 4 hours. Serve cold.

PER SERVING Calories: 95 | Fat: 0g | Protein: 0.5g | Sodium: 7mg | Fiber: 1g | Carbohydrates: 25g | Sugar: 21g

Pumpkin Spice Latte

You can have this latte ready in a flash with the Instant Pot®—and you can have it anytime. No more waiting for the fall, or for the big coffee chains to begin serving their versions, for this comforting treat!

INGREDIENTS | SERVES 4

2 cups brewed coffee
¼ cup pumpkin purée
1 teaspoon pumpkin pie spice
½ teaspoon ground cinnamon
½ cup packed light brown sugar
2 cups half-and-half
½ teaspoon vanilla extract

1. Add coffee, pumpkin, pumpkin pie spice, and cinnamon to Instant Pot®. Close lid and set steam release to Sealing, then press Manual and adjust cook time to 1 minute.

2. Once cooking is complete quick-release pressure. Open lid and stir in sugar until dissolved. Stir in half-and-half and vanilla, replace lid, and let stand on Keep Warm 10 minutes. Serve warm.

PER SERVING Calories: 229 | Fat: 13g | Protein: 3.5g | Sodium: 54mg | Fiber: 0g | Carbohydrates: 23g | Sugar: 22g

Mocha Latte

This dairy-free latte can be served hot or over ice, and it is just begging for coconut whipped cream (or regular whipped cream if dairy is not an issue) and a drizzle of chocolate syrup.

INGREDIENTS | SERVES 4

2 cups brewed coffee

2 cups sweetened almond milk

2 tablespoons cocoa powder

¼ cup packed light brown sugar

½ cup dairy-free chocolate syrup, divided

½ teaspoon vanilla extract

1. Add coffee, milk, and cocoa powder to Instant Pot®. Close lid and set steam release to Sealing, then press Manual and adjust cook time to 1 minute.

2. Once cooking is complete quick-release pressure. Open lid and stir in sugar, ¼ cup chocolate syrup, and vanilla until sugar has dissolved. Garnish with remaining syrup and serve warm.

PER SERVING Calories: 134 | Fat: 2.5g | Protein: 4.5g | Sodium: 59mg | Fiber: 2g | Carbohydrates: 24g | Sugar: 18g

Coconut Whipped Cream

This recipe is perfect for those avoiding dairy but still craving a rich treat. Refrigerate 1 (14-ounce) can sweetened full-fat coconut milk overnight. Open the can and scoop out the thick cream layer on top. Add 2 tablespoons confectioners' sugar and ¼ teaspoon vanilla extract and beat until light and fluffy, about 7 minutes. Refrigerate until ready to use.

Peppermint Vanilla Latte

Whole vanilla beans can usually be found in your grocery store with the spices. They can be a little expensive, so don't throw away the pods once you have finished cooking—there is still plenty of flavor left! Rinse them well, dry, and add to sugar for vanilla sugar!

INGREDIENTS | SERVES 4

2 cups brewed coffee

1 vanilla bean, sliced in half

1 cup heavy cream

¼ cup granulated sugar

¼ teaspoon peppermint extract

1. Add coffee and vanilla bean to Instant Pot®. Close lid and set steam release to Sealing, then press Manual and adjust cook time to 1 minute.

2. Once cooking is complete quick-release pressure. Open lid and stir in heavy cream and sugar. Stir until sugar has dissolved, then add peppermint extract. Serve warm.

PER SERVING Calories: 255 | Fat: 22g | Protein: 1g | Sodium: 22mg | Fiber: 0g | Carbohydrates: 14g | Sugar: 14g

Decadent Drinking Chocolate

This isn't hot chocolate; this is drinking chocolate. If you have never had it before, it is like drinking a melted chocolate bar. Tried-and-true chocolate lovers will go nuts for this recipe!

INGREDIENTS | SERVES 4

1 cup nondairy vanilla creamer

2 tablespoons cocoa powder

1 vanilla bean, sliced in half

1 cup half-and-half

1½ cups chopped bittersweet chocolate

1. Add creamer, cocoa powder, and vanilla bean to Instant Pot®. Close lid and set steam release to Sealing, then press Manual and adjust cook time to 1 minute.

2. Once cooking is complete quick-release pressure. Open lid and stir in half-and-half and chocolate. Whisk until chocolate is completely melted. Serve warm.

PER SERVING Calories: 492 | Fat: 31g | Protein: 5g | Sodium: 73mg | Fiber: 5g | Carbohydrates: 59g | Sugar: 51g

Classic Hot Chocolate

Cold, snowy days where the wind reddens your cheeks and nips your nose are the perfect days for a steaming mug of hot chocolate. You can add a peppermint stick for garnish—and, of course, some mini marshmallows!

INGREDIENTS | SERVES 4

4 cups whole milk

1 cup half-and-half

2 tablespoons cocoa powder

3 tablespoons granulated sugar

1 cup chopped semisweet chocolate chips

½ teaspoon vanilla extract

1. Add milk, half-and-half, and cocoa powder to Instant Pot®. Close lid and set steam release to Sealing, then press Manual and adjust cook time to 1 minute.

2. Once cooking is complete quick-release pressure. Open lid and stir in sugar until dissolved. Add chocolate chips and whisk until chocolate is completely melted. Stir in vanilla and serve warm.

PER SERVING Calories: 489 | Fat: 28g | Protein: 11g | Sodium: 135mg | Fiber: 3.5g | Carbohydrates: 54g | Sugar: 49g

Hot Chocolate

Dating back to the Mayan civilization, hot chocolate has undergone many changes over the years. From the New World, hot chocolate came to Europe, where sugar was added and it became a luxury drink enjoyed only by the wealthy due to the price of chocolate and sugar. Today hot chocolate is an affordable treat that you can enjoy anytime, anywhere!

Mexican Hot Chocolate

This hot chocolate is steeped with plenty of cinnamon and a little chili powder for a rich, earthy flavor. Feel free to adjust the chili powder to your preferred taste, but a little spicy kick is perfect with the chocolate!

INGREDIENTS | SERVES 4

2 cups whole milk

2 cups half-and-half

2 cinnamon sticks

¼ teaspoon chili powder

3 tablespoons granulated sugar

1½ cups chopped semisweet chocolate chips

½ teaspoon vanilla extract

1. Add milk, half-and-half, cinnamon sticks, and chili powder to Instant Pot®. Close lid and set steam release to Sealing, then press Manual and adjust cook time to 1 minute.

2. Once cooking is complete quick-release pressure. Open lid and stir in sugar until dissolved. Add chocolate chips and whisk until chocolate is completely melted. Stir in vanilla and serve warm.

PER SERVING Calories: 597 | Fat: 38g | Protein: 10g | Sodium: 114mg | Fiber: 4g | Carbohydrates: 64g | Sugar: 58g

Fruit-Infused Water

Have you ever been to a spa that offers pitchers of infused water? They are incredibly refreshing, and now you can have that same spa experience at home! Swap out the strawberries for your favorite fruit or add in other fruits for a medley of fruity flavors.

INGREDIENTS | SERVES 12

6 cups water

3 cups sliced strawberries, hulled

Fruity Ice Cubes

You can add an additional layer of flavor to your favorite iced beverages! Take your fruit-infused water, chill it, and then use it to fill ice cube trays. Once frozen you can use these for chilling glasses of iced tea or infused water so you don't dilute the flavor!

1. Add all ingredients to Instant Pot®. Close lid and set steam release to Sealing, then press Manual and adjust cook time to 3 minutes.

2. Once cooking is complete quick-release pressure. Press Cancel and open lid. Strain water into pitcher and chill 4 hours. Serve cold.

PER SERVING Calories: 12 | Fat: 0g | Protein: 0g | Sodium: 0mg | Fiber: 1g | Carbohydrates: 3g | Sugar: 2g

Glossary

Bean/Chili:
Programmed Instant Pot® setting that can be used for cooking dry beans and chili. Setting typically runs for 30 minutes at high pressure.

Beat:
To rapidly mix, incorporating air to make a smooth, light mixture.

Broil:
To cook under strong direct heat. Usually in an oven or grill.

Broth:
Strained liquid that meat, poultry, seafood, or vegetables have been cooked in.

Brown:
To add color to food through contact with a hot cooking surface.

Chop:
To cut food into uniform pieces of a small size, approximately ⅛– ¼" in size.

Condensation:
The change in the physical state of water from a gas (steam) to a liquid when it meets a solid surface.

Cream:
To blend softened fat with another ingredient, typically sugar, until a smooth mixture forms.

Delay/Start:
Instant Pot® function that allows for a delayed start timer to be used to schedule the start time for cooking. Not recommended for use with fresh meat or seafood.

Dice:
To cut food into uniform pieces of a small size, approximately ¼–⅓" in size.

Drizzle:
To pour liquid in a thin stream.

Fillet:
A piece of boneless meat or fish.

Float Valve:
Pressure valve that rises when Instant Pot® reaches suffcent pressure so cooking can begin.

Fluff:
To separate grains, seeds, or pasta after cooking. This is typically done with a fork.

Fold:
To incorporate a lighter substance into a heavier substance without losing volume.

Grate:
To shred food with a grater.

Inner Pot:
Removable cooking pot inside Instant Pot®.

Keep Warm:
Instant Pot® function that holds cooked foods at a safe temperature until it is ready to be eaten. Once a cooking program is completed the Instant Pot® will automatically transition to Keep Warm, or it can be manually selected using the Keep Warm button.

Knead:
To work dough to develop gluten.

Lid:
Locking cover for Instant Pot® that contains float valve, sealing ring, and pressure valve.

Manual/Pressure:
All-purpose button that can be used to set a custom pressure cooking program by adjusting the pressure level and time manually.

Meat/Stew:
Programmed Instant Pot® setting that can be used for cooking stew or braising meats. Setting typically runs for 35 minutes at high pressure.

Mince:
To cut food into uniform pieces smaller than ⅛" in size.

Mix:
To combine ingredients, usually through stirring.

Poach:
To cook food by using moist heat at a low temperature.

Poultry:
Programmed Instant Pot® setting that can be used for cooking poultry. Setting typically runs for 15 minutes at high pressure.

Pressure/Pressure Level:
Button that is used to adjust the pressure used for cooking between Low and High. Low pressure cooks at a lower temperature, and high pressure cooks at a higher temperature.

Purée:
To press, mash, or blend food until it reaches the consistency of a thick paste.

Reduce:
To thicken a sauce by simmering or boiling.

Rice:
Programmed Instant Pot® setting that can be used for cooking dry rice. This setting is fully automatic and time will adjust depending on the amount of water in the pot.

Sauté:
Referring to cooking method: to fry food quickly in a hot pan with a little fat such as butter. Referring to Instant Pot® function: heats inner pot to allow for searing, sautéing, and reducing liquids. This function should be used without the lid to avoid pressure buildup.

Sealing Ring:
Gasket inside lid designed to seal pressure inside Instant Pot® when machine is set to Sealing.

Silicone Tray/Silicone Cupcake Liners:
Silicone products that are naturally nonstick and heat resistant. Preferred for steaming as silicone does not rust, and their natural flexibility make them easy to fit into the inner pot.

Simmer:
To cook a liquid at a low temperature, usually between 180° and 205°F.

Slow Cook:
Adjustable Instant Pot® setting that can be used for slow cooking on low, normal, or high temperature settings.

Soup/Broth:
Programmed Instant Pot® setting that can be used for cooking soups and for making broth. Setting typically runs for 30 minutes at high pressure.

Steam:
Referring to cooking method: to cook food by using the vapor from the boiling liquid. Referring to Instant Pot® function: programmed Instant Pot® setting that can be used for steaming foods. Setting typically runs for 10 minutes at high pressure.

Steam Release:
Handle designed to control venting and sealing of steam. Is also used to release pressure from Instant Pot® when steam is quick-released.

Stir:
To mix ingredients by using circular motions.

Toss:
To combine ingredients by using a lifting motion.

Translucent:
The color of a food, typically cooked onion, that is no longer opaque.

Water Bath:
A large container of cold or ice water in which a smaller container of hot food is placed to speed the cooling process.

Whisk:
To mix liquids so that air is incorporated.

Wilt:
To cook a leaf or vegetable through the addition of heat and water until it is limp.

Yogurt:
Programmed Instant Pot® setting that can be used for incubating yogurt.

Zest:
The outer portion of a citrus rind where the color and citrus oil is found.

Appendix: Time Charts

FISH AND SEAFOOD COOK TIMES

Fish and Seafood	Fresh Cook Time in Minutes	Frozen Cook Time in Minutes
Crab, whole	2–3	4–5
Fish, whole	4–5	5–7
Fish, fillet	2–3	3–4
Fish, steak	3–4	4–6
Lobster	2–3	3–4
Mussels	1–2	2–3
Seafood soup or stock	7–8	8–9
Shrimp or prawn	1–3	2–4

RICE AND GRAINS COOK TIMES

Rice and Grains	Water Ratio (grain:water)	Cook Time in Minutes
Barley, pearl	1:2.5	20–22
Barley, pot	1:3–1:4	25–30
Couscous	1:2	2–3
Corn, dried, halved	1:3	5–6
Millet	1:1.75	10–12
Oats, quick-cooking	1:2	2–3
Oats, steel-cut	1:3	3–5
Quinoa	1:1.25	1
Rice, basmati	1:1	4
Rice, brown	1:1	20–22
Rice, jasmine	1:1	4
Rice, white	1:1	4
Rice, wild	1:2	20–25

DRIED BEAN, LEGUME, AND LENTIL COOK TIMES

Dried Bean, Legume, and Lentil	Dry Cook Time in Minutes	Soaked Cook Time in Minutes
Black beans	20–25	6–8
Black-eyed peas	14–18	4–5
Cannellini beans	30–35	6–9
Chickpeas	35–40	10–15
Great northern beans	25–30	7–8
Kidney beans	15–20	7–8
Lentils, green or brown	8–10	N/A
Lentils, red or yellow, split	1–2	N/A
Lima beans	12–14	6–10
Navy beans	20–25	7–8
Pinto beans	25–30	6–9

BEEF, PORK, POULTRY, AND LAMB COOK TIMES

Beef, Pork, Poultry, and Lamb	Cook Time in Minutes (per pound)
Beef, stew meat	20
Beef, meatball	5
Beef roast (rump, round, chuck, blade, or brisket) 2–3" pieces	15–20
Beef roast (rump, round, chuck, blade, or brisket) 4–5" pieces	20–25
Beef, ribs	20–25
Beef, shanks	25–30
Beef, oxtail	40–50
Chicken, breasts boneless	6–8
Chicken, whole	8
Duck, portions with bones	12–15
Duck, whole	10–15
Ham, steaks	9–12
Ham, picnic shoulder	8
Lamb, cubes	10–15
Lamb, stew meat	12–15
Lamb, leg	15
Pork, loin	20
Pork, butt	15
Pork, ribs	15–20
Turkey, breast (boneless)	7–9
Turkey, breast (whole)	20–25
Turkey, leg	15–20
Quail, whole	8

VEGETABLE AND FRUIT COOK TIMES

Vegetables and Fruit	Fresh Cook Time in Minutes	Frozen Cook Time in Minutes
Apples (slices or pieces)	1–2	2–3
Apples (whole)	3–4	4–6
Apricot (whole or halves)	2–3	3–4
Asparagus, whole or cut	1–2	2–3
Beans, green, yellow or wax, trim ends and strings	1–2	2–3
Beetroot, small whole	11–13	13–15
Beetroot, large whole	20–25	25–30
Broccoli, florets	1–2	2–3
Broccoli, stalks	3–4	4–5
Brussels sprouts, whole	2–3	3–4

VEGETABLE AND FRUIT COOK TIMES

Vegetables and Fruit	Fresh Cook Time in Minutes	Frozen Cook Time in Minutes
Cabbage, red, purple, or green, shredded	2–3	3–4
Cabbage, red, purple, or green, wedges	3–4	4–5
Carrots, sliced or shredded	2–3	3–4
Carrots, whole or chunked	6–8	7–9
Cauliflower florets	2–3	3–4
Celery, chunks	2–3	3–4
Collard greens	4–5	5–6
Corn (kernels)	1–2	2–3
Corn (on the cob)	3–5	4–6
Eggplant (slices or chunks)	3–4	3–4
Green beans (whole)	2–3	3–4
Greens (chopped)	4–5	5–6
Leeks	2–3	3–4
Mixed vegetables	3–4	4–6
Okra	2–3	3–4
Onions (sliced)	2–3	3–4
Parsnips (chunks)	3–4	4–5
Peaches	2–3	4–5
Peas (green)	1–2	2–3
Potatoes (cubed)	3–4	4–5
Potatoes (small, whole)	8–10	12–14
Potatoes (large, whole)	12–15	15–19
Pumpkin (small pieces)	4–5	6–7
Pumpkin (larges pieces)	8–10	10–14
Rutabaga (slices)	3–4	4–6
Rutabaga (chunks)	4–6	6–8
Spinach	1–2	2–3
Acorn squash (slices)	3–4	4–6
Butternut squash (slices)	4–6	6–8
Sweet potato (cubes)	2–4	4–6
Sweet potato (large, whole)	12–15	15–19
Sweet potato (small, whole)	10–12	12–14
Sweet pepper (slices or chunks)	1–3	2–4
Tomatoes (quarters)	2–3	4–5

US/Metric Conversion Chart

VOLUME CONVERSIONS

US Volume Measure	Metric Equivalent
⅛ teaspoon	0.5 milliliter
¼ teaspoon	1 milliliter
½ teaspoon	2 milliliters
1 teaspoon	5 milliliters
½ tablespoon	7 milliliters
1 tablespoon (3 teaspoons)	15 milliliters
2 tablespoons (1 fluid ounce)	30 milliliters
¼ cup (4 tablespoons)	60 milliliters
⅓ cup	80 milliliters
½ cup (4 fluid ounces)	125 milliliters
⅔ cup	160 milliliters
¾ cup (6 fluid ounces)	180 milliliters
1 cup (16 tablespoons)	250 milliliters
1 pint (2 cups)	500 milliliters
1 quart (4 cups)	1 liter (about)

WEIGHT CONVERSIONS

US Weight Measure	Metric Equivalent
½ ounce	15 grams
1 ounce	30 grams
2 ounces	60 grams
3 ounces	85 grams
¼ pound (4 ounces)	115 grams
½ pound (8 ounces)	225 grams
¾ pound (12 ounces)	340 grams
1 pound (16 ounces)	454 grams

OVEN TEMPERATURE CONVERSIONS

Degrees Fahrenheit	Degrees Celsius
200 degrees F	95 degrees C
250 degrees F	120 degrees C
275 degrees F	135 degrees C
300 degrees F	150 degrees C
325 degrees F	160 degrees C
350 degrees F	180 degrees C
375 degrees F	190 degrees C
400 degrees F	205 degrees C
425 degrees F	220 degrees C
450 degrees F	230 degrees C

BAKING PAN SIZES

American	Metric
8 × 1½ inch round baking pan	20 × 4 cm cake tin
9 × 1½ inch round baking pan	23 × 3.5 cm cake tin
11 × 7 × 1½ inch baking pan	28 × 18 × 4 cm baking tin
13 × 9 × 2 inch baking pan	30 × 20 × 5 cm baking tin
2 quart rectangular baking dish	30 × 20 × 3 cm baking tin
15 × 10 × 2 inch baking pan	38 × 25 × 5 cm baking tin (Swiss roll tin)
9 inch pie plate	22 × 4 or 23 × 4 cm pie plate
7 or 8 inch springform pan	18 or 20 cm springform or loose bottom cake tin
9 × 5 × 3 inch loaf pan	23 × 13 × 7 cm or 2 lb narrow loaf or pâté tin
1½ quart casserole	1.5 liter casserole
2 quart casserole	2 liter casserole

Index

About the Author

Kelly Jaggers is a cookbook author, recipe developer, food stylist, food photographer, and founder of the recipe blog *Evil Shenanigans* (EvilShenanigans.com). She specializes in creating indulgent recipes featuring fresh, seasonal ingredients…and lots and lots of butter! She is the author of *The Everything® Pie Cookbook*, *Not-So-Humble Pies*, *Moufflet*, *The Everything® Easy Asian Cookbook*, and *The Everything® Dutch Oven Cookbook*. When she is not developing recipes or photographing food, she teaches cooking classes and works as a personal chef and caterer. Kelly lives in Dallas.